THE WAY WE LIVED

THE WAY WE LIVED

FOREWORD

At the dawn of a new millennium, **THE EVENTFUL CENTURY** series presents the vast panorama of the last hundred years—a century which has witnessed the transition from horse-drawn transport to space travel, and from the first telephones to the information superhighway.

THE EVENTFUL CENTURY chronicles epoch-making events like the outbreak of the two world wars, the Russian Revolution and the rise and fall of communism. But major events are only part of the glittering kaleidoscope. It also describes the everyday background—the way people lived, how they worked, what they ate and drank, how much they earned, the way they spent their leisure time, the books they read, and the crimes, scandals and unsolved mysteries that set them talking. Here are fads and crazes like the hula hoop and Rubik's cube . . . fashions like the New Look and the miniskirt . . . breakthroughs in entertainment like the birth of the movies . . . medical milestones like open-heart surgery . . . and marvels of modern architecture and engineering.

THE WAY WE LIVED describes the myriad changes that have transformed all aspects of daily life during the 20th century, from coal-fired ovens to microwaves, from the first automated telephone exchange to satellite communications. In the early part of the century, people marvelled at moving stairways, daring stunts by the early aviators and canned fruit from faraway countries. By the end of the century, vacations in exotic places, frozen convenience foods, foreign television programs and computerized banking are taken for granted. Medical advances such as heart transplants and test-tube babies have given people new hope, while developments such as the family car and jet travel have given them new freedoms. At the same time, alongside the scientific and technological innovations, changing attitudes have also helped to reshape everyone's daily lives as people have questioned educational methods, social systems, mainstream religions and the very notion of the family itself.

THE WAY WE LIVED

The Reader's Digest Association, Inc.
Pleasantville, New York/Montreal

THE WAY WE LIVED
Edited and designed by Toucan Books Limited
Written by Richard Tames
Edited by Helen Douglas-Cooper and
Andrew Kerr-Jarrett
Designed by Bradbury and Williams
Picture research by Julie McMahon

AMERICAN EDITION
Edited and produced by The Reference Works
Harold Rabinowitz, Executive Editor
Ross Mandel, Managing Editor
Doug Heyman, Research
Bob Antler, Antler Designworks, Production

FOR THE READER'S DIGEST, UK
Series Editor Christine Noble
Editorial Assistant Alison Candlin

FOR THE READER'S DIGEST, US
Group Editorial Director Fred DuBose
Senior Designer Judith Carmel

READER'S DIGEST GENERAL BOOKS
Editor-in-Chief Christopher Cavanaugh
Art Director Joan Mazzeo

Copyright © 1999
The Reader's Digest Association
Reader's Digest Road
Pleasantville, NY 10570

Copyright © 1997
Reader's Digest Association Far East Limited
Philippines copyright © 1997
Reader's Digest Association Far East Limited
All rights reserved

Printed in the United States of America, 1999.

ISBN 0 7621 0258 6

An application has been made for
Library of Congress Cataloging in Publication data.
FRONT COVER

From Top: Bathing beauty, 1930s; Immigrants landing at Ellis Island, 1900s; Punk rockers, 1960s.

BACK COVER
From Top: School children at the computer, 1980s;
Women factory workers assembling aircraft, 1940s;
Rudolf Valentino and Vilma Pankey.

Page 3 (from left to right): Tango dancers, 1940s;
Punk fashions; bathing beauty; Oklahoma farmer,
1936.

Background pictures:
Page 11: Houses in Bristol;
Page 33: Well-stocked shelves at the Piggly Wiggly
supermarket, 1918;
Page 79: French students sitting an exam, 1963;
Page 123: Bathers at Coney Island, Brooklyn,
New York.

CONTENTS

A CENTURY OF CHANGE

IN JUST THREE GENERATIONS SPANNING THE 20TH CENTURY, THE WORLD HAS CHANGED MORE AND FASTER THAN EVER BEFORE

The 20th century has been a century of unimaginable change. A child born near the start of the century entered a world where no one had yet flown in an airplane or seen a television program or used a vacuum cleaner. The South Pole had not yet been reached. Yellow fever still frustrated all attempts to build a canal across the Isthmus of Panama. Even a child born nearly half a century later, in the aftermath of the Second World War, was coming into a world where

FANTASY AND REALITY   The film set for H.G. Wells' *Things to Come* (left) from the 1930s looks strikingly modern, even beside Kansai Airport, Osaka, in the 1990s.

computers were known only to a handful of scientists, the transistor had yet to be invented and the majority of people crossing the Atlantic each year did so by ship, not plane.

Imagine that the child born at the start of the century had an adult grandchild living at its close. The daily detail of their lives would have been radically different—even before either got out of bed in the morning. The child at the start of the century slept under cotton sheets and woolen blankets—not a comforter. His or her bedroom, probably shared with several brothers and sisters, had no central heating. The clock radio, shaving cream, disposable razor, deodorant spray, toaster oven, coffee machine and other gad-

gets that get the modern day under way would all have been complete mysteries to him or her.

What would this child find most bizarre about his or her grandchild's daily life? With lunch approaching, the grandchild might decide, for example, to reheat last night's leftover Chinese rice in a microwave oven made in Japan, and wash it down with some imported German beer—the very notion of these things would have been extraordinary to anyone at the start of the century. Perhaps the child of the 1900s would be reassured by the sight of a 1990s postman bringing the mid-morning mail—but maybe not. Few ordinary working-class people in pre-1914 cities received letters even once a week; even fewer received such things as income tax forms and no one would have known what a credit-card statement was. And that most vigorous of 90s phenomena, e-mail, would sound like science-fiction.

Predicting the future

Does changing the viewer change the view? What might a sophisticated, well-informed

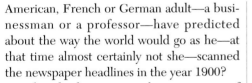

CROWDED SKIES Albert Robida's turn-of-the-century view (left) of the skies of the future cluttered with power lines and flying taxis has not, it seems, come true—yet. Most urban centers are the setting for magnificent skyscrapers, like the World Trade Center twin towers in lower Manhattan (below). At century's end, people still commuted by car, bus and train to work—even the Staten Island Ferry was still running.

American, French or German adult—a businessman or a professor—have predicted about the way the world would go as he—at that time almost certainly not she—scanned the newspaper headlines in the year 1900?

A hundred years ago, the supremacy of politics was taken for granted. Serious newspapers gave little coverage to business issues, even less to celebrities, the environment (a word then used only by scientists) or sports. Such newspapers ignored what would become known as popular culture. The first hamburger to be sold, the marketing of Kodak's Brownie camera and the first international automobile race, all of which took place in 1900, were not hailed as major portents of the emerging future.

Since it was a time of such richly and self-consciously significant cultural activity, the educated reader in 1900 would probably not be surprised to know that the names making the news that year would still be venerated a century later—in music, Puccini, Debussy, Elgar and Mahler; in literature Conrad, Tolstoy and Henry James; in art, Rodin, Renoir and Gauguin. But 1900 was also the year in which the first jazz band was formed and tennis players first competed for the Davis Cup. Readers in 1900 might have been surprised to know that their counterparts at the end of the century would still find these events of great significance.

In world headlines, little changed with the dawning of a new century. Politically and internationally, 1900 was the continuation of 1899. William McKinley was still president of the United States and Victoria was still Queen of England, though neither would survive the following year. Germany, Britain and the United States negotiated mutually acceptable terms for the administration of Samoa. All three powers, along with France and Japan, cooperated to crush the antiforeign Boxer Rebellion in China. The U.S. annexed Hawaii, and New Zealand took over the Cook Islands. Russia and Japan quar-reled over naval facilities in Korea. Persia, not to be known as Iran for another three decades, accepted a massive loan that made Russia her main creditor.

Nationalism was the great "ism" that did not become a "wasm." In the first decade of the century it was causing trouble in the Balkans and as the century drew to a close it was doing so again as ethnic tensions flared in Bosnia, Serbia and Kosovo. A liberal free-trader of 1900 might have foreseen all Europe united in a single market, though he would probably be overwhelmed by the forces of economic globalization uniting the world. Not all predictions were on the mark, however: an enthusiastic diviner writing in the *Ladies Home Journal* in December 1900 predicted that by century's end there would no longer be a *c, x,* or *q* in the alphabet.

For the most part, though, the men and women of 1900 were better informed than their parents had been. Literacy rates were as high as they had ever been, and wildly popular newspapers, like Joseph Pulitzer's *World*, William Randolph Hearst's *Journal* and the London *Daily Mail* (which had a circulation of more than a million in 1900) brought local, national and international events to the doorstep of the everyday reader. The world was on its way to becoming a smaller place.

The century of the city

"I . . . live in a little village . . . and help my father and mother, my brother and an aunt, on our little farm . . . Everything it is possible to grow, we grow. This is in order to buy as little as possible . . . Twice a week the baker comes to the village square and sells bread. A grocer comes twice a month . . . We are absolutely cut off from news . . . We have few visitors because we are so isolated . . . enclosed by our own habits and daily routines, from which there seems to be no escape. My mother has not even been to the capital of the department, 60 km [40 miles] away."

When this interview with a French peasant girl of the Isère region bordering the Alps was recorded in the early 1960s, it represented a way of life that had disappeared for most of western Europe and North America half a century before. The 20th century was replacing centuries-old isola-

FUTURE FASHION Cecil Beaton's prediction, created in 1928, of a fashion style for the year 2000 combined fantasy with nostalgia but would prove impractical for a fast-moving age.

tion with communication, self-sufficiency with interdependence. The suburb, town or city, not the village, was where most people in the Western world lived, and cities, unlike villages, are anything but self-sufficient.

In 1900, London was the biggest city in the world, with a population of just over 6 million. By mid-century it had been pushed into second place by New York, which by then had a population twice that of London in 1900. By the mid 1990s New York would be overtaken by Tokyo, with a population

PLEASE SPEAK AFTER THE TONE The first answering machine, or "mechanical secretary," marketed in 1932, used a phonograph record for outgoing and incoming messages.

more than twice as big again. London by the 1990s was no longer even in the top 20 of the world's biggest cities.

Even so, covering some 400,000 acres and embracing 12 percent of the population of the United Kingdom, the British capital was a ferocious consumer. Each week it burned enough oil to fill two supertankers. Each year it consumed 1.2 million tons of timber and an equivalent weight of metals, 2 million tons of foodstuffs and equal quantities of paper and of plastics. Each year it spewed out 7.5 million tons of sewage, twice that much waste and eight times as much carbon dioxide. Each year it was visited by almost four times as many people as actually lived there.

London was by no means an exception among the world's great cities. Together cities covered just 2 percent of the world's surface but consumed 75 percent of its resources. In the United States they were also drawing in more and more people. In 1920, for the first time in the country's history, more than half of all Americans lived in urban areas. In 1975 some 1.5 billion people lived in cities worldwide. This figure would pass 3 billion by the turn of the millennium—more than the entire population of the planet in 1960.

Science and technology

For people pondering the future in 1900 it was not hard to imagine that science and technology would transform their daily lives. The World Exhibition staged in Paris in 1900 —visited by 50 million people over the course of six months—was dominated by a Palace of Electricity, which featured a continuous movie show and the first public demonstration of the escalator. Would the same observers, however, have grasped the long-term implications of less publicized technological achievements? These included the first exploration for oil using offshore rigs, the opening of the first automated telephone exchange, controlling 10,000 lines, and the first successful transmission of speech by wireless telegraphy.

Readers brought up on the futuristic fantasies of Jules Verne or H.G. Wells knew all about the possibilities of space travel. The

TWO UP, TWO DOWN The family house of the future, 1950s style, was made from steel and welded together on site. The ladder leads to the guest bedrooms.

pioneer French filmmaker Georges Méliès even faked up a simulated Moon voyage in a backstreet Paris film studio in the early 1900s. So the visionary of 1900 would probably not have thought it too fantastic that men should be standing on the Moon in 1969. But he or she would quite possibly have been amazed to learn that large fleets of jumbo jets, which made their inaugural flight in the same year, 1969, would later be used to transport tens of millions of ordinary European and North American working people to vacation destinations all over the world. As for space travel, it has happened, and its chief impact on the way we live has been in the application of the technologies that made it possible to other areas of life. The Concorde, laptop computers, fiber optics and nonstick frying pans—all these are spin-offs of space technology.

Jules Verne and H.G. Wells enjoyed great popular success with their writings, but they were generally regarded as harmless fantasists. The most influential "futurological" writers of the turn of the century were concerned with institutional change. *Looking Backward: 2000–1887*, written in 1888 by the American Edward Bellamy, told the story of a Bostonian, Julian West, awaking at the end of the 20th century to find that squalor and injustice had disappeared, thanks to the replacement of capitalism by a benevolent state that is the sole employer. This hugely influential utopian romance actually provoked the formation of a political party in the United States to advocate its vision as a program for reform. It also inspired turn-of-the-century political groups

in Europe, notably in the Netherlands. Ironically, Bellamy died, of tuberculosis, in 1898, before his new century of transformation had even begun. The concern for social justice and change that he articulated would, however, be a constant—waxing and waning in influence—throughout the century.

Coca-colonization?

Have television, tourism and global marketing created a universal consumer culture of fast food, blockbuster films and shopping malls filled with brand-name outlet stores? Certainly there are now events and experiences that are shared worldwide in a way that was never possible in any previous century. The 1902 coronation of the British monarch Edward VII was seen by fewer than 7,000 aristocrats and ambassadors crammed into London's Westminster Abbey.

The 1981 wedding of Prince Charles and Lady Diana Spencer was witnessed by 700 million people around the world. On November 21, 1980, 450 million viewers worldwide tuned in to find out "who shot J.R.?" and 50 million watched the final episode of *M.A.S.H.* The 1984 Live Aid concert, raising money for famine-ravaged Ethiopia, was broadcast on 95 percent of the television receivers then in operation. In 1900 even some of the participants in the second Olympic Games in Paris were unaware what exactly it was that they were participating in. Few within reach of a television set could have remained oblivious to the progress of the centenary Olympiad staged in Atlanta in 1996.

Cultures and societies overlap and interpenetrate each other more than ever before, yet they retain their distinctiveness.

MOBILE SITTING ROOM One view of the future envisaged cars being guided along superhighways by electronic signal devices embedded in the road.

Characters like Big Bird, Barney and Popeye have transcended their national origins to become children's favorites in dozens of countries. But cultural exports do not receive an automatic welcome everywhere. Despite its popularity overseas, in the United States soccer still can't compete with homegrown sports like basketball or football. Kentucky Fried Chicken nearly sank without trace in Japan—until salty soy sauce was added to the batter recipe and mother-and-child-sized portions became available at railway-station kiosks.

The forces of change

This has been the century of More! and New! and Faster! Daily life in the world's great democracies has been transformed by technology and by terror, by the trivial and by the tremendous—by zippers and ballpoint pens, tampons and condoms, superglue and contact lenses . . . and the two most destructive wars in human history.

In 1900 the average life expectancy of the American male was just over 48 years. While some optimists might have believed that, as the century closed, it would be 50 percent longer, most would have been astounded that a man would have a better chance of living to 65 in Bangladesh, the 12th poorest country in the world, than in the poorer

AN EDUCATION REVOLUTION In France at the turn of the century, it was thought that by the year 2000 technology would turn schools into models of efficient learning.

COMMUNICATIONS The 1990s videophone, while more compact than one envisaged by an artist in 1905, does not enable the speakers to shake hands.

inner-city neighborhoods of American cities like Detroit and Los Angeles.

The first five years of the new era blessed the world with tea bags, teddy bears, free mail-order catalogues and powered flight. But a hunger for novelties was seldom matched by an understanding of their implications. The first newspaper reports of the Wright brothers' achievement were low-key: Only six American newspapers carried reports of the Wright brothers' flight; The

New York *Tribune* mentioned it in its sports page. It was another five years before the U.S. Army Signal Corps was persuaded to invest in an airplane. In the 1930s, after a decade of dedicated effort and the expenditure of tens of millions of research dollars, the Du Pont corporation finally succeeded in producing a new wonder material—nylon.

Technologies have proved slippery in their implications. Women pilots were commonplace in the 1930s, when new airlines were trying to take the fear out of flying. In the American Midwest some women's colleges sought to outdo more staid rivals by putting aviation on the curriculum. Newsreels of the day suggested that within a decade or two homes would have a family airplane in their driveway, instead of a sedan. But aviation has remained the prerogative of professionals.

The way we live has been changed as much by institutions as by innovations. Self-service has arrived; domestic service has all but departed. We celebrate Mother's Day in an age where the extended family headed by a matriarchal figure has been replaced by single parent families, career couples without children and fragmented families spread not just around a village but now often around the globe. The century of space travel and heart transplants has not found solutions for ethnic cleansing, poverty and road rage, and however significant the triumphs of Western science, for many people they cannot replace the wisdom of ancient religions such as Hinduism or Buddhism. As one century—and millennium—draws to a close and new ones begin, we are far less optimistic than our forebears that more and new and faster will necessarily mean better.

EN L'AN 2000

THE WORLD AROUND US

SINCE THE 1900S, THE HOME ENVIRONMENT HAS BEEN CONTINUOUSLY RESHAPED BY TECHNOLOGY, ALTHOUGH SOCIAL PATTERNS HAVE ALSO PLAYED THEIR PART. HOUSEWORK AND TRANSPORTATION WERE ONCE SERVICES THE RICH PAID THE POOR TO PROVIDE; INCREASINGLY THEY HAVE BECOME UNPAID TASKS WE PERFORM FOR OURSELVES. AND OUR HOMES AND CARS NOT ONLY MEET OUR NEEDS FOR SHELTER AND MOBILITY— THEY ALSO EXPRESS OUR TASTES AND DREAMS.

THE HOMES WE LIVED IN

SWISS ARCHITECT LE CORBUSIER CALLED THE HOME "A MACHINE FOR LIVING IN." THIS CENTURY HAS SEEN THAT MACHINE INVADED BY OTHERS

ACCLIMATIZATION In a spacious turn-of-the-century home in Brisbane, Australia, features such as gables and a veranda were used to accommodate the hot climate.

In the character of Mike Dobrejcak, the American novelist Thomas Bell recreated the experiences of his father, a Slovak immigrant, arriving in the United States in the first decade of the 20th century. Mike begins to court a young nursemaid who works in the home of a factory owner, and his first visit there comes as a revelation:

"The Dexters' [home] was the first private house Mike had ever set foot in which was wired for electricity. For that matter it was the first private house he'd ever been in that had a bathroom, a telephone, steam heat, and in the kitchen a magnificent icebox . . . Mike's interest in houses, in house furnishings, was no greater than most young men's . . . but in the Dexters' dining room, in their parlour and bedrooms, he saw furniture, dishes and silverware which were desirable and beautiful in themselves and not merely as articles of use. For the first time he perceived how graceful the business of eating and sleeping and entertaining one's friends could be, and how one could be proud of one's possessions, the way one lived. . . ."

Home comforts

Home for the well-off at the start of the 20th century was not usually as grand as the Dexters' house. But in the Western world the benefits of industry and technology meant that even those with comparatively modest means could aspire to higher levels of comfort than their forebears had ever known.

In Continental European cities the typical middle-class home was a comfortable apartment. The largest had up to a dozen rooms, including separate quarters for servants, and most had the benefit of some form of central heating. This was still a rarity in the English-speaking world, where even the rich deployed an army of screens, shawls and door curtains to fight an unending war against drafts.

In North American cities, the typical home for middle-class people was a brownstone row house; these houses were usually 2 to 3 stories high, with carved facades, a raised basement, and a rear yard, shared by several tenants. In most British cities it was a red brick terraced or semidetached house; a garden, however minute, was still regarded as an essential feature for those aspiring to a respectable status. Only the poor lived in houses whose front doors opened directly onto the street.

In Australia, New Zealand and small-town America even quite well-off people lived in houses made of wood, an almost inconceivable notion to most Europeans. In the warmer parts of those countries most houses had a wide veranda, which was often the focus of social life, especially in the evenings during the summer months, when warm or humid weather encouraged families to savor every breath of breeze.

Gas was available in most big Western cities but many women still cooked and boiled their water on a cast-iron solid-fuel range. In the rural areas of Canada, South Africa and Australia pioneer conditions prevailed. In these parts of the world, many homes of families that were otherwise moderately affluent still used kerosene lamps for lighting and had no indoor toilet. Galvanized iron had begun to replace wooden shingles on the roofs of such homes and was

TEEMING SHORE Street after street of crowded tenements were necessary to house the many immigrants who came to America in the early years of the 20th century.

sometimes used even for walls. Only time and rust would soften its patent ugliness.

Middle-class Americans definitely led the way in home conveniences in the early years of the century. Between 1912 and 1914 John B. Leeds of Columbia University in New York surveyed the living conditions of 60 American families "earning enough for decency," a figure which ranged from the $700 a year for a farming family to the $3,750 for a professional man—the average was around $1,300. No fewer than 53 of these families lived in homes with electricity and 42 in homes equipped with gas. Fifty-one homes had some form of central heating and Leeds did not even inquire whether they had a bathroom; he took it for granted that everybody did.

How people used their homes varied, then as now, from country to country and region to region. Apartment-dwelling Continental Europeans tended to socialize outside the home, in cafés or beer gardens, in parks or on esplanades. Americans and Australians sat on their front steps or verandas and chatted,

read, played board games or hailed passers-by. The English preferred to relax in privacy behind neatly clipped hedges.

The wealthy

The truly wealthy were rich enough to build new houses that looked old—assuming they had not inherited or purchased a genuinely old house. They built in pseudo-medieval, Renaissance or Neoclassical styles—or whatever combination of periods, motifs and details appealed to them.

Others could adapt existing dwellings. What the Victorian British architect William Burges had contemptuously dismissed as getting "the picturesque by any and every means" usually involved obscuring the outlines of a conventional house by festooning it with gables, dormers, scrolls, oriel windows,

DOMESTIC PALACES Large detached houses in a Vermont town (below) contrast with a Berlin apartment block (right). Even wealthy Continentals favored apartment living.

bow windows and panels of hung tiling or half-timbering and then punctuating its outer walls with asymmetrical arrangements of unusual windows—round or oval, long and narrow, lozenge-shaped or semicircular.

The largest houses were virtually palaces, the most extravagant examples including the string of ornate country mansions built in the late 19th century by the different branches of the Rothschild banking dynasty in Austria, France and England, and the vast estates (euphemistically called "cottages") built at the fashionable American resort of Newport, Rhode Island, by such families as the Vanderbilts. Mansions like these had dozens of rooms, the principal ones set aside for particular forms of leisure and entertainment: a ballroom with chandeliers and a floor specially made for dancing on, a grand dining room with a table that could seat 20 people in comfort, a salon for receptions, a music room with grand piano (at which one's daughters could

ELEGANT ILLUMINATION
A French lamp of 1902, made to a water-lily design, epitomizes the Art Nouveau style that adorned many houses of the better-off in Europe and the United States.

RICH LIVING   An English lady's light and airy boudoir (top), an American parlor (center) and the heavy opulence of a New York millionaire's drawing room (bottom) reveal contrasting styles, all fashionable in the early years of the century. Nor were individual styles confined to one country.

that was seldom discarded, though particular pieces might be relegated in large houses to corridors or less public parts of the house when they were reckoned to have become unsightly and out of date.

There was also a choice of avant-garde styles, particularly popular with the newly rich European middle classes. These styles were dominated by the heirs of the arts and crafts movement that had started in Britain in the mid 19th century, spawning imitators all across Europe. Later, in the 1890s, the

HOME WITH THE RANGE Heat for cooking and hot water is supplied by a coal-fired iron range in a "modern" kitchen in New England (top), just like its older English counterpart.

show off), a billiard room (to which the gentlemen could retreat after dinner) and finally a book-lined library and a conservatory crammed with tropical greenery—either of the last two providing an appropriate setting for genteel flirtation, depending on the weather and time of day.

More intimate rooms for family use, apart from the individual bedrooms, might include a boudoir for the mistress of the house, a dressing room or a study (or both) for the master, a breakfast room for informal meals

and a smoking room where the younger gentlemen could read raffish magazines and indulge themselves in smoking cigars without offending the ladies.

The basement was invariably the servants' realm. Here, behind the green baize door that led down to their subterranean kingdoms, the butler presided over the pantry and wine cellar and the cook reigned over the kitchen, where meals were prepared, and the scullery, where dirty cleaning jobs were done. The attics would be sub-divided into small bed-

rooms, where the female servants slept, while the younger male servants were relegated either to corners of the basement or perhaps to a room above the stables outside.

Home decor

For the wealthy, opulence was the hallmark of the period, particularly in the United States. Rich Americans were, after all, even richer than rich Europeans and had no qualms about displaying their wealth. The merely comfortably off paid more attention to more homely details, however, especially when it came to furniture.

Almost all well-to-do Americans represented, in Old World terms, "new money," but new money enjoyed old furniture. Rich and well-off Americans were eagerly collecting antiques, and not just European ones. The 1876 Centennial celebrations in cities and towns across America had renewed interest in the colonial period of American history. As early as 1883 the author of *The Hearthstone, or Life at Home* had been urging her readers to acquire homely Shaker sewing chairs for their drawing rooms, and another author suggested that it was a good idea to hang on to "one's own or someone else's great-grandmother's candlesticks."

In Europe, "old money" brought with it a ready-made inheritance of antique furniture

Belgian architect Henry van de Velde had developed the sinuous Art Nouveau style. By the turn of the century, this had spread to most other European countries under a variety of names—*Jugendstil* in Germany, *Sezessionstil* in Austria and *modernista* in Barcelona where wealthy merchants, shipping families and factory-owners were enthusiastic patrons of the new style.

The writhing curves of Art Nouveau lent themselves particularly well to metal, glass, plaster, wallpaper and textiles but were difficult to render in wood. This limited it as an overall decorative style; it tended rather to be a way of treating individual items, such as lamps or door handles. More exotic motifs and decorative items were also drawn from "Celtic" sources or "the Orient," especially from Japan, a prolific supplier of richly decorated Imari export-ware vases, lacquer chests inlaid with mother-of-pearl and delicate paper screens, painted with a variety of spiky, floral designs.

SLUM LIFE Inhabitants of New York's Mulberry Bend district, one of the city's worst slums at the turn of the century, stare into the camera of reporter Jacob Riis.

To some, this lavish eclecticism was an eyeful; to others, an eyesore. French chateaus, Romanesque castles and English manor houses sprouted up along New York's Fifth Avenue like extravagant weeds. Inside William Vanderbilt's $3 million dollar palace at 52nd and Fifth,

LIFE IN THE RAW Ragged clothes hang across the room where a Berlin mother lives with her children. On the left is a sewing machine, which she uses to earn a precarious living.

the Italian Renaissance, Catherine the Great's Russia, and ancient Greece clashed for dominance in the décor.

The struggling

The poor, who in every advanced country still made up two-thirds or more of the population, lived with very different preoccupations. Their homes were grubby tenement blocks, grimy terraces, damp cottages, leaky shanties and cabins.

In Berlin in 1901 more than 45 percent of all dwellings consisted of one or two rooms only. In London the percentage was lower, at under 35; in Paris it stood at over 55 and in Glasgow at over 70. In most of the cities of Continental Europe, Scotland and North America, the laboring poor were crammed into barrack-like blocks in inner-city areas or around port facilities. In New York, one third of the city's population lived in shamefully overcrowded tenement houses. The Danish-born journalist Jacob Riis captured the desolation of the Lower East Side's poor in his stark, unsettling book of photography, *How the Other Half Live*. Riis claimed that New York had the dubious distinction of housing the most unforgiving slums in the history of Western civilization; the city crammed in 125,000 more inhabitants per square mile than the other main contender, Dickensian London. But all the major centers of immigrant settlement in the United States— Boston, Philadelphia, Baltimore, Chicago— had their own versions of this grim underworld, blighted by lost hope, high crime, unemployment and abominable sanitation.

Housing conditions were not much better for the poor of European cities. In Berlin in 1901, more than 45 percent of all dwellings consisted of one or two rooms only. In London the percentage was lower at 35; in Paris it stood at over 55, and in Glasgow at over 70.

In most of the cities of Continental Europe, Scotland and North America, whatever architectural shell encompassed their

living space the poor lived in the closest proximity within it. Smoke, smells and noise were their constant companions. Most families consisted of an adult couple plus several children and often an aged relative and a lodger as well. This meant that overcrowding was the norm and rooms could rarely be used for one purpose only. Baths, when taken at all, were taken in the room where you ate, because that was where water could be heated. Children usually slept two or three or more to a bed, sometimes top-to-tail, divided by gender or age for the sake of "decency." Parents, and often lodgers, slept in the same room, which made passion a furtive business.

The poorest of the poor slept on rags and straw and sat on tea chests and orange boxes. Even those who were working could rarely afford cabinets or closets and kept their few possessions in chests stowed under beds, hanging on wall-pegs or ranged on open shelves if they were objects in daily use. A solid-fuel stove supplied the only heat for cooking and hot water and had to be kept going all day, even in sweltering summers.

In the tenements it was often necessary to haul both fuel and water up from street level or to use a shared wash-house built in the back yard. Washing and drying clothes was therefore a major chore and much less frequently done than in better-off households. Cooking was liable to be limited to one-pot dishes, such as soups and stews, or else to whatever could be fried up in a pan. Home economists declared that the poor could not possibly afford canned goods, store-bought bread, sausages, salted fish, cheese and other prepared foods. In fact, these often made up their basic diet because the more elaborate preparation involved in roasting and baking brought such households to chaos.

The table the family ate at was the same one at which the mother earned a few pennies by assembling matchboxes or stitching cheap garments. The same greasy towel might be used for wiping hands, windows, pans and the baby's behind. Vermin abounded—one doctor working in the Gorbals district of Glasgow at the turn of the century had to tie string round the bottoms of his pants when he visited the tenements to prevent rats from climbing up them.

With servants and without them

In 1900 the great social dividing line was between those who employed a servant of

CONDEMNED This photograph of a tenement block in Glasgow's notorious Gorbals district was taken in the 1950s shortly before the clearance of Glasgow's slums began.

some sort and those who did not. For the middle and upper classes, servants were a necessity, not a luxury. Advertisements for domestic appliances invariably showed them being used by a maid in cap and apron, rather than by a housewife herself. Anyone who could afford a carpet-sweeper could almost certainly also afford to have someone to push it around for her.

In the "middling classes" there was a clear distance between those at the upper end, who had several domestics living in, and those at the bottom, who paid for a sturdy girl to come in once a week to do the laundry, scrub the floors, clean the toilets and scour the pans. But this gap was less significant socially than the one between families who could afford even a little help and the families who sent their womenfolk out to provide it.

The First World War and its aftermath brought noticeable changes to this and other aspects of middle-class life. In Germany many middle-class people saw their way of life disappear altogether as catastrophic hyperinflation in the early 1920s wiped out the value of their property and savings. Elsewhere, the change was less dramatic, though it still made itself felt—in the so-called servant shortage, for example. Not only were fewer women willing to tie themselves to the long hours habitually demanded of them in service; but, having experienced

Life in "Middletown"

American lifestyle patterns between the wars were changing. In 1925 the sociologists Helen and Robert Lynd produced a study of the lives of 40 "business class" housewives in "Middletown" (actually Muncie, Indiana). They showed that on average these women used only about half the number of servant-hours per week that their mothers had—and paid five times as much for them. Yet, almost all of them possessed a range of labor-saving electric appliances.

Efficient washing machines, for example, enabled them to dispense with the services of a laundress. In 1932 the Secretary of the

MODERN CONVENIENCES No gadget that could help do housework was too outrageous, like the miniature washing machine (left). By the 1950s, the middle-class kitchen (above) became a virtual showroom for labor-saving electrical appliances.

wartime employment in factories and with growing opportunities opening up for them in offices, they also expected to be paid much more. In the England of 1914, £100 (about $500) a year would have paid the wages of a cook and four maids; ten years later it paid for only a cook and a housemaid.

For the very rich this made little difference, though the American model of a "service apartment" did spread across the Atlantic, where central heating did away with the need for someone to light and stoke half a dozen fires each day and even meals could be ordered from a central kitchen.

For the middle classes, however, it meant that the housewife now did more of her routine housework with her own hands and spent less time making sure that it had been done

properly by someone else. Advertisers no longer presented labor-saving devices as something one bought for the staff but as miracle-working innovations which would give back to the housewife some of the leisure hours she remembered her mother having. When General Electric unveiled the "kitchen of tomorrow" at the 1939 World's Fair in New York, one appliance was celebrated with this little ditty: "With a dishwasher so very fast and sanitary / She'd never break another dish—'twas plain / And the work she most despised / was completely modernized / when the garbage went like magic—down the drain." Sales of vacuum cleaners, electric irons, kettles and toasters boomed in response to this new demand. For the same reason new houses for the relatively affluent began to be built rather smaller; less space meant less to clean. Even having stainless-steel knives, instead of silver ones, helped, getting rid of one more messy, time-consuming job.

ALL IN A WEEK'S WORK

In 1918 the *American Journal of Home Economics* published an account of the household routine of Marion Woodbury, the wife of a university professor and mother of three small children. Describing herself as a woman who "did her own work," she did not feel that the assistance of a weekly laundress and a student part-timer contradicted this.

Mrs. Woodbury estimated that she put in ten hours' work a day, five days a week, plus five hours on Wednesdays and Sundays. Monday was her day for stripping dirty linen from beds and gathering dirty towels from the bathroom and then assembling the week's washing, which she put in to soak overnight. On Tuesday the laundress came in to do the actual washing and give the kitchen and bathroom their weekly once-over. Mrs. Woodbury meanwhile focused on darning, letting out clothes and other sewing tasks. On Wednesday the laundress came in again for half a day to iron. Thursday meant replenishing the linen cupboard and wardrobes.

Having a telephone, Mrs. Woodbury was able to order most of her groceries, which were brought to her home by an errand boy—in effect, another part-time helper. Actually going to market only took up a Friday afternoon every other week.

Mrs. Woodbury did all the cooking and ate meals with her children, but the clearing away and washing up were done by a student helper, who also baby-sat when needed. The student also did most of the dusting, sweeping and floor polishing, leaving Mrs. Woodbury to do only superficial straightening-up.

Mrs. Woodbury's housework therefore consisted more of supervising than carrying out manual tasks. It allowed her to pursue the more creative aspects of housework, such as cooking and needlework, and gave her time for social and charitable activities.

American Washing Machine Manufacturers Association announced triumphantly that for the first time ever this severely practical appliance was being offered for sale on New York's fashionable Fifth Avenue and shrewdly noted that "an entirely new class, never before directly interested in the washing process or in the details of household economics has come into the buying market . . . These housewives have the money to buy anything."

A follow-up study of Middletown in 1935 showed that 40 percent of such homes had also acquired a refrigerator. Whereas in 1910 the affluent American housewife had been a manager of people, a quarter of a century later she was a manager of technology.

Even in the booming United States the affluent were still a minority, but the urban poor did also benefit to some extent from modern conveniences. A 1926 study of the working-class population of Zanesville, Ohio, revealed that nine homes out of every ten had running water and gas; three-quarters had electricity; seven out of ten had a telephone and six out of ten had an indoor toilet and a bath. The larger electric appliances,

BARE MINIMUM Although standards of living had improved for many by the 1960s, there were still areas of great poverty, as seen in this sharecroppers' shack in South Carolina.

however, which would have taken much of the drudgery out of raising a big family, were still beyond their means. A washing machine would cost a factory worker the equivalent of an entire month's wages.

Living conditions were much worse among America's rural poor, especially in the South and among the black community. A 1934 survey of 200 Tennessee tenant farmers showed that only 4 percent could afford electricity and none had running water. Other investigations made in the same year established that four-fifths of Missouri farmhouses lacked a kitchen sink with a drain, 93 percent in Kentucky had no bathroom, and 75

STATE OF THE ART A porcelain sink of 1900 (top, left) contrasts with the sparkling stainless-steel surfaces of a 1990s Australian sink (bottom, left). The kitchen of tomorrow (above)—a 1955 vision from Frigidaire.

percent in supposedly prosperous Washington state had no flush toilet. As late as 1940 only a third of American homes had central heating, only half had a bath and only two-thirds had running water.

Ideal homes

In Europe, too, changing lifestyles from the interwar years through to the end of the century brought changing homes. The 1920s and 30s saw some notable experiments, all in their different ways attempts to rethink what made a home attractive and convenient. In the mid 1920s, in the German city of Dessau, the architect Walter Gropius—a leader of the Bauhaus movement, a later offshoot of the arts and crafts and Art Nouveau styles—built startlingly avant-garde houses, all straight lines and large glass windows, to accommodate teachers at his school of arts and design. Around the same time, the Swiss-born Le Corbusier, near the start of his career, built a model "workers' city" of 40 houses at Pessac near Bordeaux. In Vienna in the 1930s, the socialist city authorities constructed huge apartment blocks for working-class families, the most famous of which was the Karl Marx Hof built around three sides of a common garden, with a railway station next door so that people living there were just 15 minutes from the city's center.

FACE OF THE FUTURE? A housing project (top) in St. Louis, Missouri, is near completion in 1956. In striking contrast are wartime hut homes (above) near Los Angeles Harbor.

Less revolutionary in intent were the mass-produced "dream houses" put up by speculative builders, catering to people's desire for privacy and life in a respectable neighborhood. These remained a feature of both European and American cities, towns and suburbs through the rest of the century,

though the precise dimensions of the dream changed over the decades, tending to become smaller as the paraphernalia of home life became more compact. In 1919, the author of the British manual *Ideal Workers' Homes* envisaged working-class occupants having some 900–1,000 sq. ft. to move around in, not much short of the 1,100 sq. ft. typical of a 1990s four-bedroom executive estate house. The basic format was that of a cottage, with a front parlor and a back living room, with a scullery off it. The ground floor also had a pantry and storage space for a bicycle and a baby carriage. Some sample designs boasted extra fittings, such as wall-mounted drop-flap tables and built-in dressers.

The 1922 *Daily Mail Book of Bungalows*, aimed at mid-market British purchasers, assumed a 1,500 sq. ft. overall floor plan and still allowed space for a maid's bedroom and sitting room. The principal rooms in its homes were not labeled parlor and living room but more grandly as drawing room and

dining room. There were often double doors between them so that they could be used en suite. Larger models had a vestibule, to take coats and umbrellas, as well as a spacious hall, where handsome items of furniture could be displayed.

In the 1950s, a generation and another world war later, "open plan" was all the rage, with dividing walls taboo. Houses were no longer thought of as arranged sets of rigid boxes but fluid volumes of space. Many owners of existing properties knocked through the wall between front parlor and back living room to create a "through lounge"—a trend that carried on until the end of the century.

For a while, in the 1950s and 60s, period features went out of fashion in favor of streamlined modernism. Molded plaster ceilings and parquet floors were removed or covered with plastic tiling. Paneled wooden doors were disguised with hardboard and their brass handles and fingerplates were replaced with shiny new ones in plastic,

SMART SIMPLICITY Advanced taste in 1962 favored "open plan" layouts for an airy atmosphere. Even the houses were portable: a home in a 1950s Long Island suburb (below) was shifted to make way for a new road, and later reinstalled when the road was finished.

chrome or aluminum—later, in the 70s and 80s, fashion changed course again and many of these features were laboriously reinstated.

Central heating became a virtual necessity in the post-Second World War decades, as did wall-to-wall carpeting. Open-tread staircases were briefly popular but proved hazardous to families with small children. Later, as these children grew into teenagers with a fondness for loud music, the concept of

shared living space began to pall, though sliding doors helped, providing partitions when needed.

In the 1950s, American design innovations like split-level and L-shaped rooms, "conversation pits," and freestanding fireplaces swept the nation. Though most European homes were too small to indulge in these eccentricities, richer Europeans, learning about the latest fashions from American films, eagerly incorporated them into their spacious residences. Large picture windows were taken over from the American ranch house style and featured widely in European homes built in the 1960s. Later, novel devices such as solar panels for heating were tried out—though these were obvious-

HOMES FOR HEROES

In 1945, when millions of American GIs returned from World War II, triumphant, battle-weary and ready to settle down, the nation realized that there were simply not enough homes to accommodate them all. One enterprising American, William J. Levitt, knew what it would take to solve this housing crisis. By applying Henry Ford's technique of assembly line production to the housing industry, Levitt realized he could build cheap, middle-class

SOLUTION Levittown applied assembly-line techniques to the problem of creating adequate housing for GIs returning from the war.

houses fast. Levitt employed an army of construction workers, each given one of 27 specialized tasks, and in 1947, began building identical, box-like structures on 6,000 acres of potato fields 25 miles east of Manhattan. Costing less than $7,000 and heavily subsidized by the new GI Bill, these houses were perfect for young, middle-class families. In just four years, Levittown boasted 17,447 houses and 82,000 newly suburban residents.

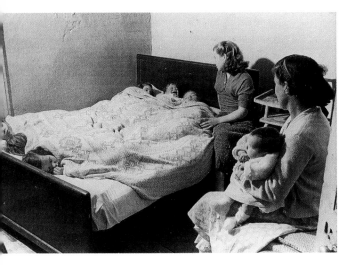

ROOM TO BREATHE? In Liverpool in the 1950s, large areas of housing were condemned as damp and overcrowded. In this household the children sleep six to a bed.

ly more suitable for the sunny southern climates than for overcast northern ones.

Late developers

Germany, Britain and the United States all saw feverish building activity through most of the interwar and postwar decades. France lagged behind, adding little to her housing stock between 1914 and 1954. A quarter of what was built in France in the interwar period was simply replacing what had been destroyed during the First World War. Rent controls, hastily introduced in 1914 to protect soldiers' families from profiteering landlords, had never been lifted, making building for renting out too unprofitable to be worthwhile and encouraging landlords of existing properties to allow them to fall into premature decay. Defeat and occupation after 1940

SUBURBAN RANCHES Ranch-style homes are firm favorites in Johannesburg's middle-class suburbs. There is room for garden barbecues and even a swimming pool.

brought such building activity as there was to a halt in France, and in the immediate postwar period industrial recovery, rather than home building, was the number one national priority.

France made gradual improvement in the following decades, though rigid regulations, local government corruption, and speculator profiteering further marred continuing efforts to rehouse the nation. In 1954, 42 percent of French homes had no running water and 93 percent had no refrigerator. A decade and a half later, in 1968, no less than 52 percent of all homes dated from before 1914, many being in an appalling state of disrepair.

The situation was much more favorable in the United States, where the building industry enjoyed greater efficiency through the use of prefabricated materials and the standardization of parts. In the decade after

LOVE OF GADGETS

America's love affair with the convenient appliance has only deepened in recent years. According to one survey, in 1993 nearly 10% of all households enjoyed internet access, 98.3% had televisions, 83.4% had radios, 77% had clothes washers, 71% had dryers, 45% had dishwashers, 84% had microwaves, and 28.5% had toasters—and the numbers were climbing in all but the last category.

1948, Americans bought some 13 million new homes. The housing market has continued to thrive in recent years. In 1995, 1,354,000 new privately owned houses were built. The average space of a one family home that year was 2,095 square feet, and almost three-quarters of them had between four and seven rooms.

At the end of the 1990s, more than half of all American homes were owner-occupied; the figure was similar in France as well, though it is well below the proportion attained in European countries like Italy, Belgium and Spain over a decade previously. In other countries of Europe, however, home-ownership was as much a matter of cultural preference as of economics. In affluent Sweden, Germany and the Netherlands, for example, almost 60 percent of the population still chose to rent their homes rather than build or buy them.

Death of the hearth

The way people lived at home was still changing as the 20th century drew to its close. In 1900 a typical home, almost anywhere in the Western world, was occupied by five, six or more people, was subject to drafts and heated by coal. Warmth in the form of an open fireplace or a stove provided the focus for family life. By the interwar period this focus had a rival in the form of the radio. A generation later the radio had, in most homes, lost the battle to the television set and solid-fuel heating had given way

MODERN AFFLUENCE Densely packed apartment blocks are still the favored style in Barcelona (left), while expensive austerity is the keynote of a Thames-side penthouse in 1990s London (right). Solar panels stud the roofs of "cube houses" in Rotterdam (below).

to gas, electricity, radiators or even ducted air circulating through grilles.

With the arrival of the phonograph and radio in the interwar years the home became a center for entertainment—a trend that was reinforced in the postwar decades by the advent of hi-fi, television, VCRs, CD players, computers, cable TV and satellite receivers. But whereas whole families had once gathered together to "listen in" after supper, increasingly the entertainment came to be provided for an audience of two, or even one, as individual members of the family started to entertain themselves separately, and as single-person households became more common, especially in big cities. Even people living

SUNSHINE CITY A futuristic house in Arizona has all the latest gadgets. In such regions solar technology may come to supply all the energy needed for domestic efficiency.

together wanted to be apart. By 1960 rent allowances to the poor in New York were calculated on the assumption that a four-person family needed a five-room apartment—a degree of luxury almost inconceivable to a family half a century earlier.

This shift was reflected in falling demand across the Western world for larger family homes and the construction of more compact residences, apartment buildings and sheltered complexes for the retired and the elderly. Most large terraced houses in inner-city areas, originally built for wealthy families with servants, were subdivided into small self-contained apartments; when the lots were large, the houses were torn down and high-rise apartment buildings built. Many residents, now living alone, became increasingly concerned about security, so homes were routinely fitted with window locks.

At the same time, greater environmental awareness and rising energy costs prompted many householders and homebuilders to invest in better insulation and double glazing. Experimental energy-efficient houses were being built and "smart" houses with computers that automatically controlled heating and lighting to optimum efficiency no longer appeared the stuff of science fiction. As the 21st century dawned, homes looked set to change even faster than they had in the past 100 years.

CONTRASTING STYLES A French family in the 1950s enjoy a celebratory drink in a rather formal home setting (left). The dinner table was the focus for most family occasions and meals were when many working families spent time together. The advent of radio created a new setting for family socializing. The programs of the 1930s and 1940s found a wide audience across the United States as people of diverse age and social status found common enjoyment of their favorite programs. The midwestern family shown listening to the radio (below, left) were typical of families across America who tuned in to hear programs like "Fibber McGee and Molly" and The Jack Benny Program. Rarely did all members of the family watch the same television programs or listen to the same music. Homes changed over the course of the century as families changed, often with more easy-going attitudes between generations—along with a loss of family cohesiveness. An "arty" New York interior towards the end of the century (below) presents a more relaxed scene.

THE WORLD ON OUR DOORSTEP

WE ARE MORE MOBILE NOW THAN EVER. DURING THE 20TH CENTURY THE WORLD ON OUR DOORSTEP HAS STEADILY EXPANDED ITS LIMITS

The family car, more probably than anything else, has transformed our relationship with the world on our doorstep, and well beyond it, during the 20th century. Apart from air travel, the transport revolution of the 19th century had already introduced most of the key forms of public transport, from trolley to

AT HOME ON WHEELS An American mother and daughter enjoy the paneled luxury of a 1905 Pullman railway carriage.

train, that are with us to this day. But none of these offered the degree of freedom to go where one liked, when one liked, at the pace one liked, that the family car would give growing numbers of people during the course of the 20th century. At the start of the century, when the motor car was still predominantly a toy of the rich, the bicycle offered many people a chance to roam more freely than ever before. The mass-produced automobile, invented by Henry Ford, would extend that

freedom to much wider horizons. It would also bring its own problems, as urban traffic congestion in the late 20th century made many people take a fresh look at the virtues of public transport.

For its part, public transport has seen refinements, improvements—and drastic changes. In 1900 there was no challenger to the railway and ocean liner for travelling long distances. This remained true for most of the first half of the century. But air travel, once properly established after the Second World War, changed all that, transforming both intercontinental travel—previously the

EARLY AUTOMATION A customer buys a ticket from a machine in London's Underground in 1928.

domain of the oceanliner—and long-distance travel within continents—previously the domain of the railway. The great liners of the past have long since gone, their successors devoted to holiday cruises. The railways, however, have fought back more successfully. Japan's highly efficient Bullet Train and France's TGV (Train à Grand Vitesse), which travels at speeds of up to 320 mph are proof of the value of modern high-speed rail links.

Local transport, meanwhile, has had its ups and downs. At the start of the century, London had an expanding underground

CAPITAL SYSTEMS The Paris Métro's first stations were built in the Art Nouveau style. New trains transformed London's Underground in the 1930s.

most long-haul journeys in the Western world for the next half century. But already electrification was promising new standards of speed, smoothness and reliability for shorter-haul journeys—the Italians inaugurated their first mainline electric service as early as 1902. Then came the diesel engine. The Germans began operating a two-car diesel service between Berlin and Hamburg in 1932. Later in the same decade, long-haul diesel engines, capable of cruising at 90 mph, were introduced on American

CABLE CARS TO THE STARS The cable cars of San Francisco turned that city into a bustling metropolis at the beginning of the 20th century (below), and continue to provide public transportation and tourist-pleasing scenes (right).

railways. The journey from Chicago to Los Angeles (some 1,746 miles) was cut from a pre-First World War average of almost 60 hours to just under 40. Other countries followed suit, though more gradually—Britain, for example, did not finally phase out its last steam locomotives until 1968.

Some long-distance rail journeys in the first half of the century could be undertaken in what were virtually hotels on wheels. Europe had its legendary Orient Express, linking Paris with Istanbul. The United States had several such services. The New York Central's Twentieth Century Limited service to Chicago, inaugurated in 1902, had two buffet cars, a library and a smoking car,

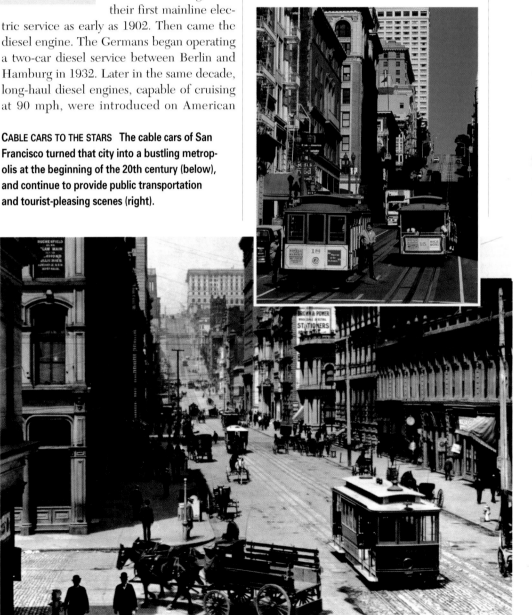

railway system, and other cities were following suit—Paris opened its Métro in 1900, Berlin its U-Bahn in 1902 and New York its Subway in 1904. In 1933 the British capital again set a worldwide trend when it created the London Passenger Transport Board, integrating the operations and timetables of all its underground, bus, streetcar and trolley lines. In recent years, as the population of cities continues to increase, the subway has become even more indispensable to their well-being. Four million New Yorkers ride it every day—more than half of the city's population. With its frequently cramped spaces and inevitable breakdowns, it has become, for many, a symbol of the convenience—and the frustrations—of urban life.

Change on the rails

Although the railways have held their own through the 20th century, just about everything about them has changed. In 1900 steam reigned supreme, and would do for

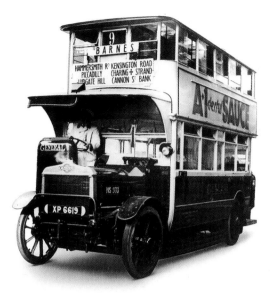

OPEN ALL HOURS The driver of this 1929 London double-decker bus still has to sit in an open cab, while the passengers are glassed in against the elements.

two observation cars and a dozen drawing-room and stateroom cars. The Santa Fe Railway's Chicago-Los Angeles service, inaugurated in 1911, had business travelers in mind, offering them the services of a stenographer, daily market reports and access to telephones at stations en route, as well as the comforts of a library, club room, barber, bathing facilities and Pullman sleeping cars with brass beds. Further refinements on the American rail network came in the 1930s with stream-lined stainless-steel carriages, complete with air conditioning.

By the interwar years, the European railways were facing a serious challenge from the roads. Trucks, offering door-to-door delivery, were cutting into much of their freight business. Charabancs (sight-seeing coaches) began to challenge them for passenger traffic, particularly for excursions and touring holidays. The railways responded with electrification and more comfortable rolling stock.

In 1936 a London-Paris overnight service was introduced which took sleeping cars right onto the Dover-Dunkirk ferry linking England and France, enabling passengers to sleep on undisturbed. Another response was for governments to take over and run the increasingly unprofitable railways as public

services. France completed the nationalization of its network in 1938, before the Second World War; Britain carried out its own nationalization ten years later in 1948. The United States did not nationalize its railroads until 1970, with the creation of the National Railroad Passenger Corporation, which later became AMTRAK.

The 1950s brought airline competition on intercity routes, beginning in North America. In 1959, American Airlines inaugurated a new transcontinental jet service that could shuttle a passenger from Los Angeles to New York in only 5 hours. These airlines first vied for passengers and soon afterwards for high-value or perishable freights. The American and Canadian railways, still privately owned, were severely pruned, while across the Atlantic, in 1963 the British government closed down 2,128 stations and a quarter of the nation's rail network. In 1995 the Canadian Pacific Railway finally closed down its transcontinental rail service—which had originally been created in the 1880s as a way of uniting the nation.

High-speed trains held the key to the railways' survival in the late 20th century. This was symbolized by the inauguration in 1964 of Japan's 130 mph Bullet Train between Tokyo and Kyoto, the two major venues for the Olympic Games that year. The opening

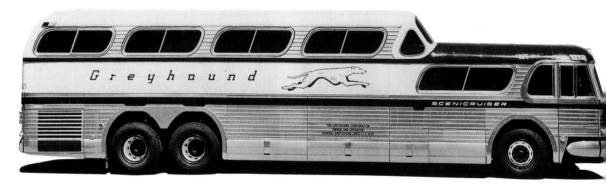

OBSERVATION CAR The design of the General Motors Scenicruiser imitated railway observation cars to give its 43 passengers a clear view on long cross-country journeys.

of the Channel Tunnel, bringing London and Paris within three hours of each other by 1995, was another milestone, allowing passengers to travel from the center of one city to the center of the other, with little bother. These long-haul journeys by rail were no

longer luxurious affairs with drawing rooms and observation cars, but in the age of executive travel they could match the airlines within a continent or country for speed and convenience.

For travel within cities in the beginning of the century, the subway was the most convenient and advanced mode of travel. The London Underground, a subsurface steam-powered system dating from the 1860s, had been supplemented in the 1890s with a true Underground system, set hundreds of feet deep and electrically powered. It could whisk a Londoner from one end of the city

KISSING AND TIMETABLES

In 1910 France banned kissing on railways on the grounds that amorous couples were delaying train departures and thereby fouling up the timetables.

to the other in a matter of minutes, avoiding the noise and congestion of the streets above for just pennies. Encouraged by the success of the British, New Yorkers began building their own underground supersystem. Inspired by the slogan, "Fifteen Minutes to Harlem," and with the rest of the city closely monitoring their progress, by 1903 10,000 workers had excavated 3,508,000 cubic yards of earth. When the IRT (the Interborough Rapid Transit) was inaugurated on October 27, 1904, 150,000 eager New Yorkers showed up for a ride. In just a decade, 726 miles of tracked snaked its way under the city's asphalt.

But only very large and wealthy cities could contemplate the expense of an underground railway. Most cities, in both Europe and North America and well beyond, relied on the vehicle running on tracks and driven from overhead powerlines that the British

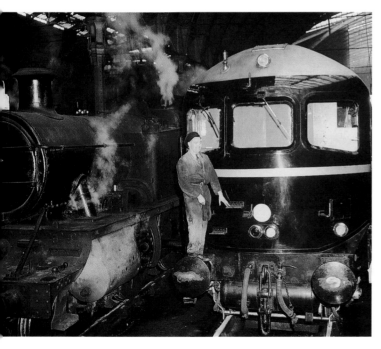

STEAM OR GAS? Gas-turbine locomotives (above) were an experiment of the 1950s. In the end, diesel and electricity won the day, replacing traditional steam power.

called a tram and the Americans a trolley car or streetcar. The trolley was then entering its heyday. By 1917 the U.S. alone had 80,000 trolley cars carrying 11 billion passengers a year. It would have been possible, if somewhat laborious, to travel from eastern Wisconsin all the way to New York, a distance of more than 1,000 miles, just by changing from one trolley system to the next at each terminal. Later, the trolley bus—electrically driven from overhead powerlines but without tracks—was introduced in many cities, notably in Italy.

The trolley made possible a new feature of urban living: the working-class suburb. Now manual workers, as well as the middle classes, could afford to commute to and from their places of work each day. The trolley also opened up the countryside to them. Indeed, trolley routes often defined the

HARD TRAVELING Early cars, like this 1925 Ford Model T (a designation often mistakenly attached to other models), shared the road with horse-drawn wagons. (Is that a shadow of a horse's head in the lower right corner?) The building of a great interstate road system in the early 1940s, which began in the east with the Pennsylvania Turnpike (top), opened the road—and America's natural beauty—to American motorists.

boundaries of a city. Where the lines ended, the countryside, by definition, began. At weekends the young and the poor could refresh their lungs simply by riding to the end of the line and then wandering off into fields and forests.

In many parts of northern Europe—Scandinavia, Germany and the Low Countries—the clatter and clang of trolleys as they rattled along their tracks would remain one of the characteristic and endearing sounds of urban life. Elsewhere, however, they were ousted by the motorbus. At the start of the century, this was a rudimentary, extremely noisy vehicle, often with an open upper deck. But in 1920 Frank and William Fageol of Oakland, California, produced a bus specifically designed for carrying passengers in comfort. It had a low floor for easier boarding, an inside seat for the driver, upholstered seats for passengers and a smooth braking system. With no overhead powerlines, the bus had the great advantage of flexibility and by

the 1960s many cities had abandoned their trolley-bus services. The bus is, however, much more of a polluter than its rivals, and as people became more aware of the dangers of pollution some cities turned back to older forms of transport.

Long-distance bus services, meanwhile, flourished. By 1933, the Greyhound company in the United States was operating a network covering 40,000 miles. Sixty years later, in 1993, American intercity bus services were still carrying 350 million passengers a year, and for 15,000 American communities bus services were the only form of public transport available to them.

The not so open road

Motoring was an adventure at the start of the century; there was virtually nothing

streamlined about it. Some manual braking systems relied on the strength of the motorist's arm to halt the vehicle. Crank-starting a car could dislocate a thumb or even bring on a heart attack. Speedometers and fuel gauges were sold as extras. Drivers and passengers, exposed to the elements, went swathed in fur-lined garments, gauntlets and goggles which could cost almost as much as a car itself. Without a net-work of filling stations (hotels and pharma-

WRAP UP!   Clothing manufacturers developed an extensive range of ingenious headgear to protect the hairstyles and complexions of Edwardian lady motorists.

cists were the earliest gasoline distributors), touring motorists were advised to strap cans of fuel around their vehicles to avoid run-ning out. Breakdowns were expected to hap-pen daily; hotels provided pits where chauf-feurs could make repairs at night.

Even so, by 1900 there were more than 8,000 Americans who owned cars, and some 40 companies competing to produce them. Whereas in the previous decade the car was a luxury affordable only to the rich—the average list price of one in 1900 was over $1,000, more than any working class family could spare—new production techniques soon brought the cost down to a more rea-sonable figure: in 1903, one could buy Ransom P. Olds's compact "Olds-mobile" for just $650. In Europe, too, the automobile revved and roared its way into respectability. British motorists were enjoying the repeal of the "Red Flag" Act in 1896, which had restricted drivers to a speed of 4 mph. France and Germany were the biggest European car pro-ducers with the names Daimler, Benz, Peugeot and Renault already prominent. Initially Britain imported most of its cars from France, but by 1914 there were some 200 British firms man-ufacturing vehicles. In par-ticular Rolls-Royce, founded in 1904, had shown what

could be done at the luxury end of the mar-ket. Its 1906 Silver Ghost set an endurance record—running some 14,000 miles without a breakdown—which stood for half a century.

But it was the United States that became the world's first motorized society. Already, the first motoring association, the American Motor League, had been founded in Chicago in November 1895—11 days earlier than its first European counterpart, the Automobile Club de France. The American Automobile Association was founded in 1902. License plates were required in Massachusetts from 1903 onwards. In the same year a Packard made the first transcon-tinental crossing by car—in 52 days (by 1909 the time was down to 21 days). In 1905 the Society of Automotive Engineers came into existence to encourage standardization of parts among manufacturers.

Then, in 1908, Henry Ford produced the first of his famous automobiles. His revolu-tionary aim was to turn out cheap and reliable vehicles that would convert the motor car from a rich person's plaything to the ordinary person's necessity. As he once vowed, the Model T "will be so low in price that no man making a good salary will be unable to own one—and enjoy with his family the blessing of hours of pleasure in God's great open spaces." To this end, in 1913 he adopted the assembly-line production method, which he had first

CARS EVERYWHERE   The automobile has inspired much engineering creativity, as in this 1940s attempt to create a flying car.

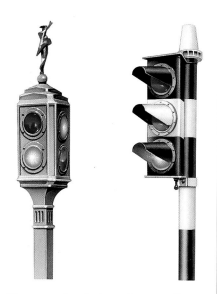

seen in action in Chicago meat-packing plants. In so doing, he transformed not only the automobile industry but all kinds of manufacturing as his methods were adopted in the production of everything from vacuum cleaners to domestic irons. Demand for the

WHERE'S THE FIRE?

In 1906, Wayne, Pennsylvania, became the first town in the United States to use a gasoline-powered fire engine. Other cities were slower to make the transition from horse-drawn carriages; the New York Fire Department retired its last team of horses in 1922. Residents lined the streets to cheer the carriages for their final, heroic run down Broadway.

Tin Lizzie, as the car was affectionately named, shot up. By 1925 half of all the cars in the world were Model T's.

Motor transport had come to stay. In 1910 an advertisement threw American businessmen and farmers the challenging query: "Can your horses deliver your goods fast enough?" It then promised that "Packard trucks can. Three tons—twelve miles an hour." A copywriter for Maxwell (later Chrysler) asserted more whimsically: "Life holds many big days. Two stand out prominently—the day a man marries and the day he buys an automobile."

Road networks expanded massively to meet the new demands made upon them. By 1914 Gulf Oil was distributing free maps to American motorists, showing the hard-surfaced routes suitable for cars. From 1916 onwards the Federal government offered 50 percent subsidies for road-building, and by 1921 the U.S. had 387,000 miles of surfaced roads. The Lincoln Highway, constructed between 1913 and 1927 to link New York and San Francisco, was the first fully paved transcontinental route.

In Europe, the Italian dictator Benito Mussolini set about building the first autostrada—at that stage, a three-lane undivided highway—in his country in the 1920s. Later, German planners came up with the idea of the dual-lane carriageway, incorporating a stretch of it in a new road between Cologne and Bonn that opened in 1932. When he came to power, Adolf Hitler quickly spotted the strategic importance of such highways and ordered the rapid construction of a 4,350 mile network of autobahns across Germany, starting in 1934. In 1940 the Pennsylvania Turnpike was completed in the United States, a divided highway which traffic could enter or leave only via interchanges.

One worrying set of statistics was the toll of road deaths. In the period from 1903 to 1907 these had averaged 400 a year in the United States alone. In 1905 the *North American Review* noted that in just five months more Americans had been killed by cars than in the Spanish-American War of 1898. Road fatalities in the United States rose steadily to an average of 1,900 a year between 1908 and 1912, to 12,500 a year from 1918 to 1922, 33,700 in 1931, and reaching 39,643 in 1939.

Danger on the roads

Obviously, better safety regulations were needed. In 1902, Minneapolis's first speeding ticket—for ten dollars—was awarded to a motorist clocked at the daredevil speed of 10 miles per hour. The French authorities had required local motorists to pass a driving test since 1893 in Paris, and since 1899 throughout the rest of France. Other countries were slower to adopt this practice. In 1903 the British Parliament rejected proposals for driving tests, vehicle inspections and penalties for drunk drivers. By 1935,

however, matters were taken more seriously. Parliament introduced compulsory driving tests that year and a number of other measures during the same decade, including specialized traffic police, standardized traffic signs, a Highway Code of traffic regulations, a 30 mph urban speed limit and "cat's-eye" road reflectors.

The first electric traffic lights, using a red and a green light (and a buzzer to warn motorists that the light was about to change) had been installed in Cleveland, Ohio, in 1914. The New York authorities introduced a system using the now-familiar red, amber and green lights in 1918. Paris had a kind of traffic light by 1923; it was a large *Halte* sign on glass with a light behind that could be switched on and off and had a gong to warn drivers that it was about to change. A system similar to the New York one was installed in London's West End in 1926. Also in London, pedestrian crossings, introduced in the late

TRAVELS WITH CHARLEY... AND JOHN

In 1962 John Steinbeck published *Travels with Charley*, an account of his cross-country road trip with his elderly pet poodle. The book is filled with Steinbeck's meditations on American life, the landscape, and the magical, sometimes frightening experience of driving :

"I sought out US 90, a wide gash of super-highway, multiple-lane carrier of the nation's goods. The minimum speed on this road was greater than any I had previously driven. I drove into a wind quartering in from my starboard bow and felt the buffeting, sometimes staggering blows of the gale I helped to make. I could hear the sough of it on the square surfaces of my camper top. Instructions screamed at me from the road once: 'Do not stop! No stopping. Maintain speed.' Trucks as long as freighters went roaring by, delivering a wind like the blow of a fist. These great roads are wonderful for moving goods but not for the inspection of a countryside. You are bound to the wheel and your eyes to the car ahead and to the rear-mirror for the car behind and the side mirror for the car or truck about to pass, and at the same time you must read all the signs for fear you may miss some instructions or orders...When we get these thruways across the whole country, as we will and must, it will be possible to drive from New York to California without seeing a single thing."

1920s and 1930s, reduced pedestrian fatalities by 20 percent.

Meanwhile, motor cars were changing the shape of cities. Suburbs continued to grow faster and spread farther throughout the 1940s as people took advantage of the new mobility that allowed them to live farther from their places of work. During the 40s, the population outside the central city core grew by over 30 percent in Buffalo and Chicago, 40 percent in Cleveland, 50 per cent in Atlanta and a staggering 70 percent in Baltimore, Dallas and Denver.

By the 1950s, the automobile represented the core of the American economy and was deemed essential to the American lifestyle. Motor manufacturers were the nation's industrial giants. A poll in 1951 showed that Americans made 80 percent of their vacation trips by car, the average trip lasting 1,400 miles, traveled over 12 days. The motel—a word first coined in 1925—had become a distinctive national institution, and the latest automobile-related novelty was the drive-in movie. By 1955, 57 percent of American families living in cities with a population of more than 500,000 owned a car. In smaller cities and towns the proportion was a third

MOBILE AUDIENCE Drive-ins, such as this one in Salt Lake City, Utah, reached the peak of their popularity in the 1950s.

as high again, and in the countryside almost four-fifths of all families owned a car.

New age, new styles
Car styles changed rapidly in the decades following the Second World War. The

THIS WAY Motorists cope with a barrage of traffic signs—elements of roads everywhere— on Route 66 from Chicago to Los Angeles.

Volkswagen Beetle set new standards of cheap reliability, overtaking the Model T as the most popular car ever produced—more than 20 million had been sold by the early 1980s. The Chrysler Crown Imperial, the first car with power steering (1951), and the Mercedes 300SL (1953), the first with a fuel injection system, attracted drivers with technological advancements, while hot-wheels like the Corvette (1953) and the Ford Thunderbird (1955) introduced the American imagination to chrome and tail-fins. In the 1970's, the international oil crises put a premium on more compact family cars and encouraged motorists to abandon their "gas guzzlers." Around the same time, the Japanese entered the world auto scene as mass-producers of inexpensive, reliable cars.

The same decades also brought more regulations. New York introduced "meter maids" in 1960 to control traffic. The wearing of seat belts became compulsory in most countries. In Britain, the Breathalyzer, introduced in 1967, cut road deaths by 23 percent within three months.

Car ownership continued to rise. By 1987 the United States and Canada both had a car for every 1.7 people. In Canada 80 percent of all journeys to work and 90 percent of all intercity trips were made by car. New Zealand ranked next in car-ownership (one car for every 2.1 people) followed by West

Germany, Australia, Switzerland and Italy.

While all this brought new freedom for millions of people, it also brought a new crisis. Congestion was so acute that a single event, such as a visit by a president or foreign dignitary, could "gridlock" city traffic, bringing it to a virtual standstill.

Despite the mushrooming of parking garages, there were often more car drivers wanting to park in the downtown areas of the city than spaces available to them. Out-of-town shopping centers or malls, with ample parking and a variety of handy superstores, became popular—but they conjured up their own nightmare vision of more and more green fields being swallowed up and coated with asphalt.

The sheer frustrations of driving, with its traffic jams and parking difficulties, induced the phenomenon dubbed "road rage." Traffic fumes, too, were a danger. In the United States in 1996, vehicles released nearly 70,000 tons of carbon monoxide into the air; not surprisingly, then, the number of children afflicted with asthma has doubled in the last 15 years to 6 million.

It seemed that the freedom of the roads that had done so much to open up new horizons was beginning to turn sour. The age of the motor car was by no means over, and researchers were busy devising new generations of vehicles such as a "cleaner" electric car, but it was abundantly clear that the whole question of transport, public and private, would have to be rethought to avert a catastrophic overload in the 21st century.

HOME ECONOMY

IN 1900 ONLY AMERICANS WORE JEANS, ONLY ITALIANS ATE SPAGHETTI AND ONLY CRAFTSMEN AND SHOPKEEPERS WORKED WHERE THEY LIVED. BY THE 1990S, PASTA, SWEATSHIRTS AND THE INTERNET HAD SURPASSED NOTIONS OF A NATIVE LAND. DIVERSITY, CHOICE, DETACHMENT AND MOBILITY WERE THE HALLMARKS OF 20TH-CENTURY LIFESTYLES, AND THE DIFFERENCES BETWEEN NATIONAL TRADITIONS IN DRESS, FOOD AND WORK PRACTICES HAVE, TO A LARGE EXTENT, DISAPPEARED.

THE WAY WE WORKED

AS TECHNOLOGY HAS REDUCED TOIL AND INCREASED PRODUCTIVITY, IT HAS HELD OUT THE AGE-OLD CHIMERA OF A WORKLESS WORLD

On Thursday, July 31, 1902, the people of Sydney were stunned by news of a coal gas explosion at the Mount Kembla coal mine. Gas had never been detected there before, so safety lamps had never been issued and miners worked by the light of naked flames. On the day of the disaster, 260 men were working underground. Ninety-four were either killed by the explosion itself or poisoned by the gas. It was the worst catastrophe in Australia's mining history. The next day's issue of the *Sydney Morning Herald* took grim consolation in the fact that: "In this country we are not accustomed to these calamitous visitations, and industrial or other accidents on a large scale of tragedy are fortunately not so common with us as they are in the United States, for instance."

The work of the miner was generally acknowledged to be filthy, exhausting and dangerous. At the beginning of the 20th century, such work was more typical than exceptional. Even in the advanced economies such as those of Australia, the United States and Britain, most work was still manual and most workers ended their day's labor both tired and dirty. Accidents were common on farms, in factories, on docksides and building sites, at sea and in the transport industries. Work involving fast-moving machinery brought with it the risk of cuts, scalping and accidental amputation. Work with toxic

PRIMITIVE POWER When the 20th century opened, the economy of much of the world still depended on the most basic technology, powered by wind, water or animal muscle.

HANDMADE In 1900 boatbuilding remained a traditional industry in Europe, dependent on a high level of craft skills.

chemicals meant the near certainty of contracting diseases of the skin or respiratory system. Miners, however, were untypical of the manual labor force as a whole in at least two respects. They were moderately well paid and usually strongly unionized.

Worlds of work—new and old

At the beginning of the 20th century, it was reasonable to suppose that if you trained long and hard enough to get "a trade in your hands," this would keep you employed for the rest of your working life. As the century closed, however, it has become virtually certain that no skill, knowledge or expertise acquired in youth would last a lifetime in the labor market.

In 1913 almost half of all Americans were still living on farms and only a minority worked in manufacturing. Most of those who did were recent immigrants. Having no family farm or store to take over, they had to be versatile and adventurous. Fortunately, demand for industrial labor in the United States was expanding rapidly. Manufacturing might mean anything from rolling cigars by hand, like the trade-union pioneer Sam Gompers, to operating massive machinery for one of the nation's newly founded corporate giants such as US Steel (1901), Ford Motor Company (1903) or General Motors (1908). To paraphrase President Calvin Coolidge, the business of the American people was becoming business; the factory was becoming the American cathedral of the new century. A new sort of economy was clearly emerging, in which firms could grow into huge companies by making such novel products as rubber tires (Firestone, 1901), cosmetics (Elizabeth Arden, 1910) and even flavored chewing gum (Wrigley, 1911).

In Britain the economy was far more industrialized than in the United States, with less than 10 percent of the population getting their living from the land. But in British industry, the level of traditional craft skills remained high, with a seven-year apprenticeship still the normal way of acquiring them. In France and Germany on the eve of the First World War, more than 40 percent of the labor force still worked as farmers, fishermen or in forestry. But, thanks to Renault, France led the world in motor-car production. Germany had the leading electrical and chemical industries, headed by new firms such as Telefunken (1903) and I.G.Farben (1904). Italy was still overwhelmingly rural, less advanced industrially than Belgium, Switzerland or Sweden, and on the same level of average living standards as impoverished Portugal. But even Italy already had Fiat, Olivetti and Alfa-Romeo.

Man and machine

In the most advanced economies, a marked decline in the number of workers in food production was already being accompanied by huge increases in productivity. In 1900 the average American farm worker produced enough food for seven people; by 1940 the comparable figure would be ten and by 1950, it was 15.5. In 1901, the U.S. Industrial Commission was told that it took 100 minutes to shell a bushel of corn by hand, but that a steam-powered machine could perform the same task in 90 seconds. A combine harvester could reap an acre of wheat 40 times faster than a man. A machine perfected by A.K. Smith in 1903 could, in one continuous process, cut off a salmon's

MACHINE AGE Men work at lathes, connected by belts to a central power source, in a typical machine shop, around 1900.

head and tail, split and gut its body, and drop the residue into hot water, constantly adjusting its operations to match the dimensions of each individual fish. Smith's machine displaced Chinese hand-labor in canneries on the west coast. The introduction in 1911 of a machine that could top, tail and core 96 pineapples a minute had a similarly dramatic impact in Hawaii. Doughnut-making was

OLD AND NEW Large numbers of women still worked in traditional jobs in domestic service (below). New occupations, such as those in business, brought greater independence for women, as well as hazards, as this 1906 cartoon (right) suggests.

automated in the United States from 1921 onwards, and potato-peeling from 1925.

White-collar workers and women

Mass education, and the growing scale and complexity of commerce, combined to increase the employment in offices and shops of workers who could read, write and calculate. They were initially referred to as "black-coated" but later as "white-collar," a term first recorded in the United States in 1921. At work, as in the street, dress signaled status. Foremen were often distinguished by brown or gray warehouse coats and usually wore a collar and tie, and sometimes a bowler hat as well. The relatively clean working condi-

tions of white-collar workers were a mark of their exalted standing above the ranks of the blue-collar masses still involved in manual labor.

Over the course of the 20th century, the proportion of white-collar workers would steadily increase until they formed the majority of the workforce, first, by 1956, in North America, and then in Australia and Britain and other western countries. The typewriter and telephone, technological marvels initially entrusted mainly to male hands, had become female instruments of labor by 1900. Telephone exchanges at first employed teenage boys as operators, on the grounds that they would be quick to learn and cheap to pay. But they were often lax on the job and rude to callers. Women were soon judged to be both more reliable and much better mannered. Female "typewriters" (the word was at first applied to the operator as well as to the machine) proved both faster and cheaper than men. Private secretarial schools proliferated to teach shorthand, typing and basic bookkeeping. In 1900, 80 percent of all American stenographers and typists were women and by 1930, so was half the nation's entire clerical workforce.

Retailing, teaching, nursing and pharmacy were other sectors in which women were strongly represented. Niche markets for the talents of the gifted female included graphic art, studio photography, music and the stage. Even in liberal countries, however, professions that were, in theory, increasingly open to women were often closed in practice. According to the United States census of 1910, there were only 9,000 women doctors in the country and only 2 of the nation's 457 medical schools admitted women; in 1970, there was still more than ten times as many male doctors as female doctors. Women were even more poorly represented in the legal profession, for which an aggressively masculine disposition was considered a necessity. Though in 1920 nearly half of all college graduates were women, only 3 percent of the nation's lawyers were. As late as 1990, only 5 percent of all partners in law firms were women.

In the industrialized countries, a number of the traditional consumer goods industries, such as textiles, pottery, hosiery and food processing, continued to recruit women by the million. But the largest single employer of

WOMEN'S WORK Scottish fishwives pose at the English port of Great Yarmouth in 1905. Their work was to gut herrings in freezing cold water and pack them into barrels.

female labor in Europe and the United States at the start of the century was domestic service. Working hours were, by definition, even longer than the waking hours of those on whom they waited. Pay was low, but servants lived untaxed, and also usually ben-

efited from tips from visitors, cast-off clothes and the occasional travel. They could also usually count on medical care being paid for by their employers.

Turn of the century feminists and labor activists had mixed views on domestic service and its impact on women. Some decried the profession as exploitative—working hours were long, pay was low, and the women often had to deal with unwanted

HOMEWORK Much female labor involved the commercial exploitation of domestic skills such as garment-making. Reformers like Upton Sinclair (right) championed workers' rights.

advances from male employers. Others, however, viewed domestic service as a way for girls from poor homes to learn the manners and housekeeping skills of their "betters" and escape poverty.

Another profession, however, unified labor activists and reformers in condemnation of its brutal conditions: sweatshop labor. Toiling in grimy workshops and dimly-lit factories, "sweated workers," many of whom were female immigrants, made clothes, trimmings, lace, packaging, artificial flowers, dolls, brushes and chains. They often worked 16-hour-days for as little as fifty cents, starvation wages enabling retailers to make huge mark-ups. On March 25, 1911, in New York City, a tragedy exposed this shameful exploitation to the rest of the nation. Blazing through its wooden frame, a fire quickly swept through the ninth floor of the Triangle Shirtwaist Factory; the owners had locked the doors to prevent theft, and the workers, mostly Jewish and Italian women, were trapped inside. As the crowd below looked on in horror, 46 women

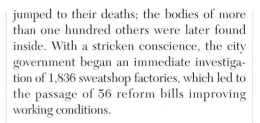

jumped to their deaths; the bodies of more than one hundred others were later found inside. With a stricken conscience, the city government began an immediate investigation of 1,836 sweatshop factories, which led to the passage of 56 reform bills improving working conditions.

Workers' rights and remuneration

Similar reform efforts were begun worldwide, as trade unionists joined forces with teachers and preachers to ban sweated and child labor by law. In 1908 an International Conference for the Protection of Labour called for the total prohibition of night work for children. Through the efforts of tireless reformers, legislation banning child labor completely passed in the U.S. Congress in 1916, but was struck down in the Supreme Court and did not become law until 1938. Significant though legislation and propaganda were, however, the gradual reduction of sweated and child labor was quite as much the by-product of new technologies, which made machines cheaper to employ than the cheapest hand labor. As a result, sweatshops have never disappeared completely. They were still commonplace in the 1990s in the manufacture of carpets in Pakistan or shirts in Thailand and Vietnam. Investigators also discovered thousands of children working in European countries such as Italy and Portugal, making shoes or garments.

Laws—often provoked by strike campaigns—were most successful in regulating working hours and conditions in large-scale, heavy industries, where huge concentrations of grown men made it easier to form unions than in trades where workers were dispersed or deeply divided by gender, age or race. In the first decade of the 20th century, major industrial confrontations were mounted by steelworkers in the United States, sailors in France, dockers in Germany, and miners almost everywhere. West Virginia miners, led by the imposing John Lewis, unionized themselves in 1920 and struck for better working conditions. The workers clashed with company police, and eventually, the National Guard had to be called in to restore order. Richard Mellon, the chairman of Pittsburgh Coal Company, grew so fearful of striking miners that he kept guards armed with machine guns in the pits as a deterrent.

Miners in Spain struck for the right to be paid weekly, rather than regularly run themselves into debt while waiting for their wages. And in 1905, British miners at last got a standard eight-hour day—although this did not include the hour or more it might take them to travel to or from the mine.

When governments and employers ganged up against them, unions responded by building their own alliances. In 1909, leaders of German and British workers met to compare conditions and to consult on common interests. In 1905, the Wobblies, as members of the Industrial Workers of the World were called, strove to create "one big union," uniting America's workers in solidarity. And in New York City, seamstresses, who had been working 10 hour days, six days a

CONFRONTING UNION STRENGTH The 1912 strike of textile workers in the wool mills of Lawrence, Massachusetts, lasted only a few days, but the use of state militia to control the strikers both invigorated and shook the union movement in the United States.

SLEEP-IN Welsh miners snatch a rest during the bitter Tonypandy dispute of 1910. Three hundred police were sent from London to curb riots with their truncheons.

week, for less than 39 cents a day, banded together to form the International Ladies' Garment Workers' Union.

Apart from limits on hours and the recognition of the right of unions to exist, organized labor also campaigned for higher standards of industrial safety and workmen's compensation for industrial injuries. In 1900 a young American lawyer named Louis Brandeis exposed the callousness of a

HEROES IN HELL

As the writer George Orwell (1903–50) observed, Britain's coal-based industrial economy rested almost literally on the shoulders of the miners, yet few appreciated the appalling conditions in which they worked. Orwell's first trip to a coal face in northern England in the 1930s left an indelible impression on him:

"Most of the things one imagines in hell are there – heat, noise, confusion, darkness, foul air and, above all, unbearably cramped space. Everything except the fire... overmastering everything else for a while, is the frightful, deafening din from the conveyor belt which carries the coal away. You cannot see very far, because the fog of coal dust throws back the beam of your lamp, but you can see on either side of you the line of half-naked kneeling men . . . driving their shovels under the fallen coal and flinging it swiftly over their left shoulders . . . It is impossible to watch the 'fillers' at work without feeling a pang of envy for their toughness . . . They have got to remain kneeling all the while – they could hardly rise from their knees without hitting the ceiling – and you can easily see by trying it what a tremendous effort this means. Shovelling is comparatively easy when you are standing up, because you can use your knee and thigh to drive the shovel along; kneeling down, the whole of the strain is thrown upon your arm and belly muscles...But the fillers look and work as though they were made of iron...under the smooth coat of coal dust which clings to them from head to foot. It is only when you see miners down the mine and naked that you realise what splendid men they are...In the hotter mines they wear only a pair of thin drawers, clogs and knee-pads...You can hardly tell by the look of them whether they are young or old...No one could do their work who had not a young man's body, and a figure fit for a guardsman at that...You can never forget that spectacle once you have seen it – the line of bowed, kneeling figures, sooty black all over, driving their huge shovels under the coal with stupendous force and speed..."

Boston laundry that not only refused to compensate a girl who had been scalped after her hair had become entangled in a mangler—a machine used in the laundry—but had deducted her wages for the rest of the day on which the accident had occurred.

Australia was widely regarded as a working man's paradise, and by 1900 most skilled men there had an eight-hour day and an average income even higher than Americans enjoyed. A Scottish Agricultural Commission in 1910 paid tribute to Australia as a country

CHILD'S WORK In 1900 in the United States, children still accounted for as much as a quarter of the labor force in establishments such as this cotton mill in the South. Moreover, they regularly worked a 13-hour day and overnight.

of "abounding prosperity . . . (where) . . . work in towns is especially plentiful and attractive," although it urged newcomers not to be put off by the isolation and long hours of farm work, because in the outback a man could still hope to have his own place one day.

Working for the First World War

When war broke out in Europe in August 1914, the industrial agenda changed dramat-

WOMEN AT WAR English women munitions workers (left) enjoyed high pay and fixed hours, and some learned marketable skills like riveting (below) and welding.

ically and in totally unanticipated ways. Both sides expected the conflict to be "over by Christmas" and thought primarily in terms of mobilizing infantry rather than industry. However, Germany had all but exhausted its military supplies as early as October 1914. Throughout the war, the Kaiser's empire struggled to supply its men for battle, breaking bottlenecks in manpower by drafting workers from conquered Belgium and Poland, and even by releasing men from the army. Both sides achieved prodigious levels

of output: Germany managed to build a new submarine every four days; and, in the course of the war, Britain and France produced 100,000 planes between them. During the Presidency of "Silent Cal" Coolidge, the United States experienced a period of unprecedented economic growth. Corporate profits in the 20's increased by more than 60 percent, and the consumer became king.

Throughout Europe, the "American system"—standardized interchangeable parts, manufactured in volume and put together on an assembly line—was widely adopted to meet the insatiable demands of war. British Dominions, cut off from imports of British industrial goods, expanded their own industrial base. In Australia, annual pig-iron production almost tripled from 130,000 tons. In Germany, cut off by Allied naval blockade from natural nitrates dug in the Chilean desert, chemists learned to extract nitrogen from the air itself, revolutionizing the production of explosives and agricultural fertilizers.

In Britain, where skilled, highly unionized engineers had long preserved their wages and privileges by requiring seven-year apprenticeships to restrict recruitment to their trade, their exclusion of semiskilled labor was roundly denounced by politicians and the press as grossly unpatriotic. The whole complex, status-bound hierarchy of boilermakers, welders, riveters, turners and fitters was shaken to its roots by an invasion of American machine tools, which were often "manned" by women.

Women also took on dozens of other tasks that tradition, convention and vested interests had deemed beyond their strength and competence, such as driving buses, trams or tractors, and operating dock-side cranes. In 1917, a major masculine bastion crumbled when London Underground's new station at Maida Vale opened with an all-women staff.

Manufacturing, marketing and management

With the return of peace, the democracies redirected their economies to the demands of the market rather than of the military. In 1923 American automobile manufacturers hit upon a new marketing ploy that had profound implications for manufacturing itself—the annual change in the style of the model. They aimed to make existing vehicles outmoded simply by proclaiming them to be so, opening the way for sales of new, slightly (but quite visibly) different models. One far-reaching side effect of such "planned obsolescence," intended or otherwise, was to impose additional production and marketing costs on manufacturers, forcing smaller com-

NEW FAD A Sunday-afternoon drive is so popular it creates serious congestion in 1920s St. Louis, while advertisements (right) emphasize the luxury status of the car.

panies out of the market and preventing new ones from entering it. Even mighty Ford, which initially held out against the trend, was forced to capitulate in 1927, closing down for five months to retool as it abandoned the Model T for the new Model A.

Increasing sophistication in manufacturing and marketing products was matched by an increasingly scientific approach to managing the employees who produced them. The father of modern management and the first self-styled consulting engineer in management was tennis champion and rose-grower Frederick Winslow Taylor (1856–1915), pio-

THE MAN WHO MADE AMERICA MOBILE

Henry Ford (1863–1947), a Michigan farmer's son educated in a one-room schoolhouse, changed the face of the United States, of the motor industry and of work itself. "I will build a motor car for the great multitude," he proclaimed. The Model T —the Tin Lizzie—"stronger than a horse and easier

READY TO GO Model T Fords are lined up for delivery to dealers. By 1925, when this picture was taken, the Model T was already nearing the end of its life.

to maintain."—was launched in 1908 and, over the 19 years of its existence, sold 15.5 million in the United States and 1 million in Canada—equal to half the world's entire output of automobiles. Over the same period, its price fell from $950 to $270.

Ford's genius lay less in his mastery of engineering than in his capacity for organizing production. He did not invent the assembly line (which had originated in Chicago meat-packing plants), but he exploited its application to the full. Whereas once it had required 728 minutes to turn out a complete chassis for an automobile, the moving-line system established at Ford's 1914 plant at Highland Park, Michigan, reduced the time to 93 minutes. Eventually, the company would be turning out a Model T every 24 seconds. In the same year, when the average motor-industry wage was $2.34 a day, Ford announced he would pay a minimum $5—and reduce the day from nine to eight hours, enabling him to introduce a round-the-clock three-shift system that maximized the use of his plant.

Ford achieved another major cost saving by dispatching cars to dealers "knocked down" into their major components. Once the parts were at the dealer's, a competent mechanic could assemble a Model T in half a day. Extraordinarily, by 1913 every town in the United States with a population over 2,000 had a Ford dealership.

neer of "time and motion" studies, which aimed to eliminate wasted effort in the workplace. The essentials of "Taylorism" were enshrined in *The Principles of Scientific Management*, which he published in 1911. Treating workers as living machines, Taylor's disciples extended their interests from employees to the working environment. In 1927, a team of engineers began an experiment at the Hawthorne works of the Western Electric Company in Chicago that would turn out to have unsuspected but far-reaching consequences.

The team focused initially on the effects of lighting on productivity, and were puzzled to find that whatever they did to change the type, arrangement and intensity of the lighting, productivity rose every time a change was made. Baffled, the experimenters turned to an Australian psychologist at the Harvard Business School, Elton Mayo. By making even more radical changes in such matters as temperature, humidity, payment methods, break times and refreshment facilities, Mayo soon determined that what mattered was not the environment at all but the fact that the

WORKERS OUTING Cadbury's, the British confectionery manufacturer, adopted a "human relations" approach to management. Here, its employees are treated to an outing, 1901.

workers suddenly felt that somebody cared about them. The unusual degree of attention paid to the employees' comfort and concerns had so increased their solidarity and morale that they had come to feel that they really mattered. It was this that had translated itself into ever-rising levels of output. Mayo proclaimed a new doctrine—a "human relations" approach that, focusing on the dynam-

QUICK-DRYING
Before 1914, Henry Ford offered customers a choice of colors. However, once he had established assembly-line production, all Model Ts were painted black—because it was the only paint that would dry fast enough to keep up with the line.

ics of informal groups, would combine efficiency with humanity. Unlike Taylor, who essentially regarded the worker as an isolated individual motivated solely by money, Mayo emphasized that the worker was a member of a group and was also motivated by such concerns as interest and dignity. A concern for "human relations" became a characteristic in many progressive businesses. Today, it is not unusual for an employer to refer to its employees as "partners," or to offer them such perks as free theater tickets, personal computers and stock options.

BOOTLACE BOY Children often sold goods on the street. This young boy was selling shoelaces in Paris in 1907.

ALL WORK AND NO PLAY At the turn of the century the UNITED STATES, the world's most advanced economy, still relied on child labor for basic tasks such as picking cotton.

In those industries where workers were still exploited, it was largely left to journalists, unions and charities to expose the scandals. In hotels and restaurants, staff frequently worked 11-hour shifts spread over 15 hours, seven days a week. Many states either specifically exempted hotels from observing the normal legal limits on working hours or simply omitted any reference to hotels in the relevant laws. A Consumers League survey of female office cleaners in New York found that only a quarter were U.S. citizens, and that most could neither write nor read English; their potential for self-protection through organization or recourse to law was therefore minimal. The long hours of harsh labor put in by sharecroppers' children on cotton plantations in the South were frequently ignored, because children under ten were not counted by the U.S. census, and therefore did not officially exist. Street-corner paperboys, working through freezing nights and early mornings to sup-plement the family income, were similarly disregarded when it came to calculating the nation's wealth—and responsibilities.

A world without work

The First World War left Germany humiliated by occupation and, like neighboring Austria and Hungary, wracked by hyperinflation. Italy, ill-rewarded for its wartime sacrifices, fell prey to a fascist experiment that promised a short cut to modernity by recalling the grandeur of ancient Rome. "Victorious" Britain, after a brief export boom led by re-stocking and reconstruction in Europe, did not see unemployment fall below 10 per cent for 20 years. France, thanks to the return of its lost provinces, Alsace and Lorraine, experienced an industrial renaissance but was tarnished by political and financial instability: between May 1924 and July 1926 alone, no fewer than 11 French governments succeeded each other. Underdeveloped eastern Europe remained severely depressed.

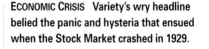

ECONOMIC CRISIS Variety's wry headline belied the panic and hysteria that ensued when the Stock Market crashed in 1929.

No European country experienced the surging, confident growth enjoyed by Americans. Even this was short-lived, however, as the Wall Street Crash of October 1929 ushered in a decade of depression. A collapse in confidence among investors, bankers and exporters plunged the world into an economic blizzard between 1929 and 1932. By 1932, 30 million were unemployed worldwide and even more on short hours and diminished wages were constantly unnerved by the fear of unemployment. In America and Australia, more than a quarter of all workers were unemployed in 1932; in Denmark, Norway and Germany, a third.

For the majority of the unemployed, whether in Baltimore, Brussels or Berlin, Manchester, Montreal or Madrid, the daily routine remained depressingly the same. Those who hadn't simply given up got up in the morning and met their former workmates. They exchanged rumors of work; lined up for the chance of a job; lined up for state handouts; lined up for charity handouts; lined up for free soup, free bread and free apples. The sociologist E. Wight Bakke, who published a study of "The Unemployed Man" in 1933, meticulously recorded the reactions offered by workless men to his inquiries. "You've heard tell that the worker today don't get no satisfaction out of his work," claimed one sheet-metal worker. "Well let me tell you something. He gets a

lot more satisfaction out of it than he does living without it on unemployment benefit." Bakke also reminded his readers that work not only filled time and generated incomes, but through the latter "gives a measure of a man's worth . . . In an earlier day, when money was not the key to most of life, money did not drive men on to exceptional effort, nor the lack of it to drink." In the so-called command economies, run on communist or fascist lines, programs of public works and

rearmament were introduced to ease the unemployment situation. In Germany, the hyperinflation of the 1920s and the economic collapse that had put 6 million out of work by 1932, prepared the way for a Nazi electoral triumph, spearheaded by the simple slogan "Work and Bread." Thanks to the building of *Autobahnen* (motorways) and state-funded rearmament, Germans could at least point to these as a sign of hope.

Working for the Second World War

The mood of the people in 1939 was very different from 1914. In Britain, the government prepared for a long haul. Learning from the previous conflict, when unrestricted volunteer recruitment had stripped the war economy of skilled men, the authorities created a category of "reserved occupations"—firemen and seamen, farmers and miners, draftsmen and dri-

JOBLESS...HOPELESS The Great Depression created more than physical hardships. It created a sense of fear and despair that those who lived through it would long remember.

vers. As 5 million men were drafted into uniform, women were mobilized to take their place. Fashion was put on hold "for the duration," as the phrase of the day put it, and some 300,000 women left the textile and clothing industries. Approximately 147,000 women went into transport services; 220,000 went into chemicals, making drugs, dyes and explosives; 480,000 performed clerical tasks in the hugely expanded bureaucracy that directed the nation's production and consumption; and no less than 2 million women went to work in factories making planes, tanks, bayonets, bullets and bombs.

In the United States, blacks and women were called upon to fill the employment vacuum created by enlisting soldiers. Millions of blacks left the fields of the South to work in the factories of the North and by 1943, nearly 16 million women had joined the workforce. "Rosie the Riveter" (possibly inspired by the figure of Rosie Bonavita, who set a wartime record by pounding 33,345 rivets into the wing of a fighter plane in just six hours), in all her muscular self-confidence, became a national icon. Even the young and the old pitched in, as eager Boy Scouts worked alongside their grandparents to dig "Victory Gardens." Buoyed by this national diligence, the country's real economic output (allowing for inflation) increased 150 percent between 1939 and 1944.

By 1942, the United States was producing more arms than all its enemies combined. Factories that had worked 40 hours a week now hummed with life for 90. U.S. output of shipping increased seventeenfold. And, despite the fact that war production was accounting for some 40 percent of total output, civilian consumption also rose by over 10 percent. This startling economic vitality did not go unnoticed by foreign leaders. When Roosevelt and Stalin met in 1943, the Russian leader proposed the toast, "To American production, without which this war would have been lost!"

The mobilization of national effort proved more complete in the embattled democracies than in totalitarian Germany where, due to the forced conscription of 14 million foreign workers, POWs and Jews, it was not thought necessary to summon German womanhood from the higher demands of "*Kinder, Küche, Kirche*" (Children, Kitchen, Church) until 1943. As a result of the administrative talents of economic minister Albert Speer, German war production reached its peak in 1944; it then fell rapidly as Allied saturation bombing took its toll and as the contraction of the Reich's frontiers deprived it of forced contributions of labor and resources from conquered regions.

In Japan the mobilization was more complete, with children in their early teens producing munitions. And the destruction was even greater. When Japan surrendered, the coun-

HYPERINFLATION   In 1923 Germany's currency collapse made 5 million mark notes (inset) common. Shopkeepers were obliged to keep cash in large chests rather than in registers, and shoppers were often seen in the streets with wheel-barrows filled with money.

ON THE BUSSES   The war had opened up employment opportunities for minorities, who were needed during the war's labor shortages.

FEMME FATALE "Rosie the Riveter" symbolized American determination to mobi-
lize its women for war work. Several
women might have been the inspiration
for Rosie; the idea for the campaign
seems to have come first.

try was on the verge of starvation. The following year, Japanese industrial production
was a mere 10 percent of what it had been
just a decade previously.

Work for all

Thanks largely to the far-sighted generosity
of the Marshall Plan to finance economic
reconstruction, Western Europe was kick-
started into recovery. Germany's "economic
miracle" tripled the country's economic output between 1950 and 1960. By the 1960s,
unemployment was no longer a problem,
and there was even an acute labor shortage,
remedied by an influx of "guest workers,"
especially from Turkey and Yugoslavia. In
Britain, hospitals and transport systems
came to rely on newcomers from the
Caribbean and South Asia.

Throughout the industrialized world, a

rising proportion of women, notably married
women, were recruited into the expanding
labor force. In the United States, female
labor, which accounted for 27.9 percent of
the total workforce in 1947, rose steadily to
reach 38.1 percent in 1970. But neither in
treatment nor opportunity did women make
much progress relative to men. They usually
got jobs that were less secure and responsible, and when they did get equal work, they
seldom received equal pay for it. The few
who did manage to succeed in business or
the professions generally got stuck on the
lower rungs of the ladder. Women lawyers
were sidelined into repetitive matrimonial or
property work, women doctors into public or
mental health. Most felt an additional pressure that seldom burdened their male colleagues—to organize the care of their
children, either by trained professions, or

informally by relatives and neighbors.

For a quarter of a century after 1945, most firms in the advanced economies grew and prospered, and so did their employees. Increasing rewards from work were not, however, necessarily matched by increasing satisfaction at work. As a Detroit automobile worker told a researcher: "The things I like best about my job are quitting time, pay days, days off and vacations."

Industrial researchers began to notice that some industries (auto manufacturing; docks), regardless of which country they were in, seemed more "strike prone" than others (railways; chemicals). Confrontation arose more frequently where workers were employed in close proximity on similar jobs, but lived in relative isolation from other workers and their own managers. Where workers experienced job variety and lived scattered throughout the community confrontation was far less common than in one-industry settings, where grievances generated at work during the day could become the staple of conversation among neighbors and workmates in the evening.

In Japan they seemed to manage the

NEWCOMERS Migrant workers from Mexico—above in California chive fields— were the backbone of that state's agriculture and were exploited until unionized by leaders like Cesar Chavez (right), who called for boycotts of California produce.

RULED OUT

In 1976 the German firm of Keuffel and Esser manufactured their last slide-rule. Recognizing that, after 350 years, this basic calculator had at last been made redundant by electronic devices, they presented it to the Smithsonian Institution in Washington as a museum piece.

human side of industry better. By the 1960s Western management experts increasingly admired Japanese manufacturers, who seemed to combine high output, high quality and high worker satisfaction. The Japanese employee was held up to the world as a model of diligence, loyalty and skill.

An era of uncertainty

The confident expansion of the advanced industrial economies was severely jolted by the "oil shocks" of 1973 and 1979, which decisively ended an era of cheap energy. At the same time, new computer-based tech-

TIGHT FIT Women, their hands more slender and nimble, installed many bomber electrical systems (opposite). They were also able to weld in cramped quarters, which could often prove the most hazardous of jobs.

nologies, offshoots of the Cold War Space Race, began to corrode old assumptions and practices, first in manufacturing and then in the service sector. As early as the 1960s, industrial analysts had predicted that computers—and the robots that were run by computers—would wipe out the jobs of millions of process workers performing repetitive industrial tasks, and then eliminate entire layers of middle management.

General Motors installed its first industrial robots in its North American factories in 1962, but by the next decade Japan, the major manufacturing nation most dependent on oil imports, was far outstripping its rivals in levels of automation in its efforts to ditch energy-intensive processes and cut labor costs. Japan, which had built its post-war recovery on steel and ships and motor cars, relocated these industries offshore in São Paulo, Brazil, or Sunderland in northeast England where land and labor were cheap-

er. In Japan itself, meanwhile, industry eagerly launched into non-polluting, knowledge-intensive, high value-added fields, such as biotechnology.

In what was now being called the post-

FACE OF THE TIGER The rapid growth of the "Tiger economies" of the Far East was fuelled by an abundance of well-educated, cheap, youthful and unorganized labor.

HIGH-TECH Robotic technology, which can perform complex tasks, replaces human workers in this Australian factory.

industrial era, new jobs depended not on manipulating materials but on information. In 1950, some 17 percent of the American workforce could be classified as information workers—clerks, teachers, lawyers, accountants and so on. Thirty years later, the figure was over 60 percent, the single largest occupational category was that of clerk, and there were more people employed full-time in

ENGINEERING THE FUTURE Biotechnology, which has been at the leading edge of industrial advance from the 1980s onwards, has provided jobs for highly skilled workers.

universities than in agriculture. Of the 20 million new American jobs created in the 1970s, only 5 percent were in manufacturing; 90 percent were in the information or service sectors. The trend was similar in other Western nations.

While the United States labor force as a whole grew by 18 percent between 1970 and 1978, the number of public officials grew by 76 percent, bankers by 83 percent, and health administrators by a staggering 118 percent. The number of engineers rose by less than 3 percent. In 1998, the three fastest growing jobs in the U.S. were database manager, computer engineer, and systems analyst.

By the 1980s, Western nations had more than Japan to worry about. Mere ministates, like Singapore, were now vying to become serious industrial competitors. Employers responded with a war on fixed costs, replacing permanent workers with part-timers, sub-contractors and the self-employed, for whose security and welfare they took minimal responsibility. Workers at all levels, who might, only a generation before, had looked forward to a lifetime of steady advancement in return for

being loyal "company men," found themselves squeezed out by younger colleagues or by machines.

By the 1990s, it was the managerial class and the knowledge-based service industries that were experiencing large-scale layoffs. In just five years in the early 1990s BP, one of the most capital-intensive, wired-up corporations in Europe, cut its labor force from 117,000 to 60,000. Even in the midst of an economic boom, in 1998 corporations laid off 103,000 workers in the United States. "Downsizing"—strictly a 20th century euphemism—cut a swathe through the ranks of whole sectors, such as banking and insurance, that had once been legendary for security of employment. And those who retained their positions often did so at the price of being expected to work harder and harder.

Yet, as the new millennium dawned, a new phenomenon emerged that may well be

PLAYING MANY PARTS

Most parents have wanted to see their children set securely in a solid trade or career and feared for the fate of those who turned out to have creative, artistic, political or entrepreneurial ambitions. Many celebrities, however, abandoned seemingly solid beginnings. Poet Allen Ginsberg was an accountant, singer-composer Elvis Costello a computer programmer and crime-writer Agatha Christie a clerk in a pharmacy. Ex-lawyers include Lenin, Gandhi, Castro, Otto Preminger, Hoagy Carmichael and Rossano Brazzi. In making their way in the world, such restless souls have often had to take work where they could find it.

Many had become familiar with the shovel: singer Rod Stewart once dug graves, while model Jerry Hall shifted manure at a stable. Groucho Marx cleaned theatrical wigs and Cyndi Lauper cleaned dog kennels. Ho Chi Minh, George Orwell and Warren Beatty were all once dishwashers, while Benny Hill, Matt Monro and Sean Connery were milkmen. Danny de Vito and Chuck Berry both worked as hairdressers. Bing Crosby, Walt Disney, Rock Hudson, William Faulkner and Conrad Hilton were employed by the U.S. Postal Service. Rudolf Valentino, James Cagney, Kirk Douglas, Peter Finch, Dustin Hoffman and Yves Montand were all waiters; and Eddie Cantor, Ramon Navarro, William Bendix and Jack Lemmon were singing waiters. Ex-salesmen include Ralph Lauren, Gene Hackman, Steve Martin and Frank Zappa.

FINANCIAL FRENZY From a London bank to the Tokyo Stock Exchange, the international nature of financial markets in the 1990s puts intense pressure on those who work in them.

the most important commercial development of recent times: the Internet and the arrival of commerce to it. Now that anyone anywhere on the planet with access to a computer and a telephone line can shop all over the world and tap into archives virtually everywhere, the only thing certain is that there is no telling what work—and life—will be like during the next 100 years.

LOOKING INTO THE FUTURE The ease and comfort with which young people deal with computers may have vast commercial implications.

THE WAY WE DRESSED

AFFLUENCE HAS BROUGHT FASHION WITHIN THE REACH OF THE MASSES AS THE NOTION OF FASHION HAS BEEN REPEATEDLY CHALLENGED

In January 1913 American poet Robert Frost gate-crashed a party to celebrate the opening of London's Poetry Bookshop and was quite astonished when a total stranger turned to him and said:

"You're an American, aren't you?"

"Yes. How did you know?"

"Shoes."

Frost was wearing wingtips, a distinctively American style, in which the soles protruded beyond the upper part of the shoe. Seen close up, they were an instant give-away—even in Bohemian circles.

In general, however, by the first decade of the present century, the nationality of the educated and propertied classes of advanced Western countries was no longer instantly detectable from a distance. American gentlemen approximated to the English ideal, wearing well-tailored jackets and pants in a dull-colored matching cloth. American ladies, like their English counterparts, took their cue from Paris.

What ordinary people wore was still much affected by their nationality, class, gender, and whether they lived in city or country. During the course of the century, these traditional and taken-for-granted influences would be undermined by the application of mass-production techniques to the clothing industry and by the influence of Hollywood films, TV programs and magazines. These forces internationalized fashion and challenged the conventional boundaries between rich and poor, town-dweller and countryman, and even male and female.

Paradoxically, the dissolution of time-honored distinctions was accompanied by the creation of new social groupings—hippies, yuppies, punks and "power dressers"—who took their sartorial cues from each other, and were intent on distinguishing

NEW FASHION The new century brought new fashions, and with it outrage for many. Below: a 1909 drawing of a woman banished from a church for her "lewd attire."

"TODAY EVERYTHING HAS TO BE MODERN"

In 1909 an East Prussian village pastor named Mosziek published a transcript of a 70-hour interview with one of his parishioners, 69-year-old Frau Hoffmann. The former maid had much to say on the subject of dress:

"Who would have thought it possible a few years ago that workers' children could go around so well dressed!... Today, if you don't have a shirt, you're stupid and lazy... Nice things are cheap today... Just stand on the corner and watch the wenches go by: they're all dressed up. And not one of the girls has a skirt made from a single piece of cloth. In a pinch they wouldn't be able to make a swaddling band from it. Around here you don't see folk costumes any more; up in Lithuania in the isolated villages you can still see them... The shoulder collars with tassels as communion coats are completely out of fashion; the same goes for head finery—the black silk kerchiefs with a bow. Today everything has to be modern... Velvet and silk aren't so expensive any more and are really beautiful. They rustle so nicely. As long as they're working at home or in the factory, the girls go around in a plain long dress; but as soon as they get off work, they change... we old people don't care much about such things anymore; but still, everyone likes to get new shoes at Whitsuntide."

themselves from mainstream society, rather than dressing, as their grandparents had, to signify their role and rank within it. Fashion changed from being a declaration of status to an expression of self. As important, it ceased to be the prerogative of the elite and became the right of the masses.

Who wore what

In 1900 the upper classes on both sides of the Atlantic were distinguished not only by the quality of their clothes but also by the size and variety of their wardrobes. The trousseau of an upper middle-class girl would include, at a minimum, a dozen each of petticoats, chemises, bodices, camisoles, drawers and nightgowns, all hand-sewn, lace-edged and monogrammed. Silk stockings could be bought ready-made from a store and were available in five sizes and 300

different shades. The wardrobe of this well-off newlywed's mother might include such exotic and expensive items as a silk kimono from Japan, cartwheel hats decorated with osprey or ostrich feathers from Africa, and dresses trimmed with exquisite broderie anglaise from Switzerland or delicate lace edgings from Belgium or Ireland.

Different occasions, places, seasons and times of day all required different modes of dress. Even a single weekend in the country might require a trunkful of outfits and accessories to meet the requirements of travel, recreation, socializing, formal dining and church attendance.

The support of a lady's maid was essential for the proper packing and care of such garments—gentlemen relied on their butlers—not to mention the arrangement of her mistress's hair into elaborate coiffures.

AT THE RACES The social elite in the United States at the turn of the century regarded elegant attire essential at sporting events, which were also occasions for display and courtship.

For gentlemen, the rules were less elaborate but no less strict or subtle. Except in high summer, dark colors and heavyweight materials were the order of the day in informal settings such as a spa or seaside resort, or on informal occasions, such as a weekend house party. In preparation for a turn-of-the-century formal dinner party (at that time, almost a tautology), a respectable American male would have to preen for hours, decking himself out in a three piece evening suit with an open double-breasted tail coat, silk lapels, and stitched cuffs, a single breasted waisted coat, creased narrow pants, a starched white wing-collared shirt, a white bow-tie, white

gloves, and black leather boots. Neither comfort nor the understatement was held at much of a premium.

Transgressions of the dress code, whether intentional or through carelessness, met with alarm, and often censure. When Britain's first Labour Member of Parliament entered the House of Commons in 1892 wearing a working man's cloth cap, he scandalized the public, press and parliamentarians alike. Nevertheless, among the working classes, having the resources to uphold rigid dress conventions was a mark of status. Only little boys and the very poorest of the poor went bareheaded outdoors. People too poor to afford formal mourning clothes still sewed black patches and armbands onto their garments. Only the most insensitive would commit the social sin of attending a funeral in brown boots or not wearing a black necktie.

Uniform codes

In the authoritarian states of Eastern Europe, this rigid and implacable sense of fashion decorum was mirrored in the prestige accorded to military uniforms. Whereas in Britain an officer would remove his military uniform as soon as his official duties were completed for the day, in the German, Austrian and Russian empires the exalted standing of the military encouraged even civilian bureaucrats to don heavily decorated uniforms. In the Kaiser's realm, even university professors chose to wear the uniform of a reserve officer instead of the flowing robes of an academic. In both types of society, democratic and authoritarian, military-style uniforms were also worn by the employees of organizations that wished to project an image of reliability and discipline, such as railway companies and the postal service.

Almost everywhere a distinction in dress between city and country was still strikingly evident. In European countries with large peasant populations, the town-country divide was honored in the elaborately embroidered costumes worn for religious festivals and family celebrations. Even in countries as advanced as France or as small as Belgium, regional identity was clearly preserved in peasant dress. In Alpine Germany, Austria and Switzerland, the origins of men and

CATALOG SHOPPING America's scattered population kept in touch with fashion through movies and mail order catalogs.

women from neighboring regions could be distinguished from the different weave of their woolen stockings, the cross-stitch on their jackets and aprons or the pattern of pleats in their headdresses.

As the English socialist writer George Orwell observed in the 1930s, it was possible before 1914 to classify the social status of any inhabitant of the British Isles instantly simply by what he or she wore. Headgear alone was sufficient for males. A stylish upper-class gentleman wore a shiny silk "topper" or tophat; the respectable middle classes a stiff bowler, or, more daringly, a soft "trilby" or the German Homburg. Working-class men wore peaked cloth caps, which first appeared in the mid-19th century as sporting caps worn by the wealthy for activities such as shooting and fishing.

CLOTH CAP The flat cap was worn by the working classes in Europe and the U.S. Gentlemen, however, attended sporting events (like the Ascot races, left) in top hats.

Dress denoted distinctions of status within classes as well as between them. In many smaller industrial towns, the mass of mill girls still clattered to work in clogs and shawls, like their mothers and grandmothers before them, but a forward miss who took the trolley to work in a shop or office might well risk provoking hostile stares from her neighbors by wearing a hat and coat. In the rural United States, the carpenter's bibbed overall was widely adopted by farmers, who could wear them over thick pants and "union suits" of underwear in the freezing winters and over

MOVING ALONG A postcard mocks the "hobble" skirt, which was replaced by loose, flowing lines (far left).

nothing at all in sweltering summers. With the aid of the ubiquitous Singer sewing machine, farm wives could readily create rough approximations of store-bought items or ones ordered through the Sears' mail-order catalog.

Breaking the boundaries

Edwardian formality was occasionally challenged by such provocative fashions as the "hobble" skirt, which restricted its wearer to a pace of 9 inches and was the height of fashion in 1910, or the exotic "harem" trousers, inspired by the stage costumes of Diaghilev's brilliant Ballets Russes, which hit Europe in 1909. But the real assault on convention came in the Twenties, when youth culture asserted itself as never before. In the United States, "Flappers" rejected notions of Victorian propriety, shocking their elders with androgynous hairstyles, leggy displays, and wholehearted embrace of frivolity. Quite literally, these women became less restrained; in one late-decade survey, more than 30 percent admitted they no longer wore old-fashioned corsets. In Europe,

TREND-SETTER Britain's playwright and lyricist Noel Coward became the personification of a casually elegant style that was admired and emulated on both sides of the Atlantic.

SHOCKER French tennis star Suzanne Lenglen stunned Wimbledon crowds in 1922 with the shortness of her skirts—but was still obliged to wear stockings when playing in front of royalty.

French tennis star Suzanne Lenglen scandalized Wimbledon with her short skirt and bare legs—and around the world newspapers reproduced pictures of her doing so. Men enthusiastically joined in the fashion follies as well, sporting extravagantly cut Oxford Bags and colorful sweaters. "Sportswear" originally developed for specific games such as tennis or golf, began to be worn casually on informal occasions and by far more people than actually played sports. The really rich could afford to play their days away. Aspirants to affluence could at least try to look as though they did.

In 1922 Paris designer Jean Patou exhibited the first-ever sportswear collection and soon after, garishly patterned loose sweaters were favored by the young of both sexes. The craze for day-long rambles in the countryside developed, under German inspiration, into a fad for more strenuous hiking trips, during which the hiker wore such informal garments as shorts, short-sleeved shirts and French-style berets. Clothes that were loose and comfortable symbolized the social and personal freedom demanded by a generation liberated from prewar conventions. As Cole Porter wisely warbled, "In olden days a glimpse of stocking was looked on as something shocking . . . now heaven knows, anything goes."

By 1926 a more definite look had begun to emerge as a small proportion of rich, young women opted for a boyish style—flat-chested, slim-hipped, with short, "shingled" hair. The ideal female silhouette was radically simplified. Fussy trimmings were banished from garments, which might now be made from previously unfashionable textiles such as knitted jersey or, more daringly, from "male" fabrics, such as tweed or corduroy. This revolution was led by the Parisian designer Coco Chanel, who made it chic to dress like the poor in black or beige or grey, adopting the workman's cap or scarf as an accessory. High fashion, henceforth, did not necessarily imply luxury.

This trend was paralleled among members of the European middle class, who had

recently been impoverished by wartime taxes and who affected to despise glamour. Chanel initiated a revolution of accessibility, and thus did for women's dress what Beau Brummell had done for men a century before, abandoning flamboyant fussiness in favor of a bold simplicity dependent on line, cut and quality. In 1926, *Vogue* magazine shrewdly recognized that Chanel's deceptively simple "little black dress" was destined to acquire classic status as the couture equivalent of the Model T Ford.

Among the young, stiff corseting was abandoned in favor of the elasticated brassiere, which gave a new freedom of movement. For the first time in centuries,

hemlines rose to mid-calf and then almost to the knee. Female footwear, now exposed, became a fashion item in its own right as shoes replaced boots. Hats, as the century progressed, lost some of their stature—literally. Millinery fashion in 1900 celebrated hats pin-cushioned with towering, jaunty plumes of ostrich and egret feathers, and even with entire stuffed orioles, wrens or owls perched listlessly on top. Conservationist zeal helped to defeat this trend, and women began looking elsewhere beside the treetops for inspiration. In 1935, the Sears

ACCENT ON YOUTH The svelte lines of Coco Chanel's classic "little black dress" favored the young and the slim.

DREAM FACTORY Hollywood supplied images of glamour (below), eagerly absorbed by a female labor force often working in anything-but-glamourous surroundings (right).

Roebuck & Co. directed their attentions westward to California, including "autographed fashion hats" from prominent Hollywood stars in their catalog.

Make up was no longer the prerogative of actresses and "floozies" as women across the world began to pluck their eyebrows and paint their nails. They took their cues from the United States, where, according to one censorious British observer, "even children of ten have their rouge pots and lipsticks."

Before 1914, a respectable wife might have employed a touch of rouge...on special occasions, lipstick and scent. Cosmetic companies such as Avon (1886), Elizabeth Arden (1910), Revlon (1932), and Estée Lauder (1940), were more than happy to provide women with the beauty supplies they desired. By the 1990s, cosmetics had become a $80-billion a year industry.

Hooray for Hollywood

If before 1914 chambermaids dreamed of looking like a duchess, 20 years later they dreamed of looking like a film star. For the first time, motion pictures—in effect, Hollywood—exerted a major influence on the fashion industry. In the 1932 film *Letty Lynton*, Joan Crawford wore 26 different outfits in the space of 84 minutes. Although the main concern of studio wardrobe departments was to make the star look good, they also succeeded in setting trends for the fashion-conscious. Costume designer Adrian distracted Miss Crawford's fans from noticing her large hips by riveting their eyes on her

NONCONFORMIST Marlene Dietrich asserted a paradoxical femininity by favoring mannish dress, but few women followed her example.

broad shoulders, which he enveloped in startling puffed epaulettes of tulle. By the end of 1932, 10,000 American women were strutting through salons in imitation Letty Lynton dresses. When tough guy Clark Gable took off his shirt in *It Happened One Night* (1934) and revealed that he wore nothing underneath, sales of undershirts plummeted.

The popularity of platinum blondes such as Jean Harlow and Mae West was good for sales of hydrogen peroxide. Their other prominent assets revived designers' interest in décolletage. German film star Marlene Dietrich, by contrast, personified a far more severe sensuousness and could make even tailored trousers look sexy.

Filmmaking was a new industry, with no traditional recruiting ground. Many early filmmakers had gained their first business experience in the garment trade, and attached great importance to high standards of costume as one of the hallmarks of a quality film. In the silent era particularly, sumptuousness had to be conveyed visually. Producers favored iridescent, diaphanous or flamboyant materials, like satin, crepe or fox fur, which looked good on the screen. The wealthy could afford to indulge their fantasies by having clothes made in imitation of those worn by the stars. By 1937, less affluent Americans could buy cheap copies retailed at one of

400 Cinema Fashions Stores. Or they could save up for garments made with new substitutes, such as rayon, sold as "artificial" silk ("artificial" in the 1930s carried the sort of connotations that "hi-tech" did in the 1980s).

Although Joan Crawford's freckles were retouched out of her publicity photographs, the sun-soaked climate of California made tanning fashionable, entirely reversing the Edwardian emphasis on a milk white complexion, which had been the clearest evidence that one did not do outdoor manual work, like a peasant. The growth of factory and office work, however, meant that even paid employees had acquired the pallor that had once been the prerogative of their employers. In Europe, "sunbathing" was encouraged by German scientists on health grounds, particularly as a way of tackling deficiency diseases. The cult of sunbathing was further reinforced by the passion among the rich for leisurely winter cruises in the Caribbean and the Mediterranean.

Depression and deprivation

The harsh economic realities of the 1930s and 1940s set limits on the ability of the masses to indulge their fashion fantasies. In the United States, the American War Production Board, responsible for regulating the manufacture of certain limited resources, banned ruffles, pleats and patch pockets in women's clothing in order to preserve fabric for the war effort. Despite Hollywood's seeming worldwide ascendancy, the economically depressed regions of Europe were oblivious to its fashions, and boots, clogs, shawls and overalls remained the standard dress of working class adults.

The spread of fascism throughout Europe in the interwar period encouraged the wearing of uniforms by a higher proportion of the population, who found themselves enrolled in militias, youth movements and labor corps. Even women's garments began to be cut with

square shoulders—a trend that was to be accentuated during the militarized 1940s. In Nazi Germany, traditional *lederhosen* and other forms of peasant garb won official approval as emblems of "Volkisch"

SUN AND SEA Changing notions of modesty and an increased emphasis on health encouraged a greater exposure of flesh in the interwar period. Tanning and exercise, along with beach holidays, became fashionable among the young, as great throngs of humanity crowded the beaches at Coney Island.

THE CENTURY OF COUTURE

Parisian haute couture was invented by an Englishman, Frederick Worth, in the 1850s, and dominated the world of female fashion until the 1950s. Before Worth, fashion was what aristocrats wore; after him, it was what couturiers said they should wear. Worth pioneered the notion of the seasonal collection, but the formal staging of annual fashion shows before press and public did not become a regular event until the early 1900s. By that

PARIS PINNACLE An outdoor show in the Bois de Boulogne in 1934 is well attended. The French capital set female styles worldwide for over a century (inset).

time, the French capital had 20 couture houses; by 1925, it had 72.

The Second World War dealt Paris a blow from which it only appeared to recover, while buyers and producers in the United States discovered and asserted their own native tastes and talents. Despite the success of Dior's postwar "New Look," haute couture became increasingly marginalized. In the 1930s, Chanel alone had employed a staff of 2,500; by 1985 the surviving 21 fashion houses would employ less than 2,000 between them and serve only 3,000 clients worldwide.

By 1975, made-to-order clothes accounted for less than a fifth of the direct profits of Parisian couture houses, and by 1985 less than an eighth. Salvation came in the shape of ready-to-wear clothing ranges—for both sexes—licensing agreements and non-garment products such as accessories, leatherware and spectacles. Lanvin, Nina Ricci and Chanel scented success elsewhere. Chanel No. 5 alone was reckoned to generate global sales of $50 million. By 1981, the overall profits of the surviving Paris couture houses from clothes and licensing amounted to 6 billion francs—while fragrances brought in another 5 billion.

authenticity. The Austrian *dirndl*, a full skirt with a tight waistband, worn by peasants, became a popular fashion in both the United States and Great Britain among the younger generation. Most German high fashion remained derivative. German manufacturers, like the Americans, were notorious for conducting more or less open industrial espionage at the annual Paris collections, employing observers to memorize the cuts and fabrics of the garments they saw, and then rush back to their hotel rooms to make drawings of them.

For the respectable classes, who were neither very rich nor very poor, managing a family's wardrobe was an important part of a housewife's skill. Women's magazines devot-

FILM AND FASHION By mid-century, motion pictures influenced fashion more and more. Couples like Humphrey Bogart and Lauren Bacall set trends as their romance captured the world's imagination.

FASHION GOES TO WAR

TOMMY The British combat uniform in the First World War was influenced by experience in India, where *khaki* blended in with the landscape.

Mass-production tailoring was pioneered by the manufacturers of military uniforms, and the wearing of uniforms accustomed millions of conscripts to novel garments which they continued to wear in civilian life. T-shirts (named for their shape) were originally introduced in the 1890s as undershirts for American sailors. In 1914 the British firm of Burberry's Tielocken waterproof of 1910 was militarized by the addition of epaulettes and rings for hanging grenades, map-cases and binoculars; it became the standard officer's "trench coat" and a postwar fashion classic. Second World War sailors keeping watch in freezing weather wore hooded coats of thick Duffel cloth which, instead of buttons, had toggles, which were easier to do up with numbed fingers.

American manufacturers were subject to restrictions imposed by the War Production Board. Belts were to be no wider than 2 inches; cuffs were banned from coats, and attached hoods and shawls from tops. Many Americans made the most of the hard times. When a scarcity of rayon and wool caused a shortage of tweed and worsted suits, men began relinquishing their vests and wore "Victory Suits," mismatching single-breasted coats and pants, to save fabric. Unable to vacation in Europe during the war, wealthy Americans headed for Latin-America and brought back some of the flamboyant styles of the sunny south. Others trekked to dude ranches on their own frontier and revived a taste for wearing denim jeans, checked shirts and high-heeled boots.

DEMOB British ex-airmen in demobilization suits at the end of the Second World War.

Across the Atlantic, beleaguered Britain also experienced serious shortages of fabric. Clothes rationing began there in 1941 and lasted until 1952. Inspired by the slogan "Make Do and Mend," housewives recycled curtains and blankets as coats and dresses. Woolen garments were routinely unpicked and reknitted. These war-years encouraged a crafty fashion resourcefulness in many citizens: the muslin cloth for making cheese was unrationed, and so could be used for making underwear—as could illegally obtained parachute silk.

ed many pages to technical instruction in the arts of dressmaking and knitting, and frequently included free paper patterns as a promotional item to boost circulation. Although the wife of a bank manager could afford to go to a personal dressmaker for "something special" for a big occasion, even she might still regard knitting sweaters and scarves as a source of satisfaction, and endless sock-darning as an unavoidable chore.

At the lower end of the middle-class spectrum, the wife of a bank clerk would pay even more painstaking attention to keeping up appearances, discreetly acquiring secondhand items at a thrift shop or flea market. She would let out a straining waistband

for her husband, run up a dress for her daughter, or revive a warm coat by retrimming its collar and cuffs.

The Second World War brought deprivation to most of the combatant countries. Frau Scholtz-Klink, head of the Nazi Women's Bureau, announced that "German women must now deny themselves luxury and enjoyment." And by 1941, the British were spending 38 percent less on clothes than they had before the outbreak of war. American servicemen arriving in the U.K. were handed leaflets warning them that the British knew how to dress well, but that rationing meant that it was good form not to do so. For the first time, perhaps, fashion took its cue from the proletariat rather than the privileged. As millions of women took over men's jobs in industry, turbans and trousers could be worn with patriotic pride. Ingenuity was at a premium when it came to maintaining a sense of style. When nylon stockings were banned during the war, American women painted lines on the back of their calves to simulate seams.

After austerity

The ending of hostilities produced a reaction to the austerities of wartime. Paris, eager to reassert its prominence in the world of fashion, responded enthusiastically to Christian Dior's striking 1947 "New Look," which rejected tight-fitting economical garments in favor of flowing lines that required an extravagant use of materials. Some of his dresses took up to 80 yards of fabric. The United States welcomed the New Look. In 1949 Dior set up his first overseas operation, a warehouse in

BRIGHTENING UP After the drabness of the war years there was a hunger in the United States for bold colors and patterns (below), which soon extended to men, who took to the Hawaiian shirt (right).

NEW LOOK Christian Dior's evening dresses in 1950 made extravagant use of materials and were elaborately decorated, in reaction to the austerity years of the Second World War.

New York, selling off-the-rack garments to trade outlets. The cutting-edge of innovation passed from haute couture to the ready-to-wear business. The following generations of designers, such as Mary Quant, Cacharel, Kenzo, Calvin Klein and Karl Lagerfeld, aimed not to create expensive couture models that could be copied in cheaper versions, but models specifically designed for mass reproduction. German and Italian manufacturers proved particularly adept in developing a "middle-class couture."

The 1950s confirmed the trend to female flamboyance, with slinky sheath evening dresses and bright cotton-print shirtwaist dresses for day wear. Shiny fabrics and dazzling floral patterns were a striking contrast to the dull, practical browns, grays and blues of the years of war and rationing. In the United States "At Home" casual clothes, such as lounging pants and flat-heeled "mules," became popular with wives allegedly reveling in stay-at-home suburban security and glued to their brand new television sets.

Women around the world eagerly embraced the concept of "separates," abandoning the conventional dress in favor of blouses, sweaters and skirts, which could be worn in dozens of different combinations and glamorized by costume jewelry. Stiffly structured brassieres with startling cone

Nylon stockings were first exhibited at New York's World's Fair in 1939, and first became available to the public in 1940, when 36 million pairs were sold. At $1.25 a pair, they cost more than twice as much as silk (at 59 cents), but eager buyers were attracted by the claims made for them: Shrink proof, moth proof, non-allergic, resists mildew, warm as wool. After the bombing of Pearl Harbor, the price leaped to $10 a pair, as nylon became a priority war material for the production of parachutes, ropes and tents.

points, pioneered by "Sweater Girl" Lana Turner, and multilayered nylon petticoats, which could easily be washed at home and dried out in a few hours, gave added allure to the female form.

Nor were American women alone in embracing these more leisurely indulgences. Men spent their weekends in tartan golfing pants, Bermuda shorts and dazzling Hawaiian shirts. The exaltation of comfort as the chief sartorial virtue soon crossed the Atlantic, and challenged the strict conventions of English men's tailors, encouraging a new trend toward a looser cut in materials of lighter weight. Over the following decades, this trend would be reinforced by the adoption of American-style central heating, which made it less necessary to wear layers of heavy garments throughout winter. Underlying this shift of emphasis was an increasing

FROM REVOLT TO STYLE A section of 1960s youth expressed their rebelliousness through psychedelic fashions. The cult model Twiggy epitomized a more acceptable style.

acceptance of informality. More profoundly, there was an unconscious recognition of "the facts of life." As "mourning clothes" disappeared, specially designed maternity wear that took the shape of a pregnant woman's torso into account made its first appearance.

Youthquake

During the 1960s, the focus of fashion switched decisively to the young: even haute couture could only react. The sensational Courreges collection of 1965 was devoted almost entirely to clothing for the teens and twenties. In 1968 Yves Saint Laurent pro-

TAKING FASHION TO EXTREMES

FROM REBELS, TO SUITED PERFORMERS, TO EXTRAVAGANTLY DRESSED ENTERTAINERS, POP STARS HAVE BEEN STYLE LEADERS FOR THEIR GENERATION

Elvis Presley led the way. Dressed in well-cut but casual jackets and pants, he soon learned that falling onto his knees "gospel-style" could be not only painful but embarrassing. So he had his pants cut specially baggy in the crotch, with padding at the knees.

With the advent of *Hair* (1967) and *Jesus Christ Superstar* (1971), rock music and theater increasingly converged. Performers who reveled in an ultra-theatrical style of presentation were the ones who grabbed the headlines. Bands like Kiss used make up in ways that would make an Avon lady blush; for them presentation was performance.

STYLE LEADERS Both Elvis Presley and the Beatles set styles of dress that could easily be imitated by their followers off-stage.

traditional tartans, paisley patterns and items of formal clothing, sports gear or military equipment.

The career of the Beatles encapsulates two transitions. Before they became famous, they wore the standard rebel uniform of jeans, T-shirt and black leather jacket. After manager Brian Epstein had taken them in hand, they became as much known for their appearance as their music. Dressed identically on stage, they were clean-shaven, with neat, "mop-head" haircuts. They wore collarless jackets, but the rest of their clothing was conventional. Their white shirts and dark ties might have been worn by an office worker, and their trousers had crisp creases down the front. That was in 1963. By 1968 tailored, uniform outfits were out. Each Beatle dressed differently—but in the same style: open-neck shirt and flared trousers, set off with an assortment of frills, velvet, furs, cheesecloth and satin. The message was clear: look as though you had begged rather than bought your ensemble—while hitchhiking from the Himalayas to Hollywood via Peru.

David Bowie drew on a succession of classic archetypes—pharaoh, medieval fool, pirate, spaceman, clown, harlequin and Japanese Kabuki actor. Not only did pop stars want to look both exotic and erotic, they also needed to look larger than life. Stiff shoulder-pads, swirling capes, stack-heels and headdresses exaggerated their basic silhouette. Stylized make-up and tattoos dramatized the face and body. Jewels, sequins and Lurex created dazzling reflections from stadium arc lighting. Clothes were often worn in layers and ultra-loose to speed rapid costume changes and to conceal pads for absorbing sweat. These stage clothes made terrific photographs for posters and album covers, spurring more demand for the musicians' wares.

For bands specializing in small-scale club appearances, where the performer and the audience are much closer to one another, detail counted and humor mattered. As a result, performers created witty costume combinations that mocked or contrasted

POP ICON David Bowie represented a trend towards fantasy fashion.

A FRENCH-ITALIAN-AMERICAN-GERMAN CLASSIC

"Jeans" was how English-speakers, 150 years ago, referred to the trousers worn by Italian sailors from Genoa. "Levis," however, perpetuate the name of their inventor, German immigrant Levi Strauss, who manufactured tough trousers, at $13 a dozen pairs, for the miners of the 1848–49 California Gold Rush.

For almost 100 years, jeans remained the distinctive garment of men doing rough, heavy, outdoor work, and as clothes they were non-fashion. Then, in the depressed 1930s, they were worn by American college students, perhaps out of sympathy for the plight of the unemployed. By the 1950s, jeans were crossing the Atlantic as Europeans acknowledged in their own midst an American invention—the teenager. Even in Europe, teenage heroes were American—James Dean, Marlon Brando, Elvis Presley—and they usually wore jeans as emblems of their defiance towards authority figures such as teachers or judges. Jeans had now become "antifashion."

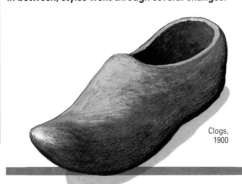

SURVIVOR A Levi jeans advertisement of 1900.

In the 1960s, jeans won universal, unisex acceptance among the young, who usually wore them skintight and often faded. Torn, frayed and patched versions were favored by those who clung to the antifashion notion of jeans—which, worn clean and neatly creased, had become high fashion.

In 1991, a jeans range was launched to accommodate the bulging waistlines and sagging bottoms of the middle-aged. They were called Dockers. In name, at least, jeans had come full circle.

claimed "Down with the Ritz! Long live the street!" perceptively observing that girls no longer wanted to look like their mothers. The youth of America had reacted to the blanket of conformity spread across the nation in the 1950s through an almost religious dedication to fashion fads, often lifted directly from Hollywood. Teenage girls begged their parents for poodle skirts and sweater sets, while boys wore motorcycle jackets and saddle shoes. A series of hairstyles, as fleeting and powerful as summer storms, swept the country: for girls, the poodle cut, the beehive, and the pageboy; for boys, the crew cut, the flat top, the pompadour, and the ducktail.

If youth culture had been simmering in the 50s, it came to a boil in the 60s, and lent its sense of extravagance and spirited rebellion to the fashion world. However, when the decade began, the emphasis was on class; Americans took their fashions cues from Jacqueline Kennedy, who in turn took hers from Paris. Jackie's bouffant hairstyle and pillbox hats bespoke elegance and grace, and appealed to the more conservative sensibilities of the nation.

Across the Atlantic, however, London was challenging Paris's supremacy, appropriating to itself the concept of the "boutique," selling cheap and cheerful clothes that disregarded the rules of good taste and many of the standards of good workmanship. Glitter, hot pants, frilly satin shirts, mini-skirts, and

MIX—BUT NOT MATCH For American punks, like their European counterparts, the fashion rule was that there are no rules. The result was an instantly recognizable "style."

MEN'S SHOE TECHNOLOGY In 1900 some European workers wore wooden clogs. In the 1990s, high-tech sneakers with air-cushioned soles were fashionable. In between, styles went through several changes.

Clogs, 1900

Spats, 1920s

Corresponder
Sportste
1920s-3C

THE ULTIMATE GARMENT The comfort of the jogging suit—derived from the athlete's track suit—made it popular with the unathletic of both genders and all ages.

bell-bottom pants appeared in storefront windows and on busy city streets. This "mod" style quickly caught on in the United States, as New York's Seventh Avenue became the center of a hyper-trendy fashion scene. Expropriating motifs from popular culture and designs from consumer packaging, and using gloriously artificial materials such as vinyl, the emphasis was on freedom, fun, and irreverence. The change was most dramatic, perhaps, in the clothing of men, who revealed themselves to be frustrated peacocks, yearning to strut in puce velvet jackets, swathed in Afghan caftans, and perched on seven-inch platform shoes. In this age, as never before, to feel good was to look good, and most probably, vice versa.

Fashion—farewell!

In the United States, a sense of tackiness and outrageousness inherited from the 60s still prevailed in the 1970s, as men relaxed in polyester leisure suits and Disco-style ultra-suede pants and women took to anything tight-fitting. In the Eighties, a sense of sobriety reentered the fashion world, as men and women began to "dress for success," attempting to evoke glamour and power with their clothes instead of freedom and exuberance. Designer logos like Ralph Lauren and Calvin Klein popped up on polo shirts across the country, and fashion magazines such as *Harper's Bazaar, Elle,* and *Vogue* instructed the lay reader as to the current fashion

whimsies of the rich and powerful. Being fit was also in as never before, as women stuffed themselves into Lycra and spandex aerobic suits. Athletic gear, in 1982 a 4.5 billion-dollar industry, became almost as fashionable as evening wear. Nike sneakers, in a myriad of styles and endorsed by the nation's top athletes, sold out at exorbitant rates; by the end of the Eighties, 400 million pairs of athletic shoes were being produced each year in the U.S. alone.

The Nineties tempered some of this flair, as people in general became less status conscious. Paris still considered itself the home of couture, but it was Milan, and designers like Giorgio Armani, that most effectively managed effectively managed to establish and exploit a link between high style and mass production. Italian designers' mastery of knitted fabrics had begun to establish their country's fashion credentials as far back as the 1950s. By the 1970s, the output of Italy's fashion and textiles business was worth more than its motor and electronics industries put together.

In the United States, fashion's ineluctable dialectic swung once again with grunge style, as teenagers emulated the sullen insouciance of such alternative rock bands as Nirvana and Pearl Jam, wearing dull flannel shirts and work boots. From rap music

came the hip-hop style, with baggy clothing and flashy athletic gear, which quickly spread from urban to suburban areas. But while they affected a casual disregard for status, these looks often denoted boundaries of cool and uncool, hip and unhip, as tenacious as those of Edwardian England.

COOL CLOTHES Male style-setting of the 1990s inverts the norms of a century ago, taking its inspiration from the streets—Below: the hip-hop group NWA. Footwear is a crucial accessory.

Casual Shoe,
1950s

Chelsea Boot,
1960s

Running Shoe,
1980-90s

OUR DAILY BREAD

INCREASINGLY COSMOPOLITAN DIETS SUGGEST THAT, IN THIS RESPECT AT LEAST, THE GLOBAL VILLAGE IS NO LONGER A FICTION

British soldiers, it was said during the First World War, could remain steadfast in the face of almost any horror—except French food. That, at least, was the opinion of the poet Robert Graves, who served as an infantry officer with the Royal Welsh Fusiliers through the four bloody years of the war. On one occasion the supplies for the British front-line troops got muddled up with those of their French neighbors. The French stared sadly at a small mountain of tins of bully beef, hard tack biscuits and plum-and-apple jam. The Welsh rejected, with contempt, the avalanche of fresh vegetables intended for conversion into stews and soups. On the other side of no-man's-land, the German soldiers no doubt munched on solid chunks of *wurst* (meat sausage) and black rye bread. While the senior officers of all three armies might have applauded the creations of a Parisian chef, the men under their command exhibited an undying loyalty to their own distinctive national diets.

In food, as in fashion, Paris represented a peak of perfection but, outside the elite, few cared to imitate it. In the course of the century rising real incomes, international migration and the common experience of travel would change all that—with the eager encouragement of a massive industry devoted to the processing, preparation and promotion of food products and liquor. Italians would learn to drink whisky, the French to relish pizza, the conservative British to wash

AT THE MARGIN The food reserves of a 1911 New York slum family consisted of a little butter, some sugar and a nearly empty can of evaporated milk.

in chemistry, botany and engineering had made agriculture scientific and, in North America and Britain especially, mechanized. Even in these countries, however, the main motive power on farms was still supplied by the horse. Thanks to the advent of railways and fuel-efficient, steel-hulled, refrigerated cargo ships, foodstuffs were among the most widely traded of commodities. Britain, in particular, relied on imports to feed its people. The British commonly ate bread made

poor of northern Europe, potatoes and bread accounted for the bulk of food intake. Proteins were largely taken from red meat, hard cheese and, less commonly, fish. Such a diet was also typical of the working class in big American cities. In 1914, the average family in Chicago's stockyard district (where there were many immigrants from Eastern Europe) spent over a quarter of their budget on baked goods, flour and meat, but only 4 percent on vegetables (mostly potatoes and cabbage) and 2 percent on fruit.

Nutritional standards were especially poor in England, where the highly urbanized working population was so far removed from country life that they often lacked even an elementary knowledge of how food was prepared. Frying was the most common method of cooking, and foods were often soaked mercilessly in grease and oil. Green vegetables were rarely eaten, and salads were virtually unknown. Children feasted on treats chosen for their flavors and not for their nutritional value—cookies and syrupy-sweet canned fruit and sausages of spicy flavor and dubious contents. Although throughout the industrialized world, more and more everyday foodstuffs, such as fruit, jams and tea, were sold in cans, jars or sealed packets, most commodities were still sold loose; this provided ample opportunities for accidental

SOLID STUFF German cuisine was varied and substantial for those families who could afford to eat well.

FRENCH FARE A soup kitchen dispenses survival rations to the needy of 1903 (top), while Paris bank employees enjoy the use of a staff canteen.

down pasta with wine, and the children of all three to eat American-style burgers.

Science, too, would play a fundamental though largely unacknowledged part in eroding traditional attitudes to food and patterns of eating, implanting a new orthodoxy of nutritional assumptions: that taste and enjoyment are not necessarily the best guide to healthy eating.

The people's diet in 1900

Food production was still the world's biggest industry in 1900, certainly in terms of the amount of manpower employed. Advances

from wheat grown on North American prairies, and meat raised in Australia or Argentina, washed down with tea from India or cocoa from West Africa, sweetened with sugar from the Caribbean.

Yet, despite advances in science and industry that might have seemed miraculous to previous generations, many of the poor in Europe and North America still suffered from malnutrition. This was largely a result of their poverty, but also partly a result of their lack of knowledge about nutrition. Malnutrition was common among the children of large families with a single breadwinner—who had to have the best of what food there was to keep up his physical strength. It was even more prevalent among their wives, who controlled the diets of both husband and children. Among the urban

contamination and deliberate adulteration, especially by retailers. The dilution of milk with water was an almost universal practice.

The French, meanwhile, refused to succumb to the joyless and unimaginative cuisine they perceived to plague England. For them, eating was not a disagreeable necessity, but was central to civilized existence, national pride and family life. A knowledge of gastronomy was by no means confined to the bourgeoisie. Even the poor knew how to make nourishing soups and hearty stews, often from ingredients that in Britain would probably have been unrecognized as edible. However, the traditional peasant recipes of the different French regions so lovingly recorded by food-writers were almost certainly for dishes eaten on festivals and holidays rather than as daily fare. Many of the poor could not afford to eat well. Jeanne Bouvier, a seamstress in Paris in the 1890s, began her day with bread and milk. At noon she bought a bowl of boiled beef and vegetables in broth, mopping up the broth with bread and saving the beef to eat in the evening with more bread. With a little cheese and thin wine, this monotonous diet absorbed half her weekly wage.

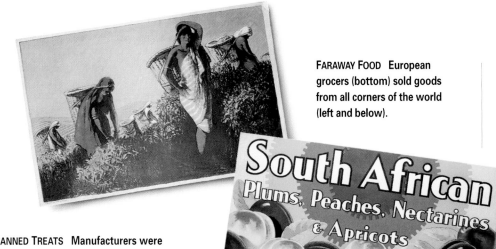

FARAWAY FOOD European grocers (bottom) sold goods from all corners of the world (left and below).

CANNED TREATS Manufacturers were quick to decorate cans with pictures of the supposedly mouth-watering contents (below).

FAIRS' FARE

The first soluble "instant" coffee, invented by Japanese-American Satori Kato of Chicago, went on sale to the public at the Pan–American Exposition at Buffalo in 1901. The St. Louis Exposition of 1904 witnessed the debut of no less than three major novelties from catering suppliers. German immigrants living in south St. Louis inaugurated a national passion by making and selling chopped beef patties under the name "Hamburg Steak." The sweltering heat gave Englishman Richard Blenchynden the chance to cash in by selling refreshing glasses of iced tea. And Syrian immigrant Ernest A. Hamwi sold wafer-thin Zabalia pastry at a fairground concession until a neighboring ice-cream stand ran out of serving-dishes and was delighted to buy rolled wafer cones from him in which to serve their ice cream.

The Germans were renowned as a nation of large, rather than discriminating, eaters. Most short-stay visitors found their diet of rye bread, beef, broth, beer, sausage and potatoes cooked in 20 different ways, filling but boring. They lamented the absence of tea, mutton and fresh fish. Those who stayed longer, however, discovered the delights of smoked eel, roast goose, asparagus omelettes, hare basted with sour cream, pickled cucumbers, paper-thin noodles, chocolate with whipped cream, and tarts and cakes in infinite variety.

Lands of plenty

Posters aiming to attract European immigrants to the unfarmed lands of North America, Australia and New Zealand frequently featured pictures of families around tables piled high with food. It was a shrewd marketing ploy, and by no means misleading. The peoples of these pioneering societies ate well, if not always wisely. The sort of breakfast served by the Union Pacific railway at North Platte, Nebraska, in the 1890s, before dining cars came into regular service, would have seemed like a foretaste of heaven to many a newly arrived immigrant: ham and eggs, fried oysters, fried chicken, sausage, fried potatoes, hot biscuits, corn bread and hot cakes, all served with syrup and coffee.

But American obsessions with health and hygiene were already exerting a powerful influence on the nation's diet. The militant vegetarianism preached by Dr. John H. Kellogg and his brother, Will, gave birth to

peanut butter and to cornflakes, the first of the cold, dry breakfast cereals, whose success rapidly inspired rival products such as Shredded Wheat and Grape Nuts. Dry cereals required no preparation and were preferred by children to the hot, gluey oatmeal that left mothers with sticky saucepans to wash. The food value of the cereals was low, but the milk and sugar eaten with them made up for that.

A parallel health-inspired fad was the consumption of citrus fruits from California and Florida. Those who balked at fresh fruit substituted stewed prunes to combat the supposed American national curse of constipation. Salads were another American preoccupation. Coleslaw had long been known wherever the influence of the Pennsylvania Dutch had penetrated. Lettuce was grown widely, to be eaten raw with sugar and vinegar, or wilted, with the same ingredients, plus hot bacon fat. The French-style compote of mixed greens dressed with oil, vinegar, salt and pepper, was initially known only in smart city restaurants or on the dinner tables of the well-traveled upper class of the East Coast. From such rarified circles the principles of sound salad-making were spread by that temple of stylish nutrition, the Boston Cooking School, source of the Fanny Farmer cookbooks. The Puritan heritage of the average American housewife, however, often tended to make her equate simplicity with idleness rather than elegance. Thinking vinegar vulgar, she substituted lemon juice. Tempted by ready-made mayonnaise, she used it to dress lettuce. She also spiked the mayonnaise with ketchup or chili sauce to produce colorful or spicy variants.

All across America, and especially in the South, grocerterias, self-service precursors to supermarkets, sprouted, laden with brand name pre-processed goods, such as Campbell's Soup (1899) and Kraft cheese (1915). The Piggly-Wiggly chain grew from 500 stores in 1920 to 2,500 stores in 1929. F.W. Woolworth opened up his first five-and-ten store in 1879 in Utica, N.Y., and by 1910, had over 200 across the country. The Irish-born Thomas Lipton

introduced these American-style retail stores overseas. Recognizing that the working-class diet meant that four-fifths of a grocer's turnover came from the same dozen or so basic items, he pared down the stock in his shops to concentrate on bulk-buying flour, tea, sugar, butter, eggs, lard, cheese and other such daily necessities, passing on

JUST LIKE MOTHER BAKES

In 1910, 70 percent of the bread consumed in the United States was still baked at home; by 1924 the figure had plummeted to 30 percent. In 1930 the first pre-sliced loaves went on sale in the U.S.—three years later sliced bread accounted for 80 percent of all bread sold.

economies of scale to the customer in the form of lower prices.

Food—war's most decisive weapon

When the First World War broke out in 1914, neither side had prepared plans for

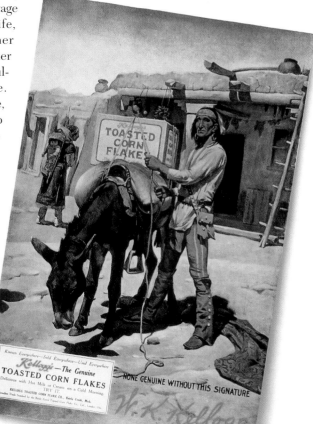

AUTHENTIC PRODUCT Reputable manufacturers emphasized the authenticity of their products to play on consumer fears of impurities in inferior imitations.

WAR SHORTAGES Germans bear sacks of potatoes away like treasure, and buy loaves that have been dusted with chalk to make them look more appealing (above).

FORTIFYING THE INNER MAN

Franz Rehbein (1867–1909) worked as an itinerant farm laborer in northern Germany until he lost a hand in a threshing machine and turned to journalism instead. His autobiography reveals the major part that was played by food and strong drink in the lives of the machine-gangs who progressed from farm to farm threshing the harvest:

"The machine master's first task in the morning is to give all his men a shot of schnapps. Because of the short night's rest, a little bad liquor has to revive your flagging energy... Many farmers give the crew the worst possible food... They reckon that where there is bad food the crews will work as fast as they can in order to get away from there fast. So it can happen that every noon for a whole week or at least five days, you get the notorious dumplings with gravy. When you consider that breakfast and supper are always the same anyway—milk and bread or beer and bread—then it's understandable how this miserable slop finally makes your whole body feel sick...

"I already mentioned the schnapps that every threshing-machine worker drinks on an empty stomach first thing in the morning. But this isn't the only time. Rather, schnapps is given out at regular 2 hour intervals... It is, so to speak, the life elixir of the machine personnel... Besides, what else were we supposed to drink? Granted, for the usual thirst, the landlords handed out flat thin beer or buttermilk. As long as the buttermilk is halfway fresh, it agrees well with your stomach. But if it's old and sour... then you can feel the effects right away when the seat of your pants billows out violently... You also get an evil slimy aftertaste in the mouth that not even chewing tobacco can get rid of. Then you really long for a drink that can clear out your throat... and, unfortunately, the only thing available for this is schnapps."

the maintenance of food supplies because both expected the conflict to be bloody but brief. After a year, however, the civilian population in Germany was experiencing an alarming rise in the incidence of rickets, tuberculosis and influenza. The lightning conquest and exploitation of fertile Romania in 1916 relieved the situation temporarily, but by 1918 near-starvation had undermined the German nation's will to battle on. In Germany's ally, Austria-Hungary, the situation was even worse, with outbreaks of scurvy and deaths from hunger.

In 1916, Germany's campaign of submarine warfare had brought Britain within weeks of starvation, but the British Government was reluctant to introduce rationing. When this did become inevitable, it was introduced piecemeal, with a different impact in different parts of the country. "War bread," made from flour with a high proportion of husk milled in, was, however, universally disliked and regarded as dirty.

The experience of war stimulated scientific research into food-preservation techniques and the links between health

times as much. Leftover macaroni and cheese, ham and remnants of so-called Spaghetti Italienne could be rehashed into what the trade called "work-overs" and sold under another name the following day. Public suspicion of these practices opened yet more avenues for the enterprising. Entrepreneur Frank G. Shattuck carved a profitable niche in the market by promoting his chain of Schrafft's restaurants as suppliers of genuine home cooking. This ploy was based on his realization that "Mothers today . . . aren't particularly interested in pies. Their time is now taken up with all sorts of other things— movies, bridge par-

RETAIL REVOLUTION Grocers in Britain, such as Sir Thomas Lipton, got the idea for their food stores from American grocers like the one above, down to the white uniforms.

and nutrition. In 1928, a Polish-American biochemist, Casimir Funk, discovered Vitamin B, and was able to demonstrate that its absence was the cause of the disease beriberi. This insight led to a greater understanding of vitamin deficiencies in general, including the discovery of Vitamin C in 1928, which was linked to scurvy. In 1932, Vitamin C was first synthesized in a lab artificially, resulting in the near eradication of scurvy throughout the Western world.

Novelty and nutrition

By the 1920s, improvements in refrigeration, transportation and communication were blurring regional differences in American cooking and fostering the emergence of a national cuisine. In 1928 home economist Christine Frederick complained that: "I have eaten in

Florence, Alabama, in Logan, Utah, in Mansfield, Ohio, and Penobscot, Maine. Is there any difference in the meals served in one locality from another? No. The customer . . . sit[s] down to the same old steak, or canned beans, bottled catsup, French fries or Adam and Eve on a raft. Where, I ask you, is the sweet potato pone of Maryland for a slice of which General Lee would walk a mile? Where is the genuine clam chowder of New England? Gone, or rapidly disappearing."

One of the reasons for this standardization lay in the fact that restaurant chains could be very profitable if they were organized on industrial lines and used commercially prepared foods that could be assembled by unskilled, underpaid labor. In 1929, canned soup costing 3 cents a serving could be sold for five or even seven

FOOD ON THE MOVE The ability of Americans to travel across the country made the roadside diner a favorite place to grab a meal.

NOR ANY DROP TO COOK WITH

America's experiment with Prohibition, which was introduced in 1919 and not repealed until 1933, had a dramatic effect on the nation's eating habits, especially among the elite. French chefs emigrated in droves. Smart New York restaurants such as Delmonico's and Sherry's closed their doors, unable to offer fine food at relatively modest prices because they were no longer able to subsidize the meals by selling wines and spirits with high margins of profit. Redundant bars were turned into cafés or ice-cream parlors, and bar tenders were replaced by soda-jerks. In California, the vineyards were turned to growing raisins. And at one teachers' college, an instructor managed to produce a volume on *French Home Cooking* that not only omitted wine from many of the recipes for which it would have been deemed essential in any French home—but even omitted to say that the wine had been omitted.

DO YOU COME HERE OFTEN? American sailors take their girlfriends to a soda fountain—Prohibition's respectable alternative to a public bar or tavern.

ties and automobile rides. A young man contemplating marriage no longer asks whether a girl is a good cook; he wants to know whether she is a good sport."

Technological changes in processing and packaging also had their impact on food in the home, as an account of the "Grocery Revolution" in the *Ladies' Home Journal* enthused: "Every day sees some ingenious new wrinkle [ploy] devised to lessen labor . . . You don't have to clean up tea grounds; tea comes in individual bags, made possible by new packaging machinery . . . You don't have

to prepare the morning grapefruit any more; if you wish you can get all the meat of the grapefruit in cans or glass containers ready for the hurried commuter's breakfast . . . There are few things except soft-boiled eggs that you can't buy almost ready to eat today."

Department of Commerce surveys revealed that respondents still believed overwhelmingly that fresh foods tasted better and were more nutritious than canned goods—but canned goods were so much more convenient. Paradoxically, they were valued less in winter than in summer, when social and other activities such as gardening left the housewife with less time for lengthy food preparation. Should she be so pressed that she even forgot to shop for her canned goods, she could always find salvation in such handy recipes as Emergency Cream of Tomato Soup—one cup of diluted condensed milk, plus three tablespoons of bottled ketchup.

In the 1920s, American-style "convenience foods" began to penetrate Britain, although they made little headway in mainland Europe. During the First World War, many women had swapped the long hours and confinement of domestic service for well-paid, if noisy, factory work. The result of this change in occupations was a postwar shortage of servants, which in turn obliged many middle-class British housewives to do far more of their own cooking than they had previously done. They welcomed the short cuts represented by products such as custard powder and sandwich spreads. The range of canned goods, previously confined to soups, fish, corned beef and Californian fruits, increased enormously. Tempting advertisements for Heinz canned soups taunted the housewife—"Would you buy a plump young chicken just to make soup? Would you make soup with rich cream? Would you take new peas, choice asparagus and expensive mushrooms and put them into soup? Perhaps—if you were a millionaire! But that's just what Heinz does."

Giant manufacturers, like H.J. Heinz, Kellogg, Nabisco, and in Great Britain, Crosse & Blackwell, quickly came to dominate the food trade. Though the main streets of large cities were still crowded with grocers, butchers, and bakers, by the 1930s, many small shopkeepers were being reduced to the role of an agent, selling the branded,

packaged goods supplied by big firms rather than blending their own teas, curing their own hams, or weighing out butter produced on a local farm.

Just scraping by

The leanness of the Thirties curbed much of the prosperity of the earlier decade, and men and women struggled to feed their families with often meager provisions. In many countries, nutritional standards suffered accordingly. In Britain, an influential survey of eating habits, conducted in 1936 by Doctor John Boyd Orr, caused

CUSTOMER CARE Higher wages in the United States encouraged the development of labor-saving self-service in groceries (left). In France the customer was still helped by an assistant.

considerable alarm with its contention that half the population still did not have a diet adequate for optimum growth and health. These findings were confirmed indirectly by British army recruitment figures: in 1935, 62 percent of would-be volunteers were rejected on medical grounds.

By the end of the decade, Britain began to recover, and nutritional standards began to rise. A 1938 survey revealed that even the poorest British families usually began the day with a hot meal. More than half the families still had a substantial midday meal at home, usually consisting of meat and vegetables. In the evenings, another cooked meal was eaten, except by the poorest, who were more likely to make do with bread and jam, cakes and biscuits.

In the United States during the Depression, the poor were said to have "starved in the midst of plenty." There were bread lines and soup kitchens, localized hunger and malnutrition even among the rural poor. During the Depression's worst years, New York City alone harbored 82 bread-lines, providing 85,000 meals a day. For those accustomed to American abundance, such deprivation was difficult to

A NOTRE SANTE

During the 1932 Los Angeles Olympics, the French national team successfully managed to gain exemption from Prohibition by claiming that wine was an essential part of their national diet. The team won several medals, including four for cycling and three golds for weightlifting.

BREAD LINES The unemployed lined up for handouts in New York's Times Square in the early 30s. Left: Many survived on soup, bread and coffee with the occasional apple.

accept, and at times led to fits of frustration and violence. In 1930, 1,130 discouraged men waiting in a bread-line, on seeing truckloads of food being delivered to a nearby hotel, surrounded the truck and ran off with the food. But despite the overall sense of desperation, there was no indication, in mortality or other statistics, of an overall deterioration in the health of the nation. As President Hoover resolutely asserted, "Nobody is actually starving. The hoboes, for example, are better fed than they have ever been. One hobo in New York can easily get on line for 10 meals in one day." Even in Southern mill towns, the poorest workers still ate better than their counterparts 20 years previously.

Research by anthropologists revealed that cultural attitudes as much as material factors determined food preferences. A study of the rural poor in southern Illinois reported that taste and economy were far less important than status. Fish and greens, for example, were disparaged as poor people's foods. What country folk aspired to was the canned

BREAD INTO DUST In the Midwest, long-term erosion caused by inappropriate farming practices, compounded by natural disasters, stripped topsoil from the land.

salmon and hamburgers they associated with their city cousins. Another study of farmers in the southeast in 1940 revealed a strong preference for processed foods over home-grown ones, even though the latter were both cheaper and more nutritious.

Guns before butter

Elsewhere in Europe, conditions improved slowly as well. In the 1930s, the average German family spent almost half its household income on food, with bread the single largest item. Between 1932 and 1938, as Germany pulled out of the depths of the depression, bread consumption increased by about a sixth. During the Second World War, bread was rationed, bulked out with bran, and was generally sold a day old because this meant that the bread required more chewing and went further.

Average German meat consumption in the 30s stood at about 119 lbs. a year, markedly lower than in the United States (125 lbs.); and over half was in the form of pork. Germans also consumed only half as many eggs and half as much sugar as Americans and Britons did—but roughly twice as much cabbage and potatoes, and three times as much wine. During the war, meat consumption fell to just 35 lbs. a year—but that was still more than twice as much as the average Frenchman or Pole.

Propagandists urged consumers to accept shortages cheerfully. When lemons became unobtainable, they argued that German-grown nutrients benefited only the body of a pure-blooded German, so patriots should be glad to consume home-grown rhubarb instead of foreign citrus fruits.

In postwar Germany, unprecedented prosperity, foreign travel and immigrants from Turkey, Yugoslavia, Greece, Italy and Spain, combined to revolutionize eating patterns. The "economic miracle" of the 1950s was accompanied by a *Fresswelle* (wave of guzzling), as the nation attempted to bury memories of wartime hunger under an avalanche

WAR-TIME FOOD RATIONING

A SCARCITY OF SOME FOOD ITEMS IN EUROPE LED TO WORLDWIDE RATIONING, BUT AMERICANS, FAR FROM THE FIELDS OF BATTLE, CONTINUED TO HARVEST

Roses are Red, violets are Blue/ Sugar is sweet. Remember?—So went Walter Winchell's wry take on the food rationing enforced by the U.S. government during World War II. Ships that had once carried sugar from Cuba and coffee from South America were suddenly appropriated for the war effort, and to budget the nation's limited supply, sugar was rationed in May of 1942, and coffee in November. As the naval threat posed by German U-boats diminished, the restrictions on coffee and sugar were relaxed. However, in February 1943 the country scrambled to feed its soldiers overseas, and canned meat and fish were added to the list as well. They were followed the next month by fresh meat, butter and cheese.

The rationing system was implemented through the distribution of coupons. Each month, every American man, woman and child was given two books, one of blue coupons for canned goods, and the other of red coupons, for meat, butter, and cheese. In 1942, these coupons allowed Americans 2 pounds of canned fruits and vegetables, 28 ounces of meat, and 4 ounces of cheese a month.

Depending on the national supply of certain foods, these allotments rose and fell throughout the war years. However, in some areas, a de facto rationing prevailed, as regional shortages meant that even unrationed foods were unavailable in stores.

As they did with fabrics and gasoline shortages, Americans dealt with food rationing with a mixture of resignation and ingenuity. In a version of culinary car-pooling, mothers made casseroles and stews from leftovers, and pork and fish became substitutes for beef. Coffee drinkers, following President Roosevelt's advice, even rebrewed their grounds. To deal with a shortage of many vegetables (caused, in part, by the forced internment of the nation's Japanese-Americans, who produced two-thirds of California's produce) Americans turned to gardening. "Victory gardens" sprang up all over the country, and by 1943, produced more than one million tons of vegetables each season, satisfying forty percent of the nation's needs. Many Americans continued nursing their green thumbs even after the rationing was ended in 1946, and the nation's collective stomach issued a loud, rumbling sigh of relief.

RATIONING AND THE WAR Rationing in the U.S. (below, ration stamps) was a very different affair than in Europe, where combatants, and even POWs, usually ate better than civilians. In the U.S., rationing served more as a way of involving Americans in a war halfway around the world.

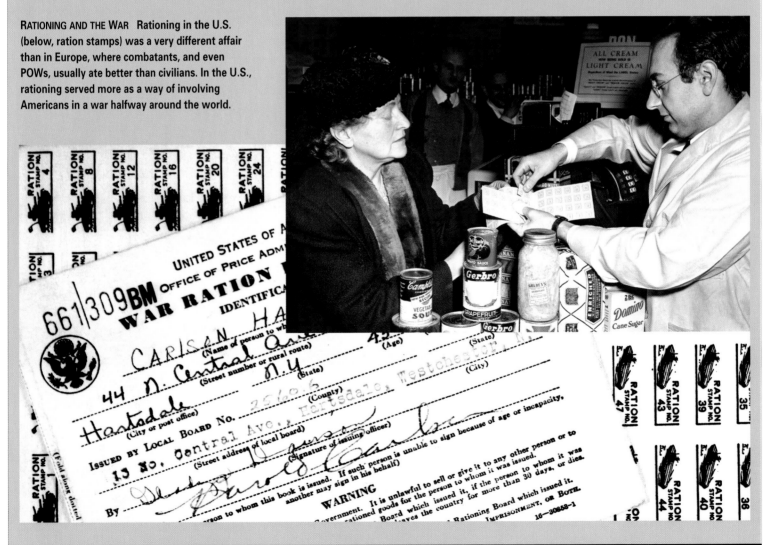

FAIR SHARES In England, the poorest families were better fed after the imposition of wartime rationing than during the 1930s.

of food. By the early 1970s, medical statistics proclaimed that 10 million Germans were overweight, including a quarter of all children.

In the Post-War years, Americans and Europeans began to develop a dual attitude toward foods. Day-to-day eating became more casual and perfunctory, with a greater usage of convenience foods, more snacking and much less genuine home cooking. The commercial microwave ovens, first available to the public in 1967, allowed men and women to thaw out a pre-packaged meal in just a matter of minutes. Fast-food restaurants like McDonald's, nationally franchised in 1955, provided cheap, if nutritionally suspect, fare, selling billions of burgers and untold quantities of greasy fries. But this high valuation of convenience was offset by a striking increase in the time and money spent on occasional meals in restaurants or at dinner parties. Americans spend over $272.2 billion each year dining out, and in Europe, the figure is nearly as high.

The last bastion

The French, too, experienced wartime hardship and postwar austerity—but the term is relative. French women's magazines assumed that their readers were willing to take a great deal of time and trouble over preparing meals. The Christmas 1945 issue of *Elle* magazine suggested how to make a turkey

RICH REWARD Germany's postwar economic recovery was celebrated by a general indulgence in the sort of fatty foods unobtainable in wartime.

last five days—as turkey stuffed with chestnuts, turkey giblets with carrots and celery, turkey croquettes, turkey risotto and turkey soufflé. Few British housewives could have risen to making a soufflé—or would have dared to set a risotto in front of their husband. But the problem was largely theoretical: in the Britain of 1945, it was extremely hard to acquire a turkey in the first place.

The resurgence of France in the 1950s and 1960s was matched by a gastronomic renewal along largely traditional lines. Fine food had been an essential element of French national identity and pride since the 17th century, and the French were slow to accept the products of modern food technology, such as frozen TV dinners. In the early 20th century, however, the advent of the automobile enabled "gastronomads" to drive from province to province, celebrating the delights of French regional

LEISURELY MEAL A British family in the 1960s enjoy a traditional day out with a picnic on a beach in Wales.

cookery and publishing their findings in guidebooks. The venerable Larousse dictionary was complemented by a *Larousse Gastronomique* from 1938 onwards. The *Guide Culinaire*, published in 1903 by master-chef Georges Auguste Escoffier (1846–1935), was a central text for trainee chefs three-quarters of a century later.

Escoffier, chef to the great hotelier César Ritz, was essentially modern in his outlook. He conceded that the traditions associated with his eminent predecessor, Antonin Carême (1784–1833), with their elaborate sauces and ostentatious presentation, might still be appropriate for an ultra-formal state banquet, but argued that they were quite unsuited to the atmosphere and practical requirements of the fashionable hotel or successful restaurant. Escoffier reorganized kitchen routines along production-line principles, anticipating the time-and-motion-study approach

which the American management theorist F.W. Taylor would apply to manufacturing. By the 1950s Escoffier's revolution had run its course and was to give way to what the high priests of food-writing, Henri Gault and Christian Millau, dubbed "nouvelle cuisine."

In 1964 a group of French chefs returned from the Tokyo Olympics impressed by Japanese cooking and its simplicity, lightness, healthiness and artfully aesthetic presentation. These principles were the hallmark of a new orthodoxy. Rich, heavy, flour-based sauces were abandoned in favor of dressings made with herbs, ginger, vinegar or lemon juice. Cooking times were reduced to reveal "forgotten flavors." Steaming was rediscovered, to become the favored method of cooking delicately flavored seafood and vegetables. The truly excellent restaurant presented its patrons with a short menu, offering dishes prepared from the freshest ingredients available from the market on that day. The preserved products created by modern food technology were regarded as anathema. The leading chef also changed his location and status—from imperious master of the kitchens of an international hotel to proprietor of his own restaurant in a provincial town.

A startling, and savory, culinary cross-pollination defined the 1970s and 1980s. Even the French, so defiantly rigid in their eating habits, came to accept, and even celebrate, fast-food. Meanwhile, encouraged by the indefatigable crusading of food-writer Elizabeth David, the English middle-class shed their mistrust of French food and adopted Continental European styles of cooking even in their own homes. In the United States, French restaurants defined the pricey pinnacle of gustatorial excellence; First Lady Jacqueline Kennedy even introduced a French chef to the White House.

Increasing cultural awareness, and the burgeoning popularity of international tourism, sparked an interest in "ethnic" cuisine. Chinese, Japanese, Thai, Tunisian, Indian, Vietnamese, Swedish, Mexican and Middle Eastern restaurants opened across the United States to rave reviews. On supermarket shelves across the world, pita now jostled for space alongside ingredients for polenta or paella. But, of course, there were limits. Garlic and hot peppers were toned down in mass-market products. A range of authentic Mexican foods was reassuringly "adapted" to suit Canadian tastes. In

EAST MEETS WEST Westerners have accepted Japanese cuisine (right) as a mark of their sophistication. Some, however, still prefer to eat in a traditional French brasserie (below).

GLOBAL GOURMETS

THE PEOPLE OF THE WORLD'S AFFLUENT NATIONS CAN CHOOSE FROM AN EVER-EXPANDING VARIETY OF NATIONAL AND CROSS-CULTURAL CUISINES

INSPIRATION Traditional national dishes, such as *escargots* (snails, top left), spaghetti (top right), raw fish (bottom left) and sausages and sauerkraut (right), have become increasingly popular outside their countries of origin, not only in restaurants but also for cooking at home. Meanwhile, 1970s nouvelle cuisine (above), which stressed light cooking and elegant presentation, made use of a diversity of ingredients from around the world.

C ritics have called the process Coca-colonization—the Americanization of popular tastes and lifestyles. Since 1945, the expansion of American-based food-service chains has been awesome, giving the world such global products as Burger King (1954), McDonald's (1955), Kentucky Fried Chicken (1955), and Häagen-Dazs (1959). The traffic in food fashions, however, has not been all one way, and in some counties, individuals have been influential along side the big corporations.

After the Second World War, French cuisine retained its cachet among the elite of the English-speaking world. In the 1950s, Brits were encouraged to forget their previous grumbling over French food by the doyenne of food-writers, Elizabeth David. Julia Child, who had trained at the refounded Cordon Bleu school in Paris, pointed the palettes of Americans in a similar direction. Her PBS series, "The French Chef," first aired in 1962, and millions of viewers, enamored with her accident-prone charm, licked their lips as she prepared her beef bourguignon. Child's *Mastering the Art of French Cooking* (1961) sold nearly a million copies in its first decade in print, and joined such other culinary classics as *The Joy of Cooking* (1931) on the shelves of countless kitchens across the country. Her success on television inspired other chefs to cook on camera, and by the 1990s, there were entire cable channels devoted to making the American's mouth water.

In the post war years, America came to enjoy a range of gourmet choices once undreamed of, even in a nation built on the concept of affluence. The first restaurant to serve uncompromised Japanese food in the U.S. opened in New York in 1963. Hollywood's first Thai restaurant opened in 1969. By the 1970s, American demand for instant noodles and soy sauce was so great that Japanese manufacturers had set up plants to manufacture them in the United States—and a nation slowly but surely learned to use chopsticks.

The food industry, guided by its usual instinct for self-preservation, caught on quickly and churned out newly packaged versions of conventional items that claimed to be low on calories, sodium, fat, cholesterol or caffeine, and high on protein, fructose, calcium and fiber. In the United States, health food sales grew ten-fold in the 1970s, becoming a $1.6 billion business by the 1980s. Slimness came to signify healthy living—and as desirable in men as in women. According to advertisers, it really was possible for men to be as "Lite" as what they drank or ate—although a six-pack of reduced-calorie beer still contained a huge number of calories. The result was a wonderful marketing paradox—people spent more money on food that promised to give them less.

Meanwhile, restaurant goers seemed to want more than just food when they dined. At the close of the century, theme restaurants and celebrity bistros opened around the world to great fanfare, though no one could be certain they weren't witnessing just another passing food fad.

SPOILED FOR CHOICE   In the 1990s Californian shoppers could enjoy an opulent adventure in a luxury superstore (above); in Britain, discount superstores offered value for money on a bewildering range of products.

ural and normal were suddenly regarded as noxious. Concern over cholesterol caused the consumption of dairy products, eggs and whole milk to fall. The American Heart Association announced that in 1987, heart and blood pressure diseases killed nearly a million Americans—more than cancer, accidents, pneumonia and influenza combined.

London, Anglophile Americans eager to sample "pub grub" drew the line at steak and kidney pie, and publicans obliged by substituting mushrooms.

THE PRICE OF A BOTTLE

In 1970 it was estimated that one in 15 adult French males drank more than two bottles of wine a day, and three times as many drank more than one bottle. Two thirds of the nation's mentally handicapped children were born of registered alcoholic parents. Delinquency, ill-health and road accidents, caused by excessive alcohol consumption, were reckoned to cost the French state three times what alcohol raised in taxes.

The craze for jogging and fitness focused the minds of the baby-boomer generation on the links between diet and health. Foods that had for centuries been looked on as nat-

CHANGING TIMES   Two popular food choices that began in the U.S. and spread throughout the world in the 1990s: the food court (left in China, but the scene could be anywhere in the world); and the theme restaurant—above, inside New York City's Harley-Davidson Cafe.

FROM CRADLE TO GRAVE

OUR GREAT-GRANDPARENTS SWORE TO MARRY "UNTIL DEATH US DO PART"—WHICH OFTEN OCCURRED LONG BEFORE EITHER HAD REACHED OLD AGE. LIFE EXPECTANCY INCREASED DRAMATICALLY DURING THE TWENTIETH CENTURY AND SO HAVE LIFE'S EXPECTATIONS—PERHAPS BECAUSE THE CERTAINTY OF AN AFTER-LIFE IS LESS WIDELY SHARED. HEALTHCARE AND EDUCATION ARE NOW REGARDED AS RIGHTS RATHER THAN BENEFITS, BUT POVERTY REMAINS.

TO LOVE AND TO CHERISH

CHANGES IN MEDICINE, MORALITY AND TECHNOLOGY HAVE COMBINED TO POSE UNPRECEDENTED CHALLENGES AND DILEMMAS FOR THE FAMILY.

TRUE LOVE A British postcard gives an idealized view of middle-class courtship – a protracted business at the start of the century.

Many moralists at the beginning of the 20th century feared for the conventional family, even predicting its demise. In France, self-appointed crusaders formed themselves into bands for its defense—such as the League for Public Morality and the Central Society against License in the Streets. The Archbishop of Paris waged his own war against trends that he, like many others, saw as a threat to family values. Among other things, he inveighed against the couturiers of the world capital of style for producing "indecent and provoking fashions"—a cry that would be repeated many times during the course of the century against a succession of fashions that would make those the bishop disapproved of look tame indeed.

In the United States, where the divorce rate in 1900 was the highest in the world, individual states, alarmed at this record,

THE POOR MAN'S RICHES A Berlin working-class family, with attendant grandmother, pose in their one-room home in 1907. Privacy was almost unknown to slum-dwellers.

began to make divorces more difficult to obtain. Some American commentators spoke out against a new breed of young women who wanted to be educated, take part in vigorous sports, ride bicycles, smoke, wear make up, vote, go out to work and live apart from their families. The pundits claimed to see all too clearly where such trends would lead: an erosion of the ideals of premarital chastity and monogamy—and they may not have been entirely wrong. The psychologist Lewis M. Terman, working in the 1930s, found that of the American women he surveyed 90 percent of those born before 1890 were virgins at marriage. For the next decade, 1890–1900, the proportion slipped to 74 percent. Among those born between 1900 and 1910, 51 percent were virgins when they married; of those born between 1910 and 1920 the proportion fell to just 32 percent.

In fact, family life by the late 20th century would probably have confounded the most far-sighted commentator of 100 years ago. Gay then still meant happy. Test tube babies and surrogate motherhood were not even the stuff of science fiction. The notion that children might move to divorce their parents would have seemed not just revolutionary, but beyond belief. In the eyes of French law in 1900, women were still not allowed to be official guardians of children—things changed only in 1917 after the slaughter on the Western Front had decimated a generation of husbands.

Unease about the state of the family would grow throughout the century—as would challenges to its traditional norms. Two world wars, causing devastating loss of life on the one hand, but opening up new horizons and freedoms for servicemen and women on the other, had their effect in relaxing many people's adherence to the old values. The 1950s brought the golden age of the suburban nuclear family, especially in the United States; the 1960s inaugurated its deconstruction as young baby boomers—born in the postwar baby boom of 1947–57—questioned many of its assumptions. In Catholic southern Europe, the extended family retained its hold, but even there more and more families were uprooted from their networks of relatives in the search for work, while young people increasingly broke free from the family embrace to set up on their own.

By 1977 a Gallup poll found that almost half of all Americans believed family life had deteriorated in recent years. The next year, a White House conference on the family generated not consensus but a heated debate that revealed how contested the whole notion of "normal family life" had become. Social scientists noted that many conventional families now consisted of remarried parents with children from previous relationships.

Family values

Foreign visitors to Britain around 1900 frequently commented on the apparent national passion for family life. The aged Queen Victoria was revered beyond the British Empire as an icon of motherhood, whose immediate offspring

united the royal houses of Germany, Denmark and Russia. But while domestic bliss arising from the marital state was celebrated in sentimental ballads and memorialized in albums with photographs of weddings and christenings, the realities of family life were more complex.

Victoria had nine children. By the end of her reign in 1901 the average British family had only three or four. One-person households were still rare, but single women were common. One in six women remained unmarried throughout their lives. More girls than boys survived infancy. Women, less vulnerable to industrial accidents than men and not liable to be killed in colonial wars, lived longer. More important still was the huge

exodus of young single men to the "empty" lands of the Empire, such as Australia or Canada. In the Catholic countries of mainland Europe many such unattached women might join a religious community. In Britain they were destined, according to their class, for domestic service or a subordinate position in the home of a married sibling.

In rural areas such as parts of the American Midwest, Ireland and much of continental Europe it was still common for extended networks of kin to live in a single home. In old-established industrial communities, although relatives no longer inhabited the same homes, they still often lived in the same tenement block, courtyard or street and supported each other with gifts and help. In new industrial communities, in mining or logging camps, by contrast, even nuclear families were a rarity and many single males lived in lodging-houses or dormitories.

In the families of the comfortable classes on either side of the Atlantic there was usually only one breadwinner. A grown-up son frequently lived under his father's roof until he had established himself in a chosen pro-

FOR THE ALBUM A cheerful, relaxed group from 1900 (left) contrasts with the carefully composed studied informality of Queen Victoria's brood (below).

fession. During this time the father would customarily pay his son an allowance to finance personal indulgences—in return for which he expected the son's continued obedience. After his death parental control might still be exercised by a matriarch. Franklin D. Roosevelt's mother controlled his personal finances even when he was president. The working-class or peasant family was far more of a collective enterprise. The contributions of offspring, in cash or labor, were the best hope such families had of raising themselves above subsistence.

After Armageddon

The impact of the First World War on every combatant nation was profound and enduring—but not universally negative. The absence at war of millions of men obliged a corresponding number of wives to take on the role of head of the household, handling its budget, disciplining its members and representing its interests when dealing with figures of authority—the doctor, the teacher, the priest or the policeman. When the warrior returned to resume his accustomed place in such a household he could no longer be master in quite the same old way.

The major impact of the war, however, was the immense loss of life, with junior officers having the highest death rates of all in combat. Drawn mostly from the educated classes, they were often eldest sons, destined to take over the family firm or farm. The bright futures once imagined for a million such enterprises lay cold in the European soil or beneath the icy waters of the North Atlantic. Gray-haired, grieving parents stared at a blank tomorrow. Spinsters faced the prospect of a lifetime without a partner. In Germany alone there were a million unattached women at the end of the war.

In France, which had lost 10 percent of its male population, various policies were launched to repair the demographic disaster. Laws passed in 1920 banned all publicity for birth control and prohibited the sale of contraceptive diaphragms. A *médaille de la famille* was instituted to celebrate the fertility of mothers producing four or more children. In Italy, the Fascist dictator Mussolini, who came to power in October 1922, aimed to raise an army of "Eight Million Bayonets." He made abortion a criminal offense and required all males in state employment, from teachers to postmen, to marry or face losing their jobs. Despite these initiatives, the size of families continued to fall in many countries.

Thanks to wartime service in the military, where the use of condoms had been encouraged to limit the transmission of sexual infections, knowledge of birth control was far more widespread among the working classes after the war than it had been before. Fear of unemployment caused many to postpone marriage and limit their families to one or two children.

For some, the sanctity of marriage, previously indisputable, was itself called into question. As American novelist Fannie Hurst wrote, "[The institution of marriage] is drafty, it's leaky, the roof sags, the timbers shake, there's no modern plumbing, no hard wood floors, no steam heat. We don't feel comfortable in it. We've outgrown the edifice."

As families had fewer children, each child became more precious, the focus of affection, attention and anxiety. At the same time, many businesses shortened the work week from six to five days, granting their employees an extra half day off on Saturdays. This gave families more time to spend with each other, and increasing prosperity meant more money to spend on the kids. Birthday parties, trips to the movie theater, the purchase of comics and the giving of regular pocket money became commonplace among families who could afford such indulgences. The sharing of parental bedrooms with children became a badge of poverty, with implications of shame and degradation. Far fewer children were required to address their parents by formal titles. Mother's Day, first celebrated in the U.S. in 1907, reached Europe in 1923.

Decade of depression

Economic instability inevitably left its mark on family life. In the early 1920s, defeated Germany suffered its period of excruciating hyperinflation when, at its worst in November 1923, one U.S. dollar bought 4,200 billion marks. Later in the decade came the Depression. Between 1929 and 1933 average American incomes fell by almost half. Official statistics revealed that in 1933 at least 29 people died of hunger in New York City; in 1934 the figure was 110.

PAYMENT IN KIND A German family used food to buy seats at a circus during the inflation of 1923. Economic hardship brought some families close but destroyed others.

Britain, where unemployment pay was calculated in relation to a means test based on total household income, younger, employed family members left home, withdrawing their contribution, so that their parents could qualify for "the dole." The traditional authority of the father as provider was inevitably undermined in situations where the wages of an employed son, or worse still a daughter, in effect paid for his cigarettes, beer and betting.

The family at war

The Second World War subjected families to new strains and terrors. Aerial bombing accounted for some 55,000 civilian dead in Britain and about ten times that number in Germany. In France the number of civilians killed by bombing was a little higher than in

Britain. As many French people, however, died as a result of military operations, and almost as many more as a result of Resistance activities. Some 200,000 French men and women—more than all three other categories added together—died as a result of being deported to Germany for forced labor or execution because of their race or political activities. Poland lost a fifth of its entire population during the war, Greece a tenth—more than half from outright starvation. And millions of Jews lost parents, spouses and children in Nazi concentration camps.

FACE OF POVERTY Children in a center for migrant workers on Long Island (above) in the 1950s, echoing the 1930s Depression. A farmer's family in Alabama (right) faces debt and ruin in 1935.

The poorest American families were reduced to living in dilapidated freight cars, sewer pipes, tar-paper shacks and even in caves. Less spectacularly, in all countries afflicted by severe unemployment, families unable to pay their rent were forced to move in with relatives. In such circumstances, it was not surprising that people postponed marriages or having more children.

Divorce rates, on the other hand, declined during the Depression as families pulled together in their battle for survival. With less money to spend on going out, family members often spent more time with each other. Party-going declined. A local newspaper in Muncie, Indiana, pronounced piously that "many a family that has lost its car has found its soul". Many families sacrificed from what little they had to help out elderly relatives who had even less. In 1930, 60 percent of elderly Americans had been self-supporting; by 1940, two-thirds relied on public relief, private charity or support from relatives.

Divorce may have declined but rates of desertion soared as men left their families to search for work and lost touch with them. In

BLEAK OUTLOOK An Oklahoma farmer in 1936 contemplates burnt-up crops in drought-stricken fields.

Invasion and defeat forced huge numbers of people out of their homes. Between 1939 and 1945 an estimated 40 to 50 million Europeans experienced what it meant to be a refugee. For millions their exile became permanent. If they eventually returned to their own communities they were highly unlikely to find their previous network of neighbors and kin undisturbed. Disruption of family ties was also caused by recruitment into the armed services and industry. Over 7 million American men served overseas dur-

ing the war, and their absence was keenly felt by their wives and children. As soldiers prepared for demobilization once the war ended, one U.S. senator received 200 pairs of baby booties in the mail, all carrying the same message, "I miss my daddy!"

Death, danger, disruption and deprivation took their toll on those who survived as well as those who succumbed. In 1950 John Bowlby published a widely influential study of English children's reactions to wartime bombing—*Maternal Care and Mental Health*.

This supported an emerging consensus among health-care professionals and social-workers that having a mother at home full-time was indispensable for the healthy development of the child. The absence of adequate maternal attention was identified as a potential cause of retardation and disorders ranging from bed-wetting and thumb-sucking

HOMEWARD BOUND Two American children at the dockside in Galway harbor wait to return home to the safety of the United States in 1940.

VACATION
The most amusing ever
CARD GAME

G EVACUEE
Nancy N...

T TEACHER
LET X = 10
XYZ = 0

G EVACUEE
Fanny Fuzzy

WHERE TO? A 1940s card game makes light of the trauma faced by British evacuee children (left) and other refugee children (below).

HOMELESS Defeat condemned millions of Germans to flee their homes. Exhausted arrivals rest in Berlin (above) while Russians (below) subsist on little more than bread.

to insomnia, truancy and aggressive behavior.

As prosperity returned in the 1950s people set about realizing their domestic dreams. In the United States marriage rates reached an all-time high; the age of marriage fell to a record low, and the population grew almost as fast as it did in India. Only one in ten women, according to a poll taken by McCall's Magazine in the mid-1950s, thought "an unmarried person could be happy." There was nothing more enjoyable than spending an evening crowded around the television set with one's husband and children, watching a program that often depicted an idyllic family life.

In France Charles de Gaulle called for "12 million beautiful babies" to be born in the decade 1945–55. The French got two-thirds of the way towards his target. Partly, no doubt, this was a response to the optimism and expansion accompanying postwar reconstruction. But many pregnancies were still unwanted. France's first birth-control clinic did not open until 1961. At that time, two-thirds of all couples were relying on withdrawal to avoid conception. Abortions were estimated to run at around 500,000 a year, many performed with the help of a medically unqualified friend, resulting in an estimated 20,000 maternal deaths a year.

Childbearing remained the priority for many American women in the 1950s. Almost one in three was having her first child before she was out of her teens. Two out of three women entering college dropped out before graduating—either to marry or because they feared that graduation might damage their marital prospects. The supposedly progressively minded politician Adlai E. Stevenson told the 1955 graduating class of the elite Smith College that their mission in life was to "restore valid, meaningful purpose to life in your home" and back up their husbands and sons as they battled their way in the world.

The Easter 1954 issue of *McCall's*, featured the lifestyle of an "ideal" family living in a New Jersey suburb, whose routines revolved around family mealtimes, playing in the garden, shopping at the supermarket, carrying for the children and beautifying the home.

> At the time of Dr. Benjamin Spock's death in 1998, *Baby and Child Care* had sold nearly 50 million copies and had been translated into 29 languages, making it the biggest bestseller ever written by an American.

"Togetherness" became the slogan for the decade and those who did not subscribe to it were likely to be condemned as immature, selfish, afraid of responsibility or quite possibly repressed homosexuals.

ME AND MY DAD The suburban ideal of 1950s America was a nuclear family, with executive father and a mother who brought up the children, did the housework and was always beautifully dressed.

The pediatrician Dr. Benjamin Spock's revered manual on baby and child care, first published in 1946, replaced routines with relationships as the key to success in parenting: "Children raised in loving families want to learn, want to conform, want to grow up. If the relationships are good, they don't have to be forced to eat, forced to learn to use the toilet." *Housewife* magazine agreed: "firmness is one of the least useful attitudes of a good parent and certainly not nearly as important as sympathy, understanding, patience and skill."

But the suburban scenario soon spawned its own critics who charged it with fostering mindless conformity and undermining true community and family feeling. Fathers, commuting ever farther to work, saw their offspring only at weekends. While *McCall's* celebrated fathers who pitched in with bathing, feeding and playing with his children, a contemporary survey showed that, in reality, of 18 typical household chores husbands routinely undertook only three—

FAMILY AND FREEDOM—MARGARET SANGER, FIGHTER FOR BOTH

When Margaret Sanger (1879–1966) came to New York in 1902 as an obstetrical nurse, she saw first hand the damage done by unwanted pregnancies: child abuse and neglect, and the deaths of countless women through unsupervised self-induced abortions. Perhaps equally inspired by the example of her own mother, who gave birth to 11 children and suffered from chronically weak health, Sanger realized that, "no woman can call herself free until she can choose consciously whether she will be a mother." Sanger dedicated herself to educating the nation on birth control. At the time, however, that term did not exist; Sanger had to coin it herself. Doctors were forbidden by law to broach the subject, and it was illegal to sell contraceptive devices. But Sanger, determined to raise the subject "out of the gutter of obscenity...into the light of intelligence and human understanding," fought the censorship with a zealous ferocity.

In 1914, she founded the militant feminist journal, *The Woman Rebel.* She was immediately indicted under obscenity laws and on the eve of her trial fled to Europe, where she studied family planning in several different countries. When she returned in 1915, the charges had been dropped. The following year, in Brooklyn, Sanger opened the nation's first birth control clinic, with her sister, Ethel Byrne. In the first nine days, the clinic served the needs of over 500 women, but on the tenth day, the police arrived, closed the clinic down and arrested Sanger. Out of her controversial arrest came a landmark court ruling that allowed doctors to give their patients advice on contraceptives. Encouraged by the decision, in 1921 Sanger founded the American Birth Control League, which later became the Planned Parenthood Federation of America. In 1923 she established the Birth Control Clinical Research Bureau, which trained doctors and performed the first ever systematic test of the effectiveness of various birth control methods. By 1938, over 300 such clinics had been established. In her later years, Sanger focused her boundless energy on another area of public concern; in 1926, she published *Happiness in Marriage*, a manual on maintaining a healthy sexual relationship.

JUST YOU AND ME Single-parent families became increasingly common from the 1970s.

locking up at night, clearing up outdoors and fixing broken things. Everything else was left to the wife, who was also expected to act as a glamorous and imperturbable hostess on the social occasions deemed essential to securing advancement in his career. Chasing better pay or a promotion also meant moving on to yet another new suburb in a new city before a family had ever really settled in where it was before. Each year during the 1950s roughly one-quarter of the entire population of the U.S. was involved in moving. The local neighborhood became a support group for subur-

ban mothers, plucked from one community to the next, supplying them with willing confidantes, babysitters and bridge partners.

Realities failed to match ideals. Between a quarter and a third of 1950s American marriages ended in divorce. Two million marrieds lived apart from one another. Pollsters determined that a fifth of all couples living together considered themselves unhappy in their marriages. Alfred Kinsey's pioneering 1953 study, *Sexual Behavior in the Human Female*, revealed that a quarter of the married women interviewed in his sample admitted to having had extramarital intercourse. Perhaps the rest were too preoccupied with driving their children from one club or lesson to the next or simply too exhausted by their chores.

NEW MAN? Social expectations required more active parenting from fathers (below). A fanciful poster shows a pregnant father to encourage men to be more responsible sex partners (below right).

MOTHERHOOD: A CARAVAN OF COMPLICATIONS

Anne Morrow Lindbergh, wife of the pioneering aviator Charles Lindbergh, meditated on the rigors of modern suburban motherhood in her book *Gift from the Sea*, published in 1955:

"I mean to lead a simple life, to choose a simple shell I can carry easily—like a hermit crab. But I do not. I find that my frame of life does not foster simplicity. My husband and five children must make their way in the world. The life I have chosen as wife and mother entrains a whole caravan of complications. It involves a house in the suburbs and either household drudgery or household help that wavers between scarcity and non-existence for most of us. It involves food and shelter; meals, planning, marketing, bills, and making the ends meet in a thousand ways. It involves not only the butcher, the baker, the candlestickmaker, but countless other experts to keep my modern house with its modern 'simplifications' (electricity, plumbing, refrigerator, gas-stove, oil-burner, dish-washer, radios, car, and numerous other labor-saving devices) functioning properly. It involves health; doctors, dentists, appointments, medicine, cod-liver oil, vitamins, trips to the drugstore. It involves education, spiritual, intellectual, physical; schools, school conferences, car-pools, extra trips for basketball or orchestra practice; tutoring; camps, camp equipment and transportation. It involves clothes, shopping, laundry, cleaning, mending, letting skirts down and sewing buttons on, or finding someone else to do it. It involves friends, my husband's, my children's, my own, and endless arrangements to get together; letters, invitations, telephone calls and transportation hither and yon."

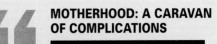

Women's lives, it turned out, were busier than ever. Despite the acquisition of a washing machine, refrigerator, vacuum cleaner and food blender, the American housewife was actually spending more time on housework than her mother or even her grandmother had. Rather than releasing women from household chores, new gadgets simply brought higher standards. Families expected more varied meals and changed their clothes more often. People were increasingly aware of the importance of hygiene, hence homes had to be kept cleaner than ever.

Equal rights?

There was increasing talk of equality between the sexes, but again reality lagged behind

the traditional status of woman as homemakers and wives. Books such as Betty Friedan's *The Feminist Mystique* articulated the submerged but roiling sense of discontent that tormented many housewives. The book sold millions of copies and Friedan, along with other prominent feminists, went on to form the National Organization for Women, the leading advocacy group for women's rights.

The radicalization of family life spread to Europe, as even conservative countries like England experimented with a more liberal attitude; in 1964, the first Brook Advisory Centre opened in Britain to give birth-control advice to the unmarried. By 1969, 37 percent of all first children born in Germany had been conceived before marriage.

TWO SHALL BE ONE Marriages between the races have helped to ease tensions in multi-ethnic societies like the United States and, increasingly, in many European countries.

Divorce and even illegitimacy began to lose some of their traditional stigma. Far fewer couples felt pressed to remain together in loveless unions. In 1920, there were 13.6 divorces per 100 couples in the United States;

PARTNERSHIPS Danish homosexuals (above) celebrate their marriage—a legal formality still denied in many countries. A lesbian couple (right) march in a British Gay Rights demonstration.

many people's hopes. In West Germany the new 1949 constitution proclaimed the equality of men and women before the law, but legal recognition of equal rights over marital property had to wait until 1957. It was another 20 years before wives were allowed to take a job outside the home without, in theory at least, having to ask their husbands' permission and assure them that the job would not interfere with domestic duties.

The 1960s proclaimed itself a decade of sexual liberation. In 1962 Grossinger's resort in the Catskill Mountains of upstate New York ran its first "singles only" weekend. The post war baby boom in the United States—half the population was under 30—spurred an aggressive youth culture that challenged

CARE COSTS Sitters in Mississippi (above) and Seattle (right) provide an essential service for many working mothers but remain beyond the means of others.

by 1990, that number had skyrocketed to 48. But there were undoubtedly losses as well as gains. Rates of reported sexual crimes and family violence rose sharply, as did deviant behavior among juveniles, from truancy to drug-dependency, alcoholism and prostitution. Those to whom much had been given wanted yet more. The couples who married in the 1940s and 1950s, having grown up through Depression and war, were largely content to make their goal the sort of family life their own parents had rarely been able to enjoy. Thanks to decades of more or less full employment, that goal was generally attainable. Their children, who grew up in the 1960s and 1970s, enjoyed unprecedented affluence and undreamed-of opportunities for education and travel—two potent parents of discontent. One no longer grew up to settle down or even get on but to discover oneself and fulfill one's potential.

Most people paid lip service at least to the core ideals of the traditional family, but a few denied even these. In 1960 seven out of ten American households still had a Dad who was a full-time breadwinner, a Mom who was the homemaker and their kids. By the mid 1980s, fewer than one in seven American families fitted this pattern. Throughout the industrial world "families" had increasingly come to embrace single parents bringing up children without a partner, couples living together without the formal tie of marriage, or "blended" families of remarried couples with offspring from previous relationships. In the United States, the number of households headed by unmarried women soared to 12.8, including an astonishing 46.7 percent of all black households.

An unprecedented number of individuals were living alone, either because they were students or widowed or divorced or still unmarried—or simply preferred to. Gay men and lesbians found it increasingly possible to live openly as couples and in the Netherlands and Denmark won legal recognition of committed relationships. "Paternity leave" became institutionalized in numerous West European states including West Germany from 1986.

Interethnic marriages also became more accepted throughout the world; there were three times as many such marriages in the United States in 1993 as there had been twenty years ago. These relationships challenged boundaries not only of language and color, but of caste and creed as well.

Whither the family?

The family was changing profoundly. In North America and Britain, by the 1980s almost half of all children could expect their parents to divorce before they themselves had attained the age of majority. As average family size dwindled, owing to later marriage and the increased use of contraception, fewer children grew up with siblings—although more grew up with step-parents or half-siblings.

Increased mobility meant less contact with relatives. Only one American child in 20 saw a grandparent regularly, though four out of ten now had living great-grandparents. The enlarged role of women in the work force meant children were likely to spend some of their preschool years in the care of a non-relative. By the end of the century, the family had undergone—for better or for worse—the most radical transition in its history.

IN SICKNESS AND IN HEALTH

RISING STANDARDS OF MEDICAL CARE HAVE CHANGED OUR PERCEPTION OF HEALTH, FROM SEEING IT AS A BLESSING TO SEEING IT AS A RIGHT

Germany stood at the forefront of medical science at the start of the 20th century. Its medical schools were regarded as the best in the world—the German state made sure that they were also the most generously funded—and it boasted some of the most innovative medical scientists of the age. They included such figures as Paul Ehrlich, the inattentive scholar whose early teachers had regarded as a dunce but who went on to win the Nobel prize for medicine in 1908. His pioneering work in immunology (the study of immunity to disease) and chemotherapy (the treatment of disease with chemicals or drugs) laid the foundations for many later breakthroughs in the treatment and control of infectious diseases. He also discovered Salvarsan and neosalvarsan, used to treat syphilis before the discovery of antibiotics.

Medicine has been a field of heroic activity throughout the century. Already in the late 19th century scientists including the Frenchman Louis Pasteur and the German Robert Koch had studied the activities of bacteria and other microorganisms and dramatically expanded our understanding of what causes disease. The 20th century would see that process taken steadily farther—and people's expectations of a healthy life transformed accordingly as vaccines and other treatments were developed to control and even eradicate notorious blights. The BCG antituberculosis vaccine, first developed in France in 1927, was a case in point. Thanks to BCG (Bacillus Calmette-Guérin, after the two French scientists who developed it), infant deaths from TB in Sweden fell from an average of over 400 per 100,000 between 1912 and 1921 to around 50 by the 1930s. The World Health Organization, a United Nations agency established after the Second World War, carried the fight against disease a stage farther. It promoted health education and vaccination campaigns in countries of both the developed and developing worlds and had notable success against such threats as cholera, yellow fever and malaria. In 1977 it was able to announce that smallpox had been eliminated globally.

The results of such campaigns are all around us. In the Western world, people at the end of the century are unquestionably more healthy than they were at the beginning. On average, they live longer, grow taller and can expect more pain-free lives. Increased prosperity has struck at the roots of much ill health: poor hygiene and poor nutrition. National health schemes developed in most Western countries since the Second World

NO COVER The unhygienically bare heads and hands of these early 20th-century surgeons—English (left), French (above)—would horrify their modern-day counterparts.

War have brought wider access to up-to-date forms of treatment and health care. Medical and surgical science, meanwhile, have continued to open up new frontiers—from heart transplants, pioneered by the flamboyant South African surgeon, Dr. Christiaan Barnard in the 1960s, to techniques such as arthroscopic surgery, enabling a surgeon, equipped with a viewing tube and remote-controlled instruments inserted through tiny incisions, to remove, say, a gallbladder, without cutting the patient open.

But ill health has also proved a slippery foe to fight. The diseases of dirt and deprivation,

BETTER HEALTH In 19th-century Europe, disease was often spread by shared drinking utensils. A dental hygiene class in the early 1900s (below) promotes better health care.

from typhoid to diphtheria, have yielded ground or even virtually disappeared in the Western world, but the diseases of affluence, from heart disease to cancer, have gained ground. At century's end, an American male has a 50 percent chance of developing an invasive cancer some time during his life; every year, 150,000 Americans die from strokes. Old diseases such as malaria, thought to have been controlled, have started to make a comeback; new diseases such as AIDS have struck down millions. As the 20th century draws to its close some people have even started to lose faith in the scientific basis of Western medicine, turning to various brands of alternative medicine instead, from homeopathy to acupuncture to aroma therapy.

Living at risk

Public health presented a mixed picture at the start of the century. Infant mortality was a major preoccupation in advanced countries, increasingly concerned at any wastage of a precious resource—their own populations. The statistics were not encouraging. In New York City slums at the turn of the century, one third of all babies born died before their first birthday. In Britain, that number in 1900— 140 deaths per thousand births—was more or less what it had been 60 years earlier in the

THE HEROIC CURE

In 1901, an American commission traveled to Cuba to find the cause of yellow fever. A few brave volunteers allowed themselves to be bitten by mosquitoes known to have already bitten yellow fever victims. When one of those men died, the commission could confirm its suspicion that the disease was indeed spread by that insect.

"Hungry Forties"—the decade of such disasters as the Irish potato famine.

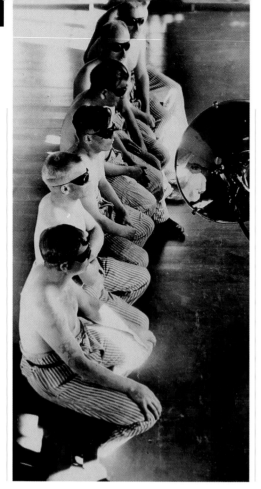

The French had taken the lead in combating the problem. Contaminated milk had been identified as a major source of infantile disease, and so *gouttes de lait* (milk stations) were set up in Paris and other cities in the 1890s to ensure that mothers had a reliable source of uncontaminated milk. Later, figures such as the Parisian obstetrician Pierre Budin established the first child welfare clinics offering care and guidance for mothers with babies. By 1907 there were 497 such clinics in France and 73 in Germany. The next year the New York City authorities put things on an official footing when they established a Division of Child Hygiene headed by a redoubtable champion of child welfare, Dr. Josephine Baker.

For the rest, most people in the Western world in 1900 could expect to live a decade

SHUT AWAY In 1930 German convicts with TB receive ultraviolet treatment (left). Isolation wards, such as this military facility in Dayton, Ohio (below), were also used for TB sufferers.

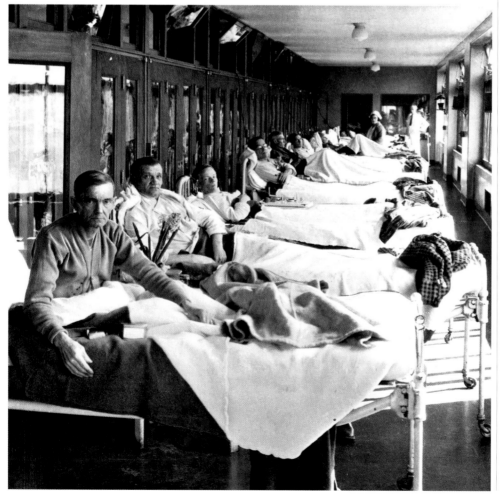

or so longer than their ancestors around 1800, though this had more to do with the engineer, builder, government inspector, and farmer than the doctor. Thanks to steam-powered systems for distributing clean water and disposing of wastes, people were far less vulnerable to cholera, typhoid, and other water-borne diseases than before. Improved housing and working conditions meant less risk of tuberculosis and respiratory diseases. More rigorous inspection meant less food infection, while better diets led to greater resistance to illness in general.

Hospitals, too, had improved. By 1900 there was a relatively high probability that if you died in a hospital it would be from whatever you went in with, rather than from something you caught there or as a result of your treatment. Hospitals had ceased to be primarily prisons for the deviant and depositories for the dying and had begun instead to resemble agencies for curing the sick. Even so, they still catered primarily for the poor, who had no alternative but to trust them. The rich were usually treated at home. When Britain's King Edward VII was stricken with appendicitis just two days before his coronation in 1901, he was operated on at Buckingham Palace, climbing onto the operating table himself, with Queen Alexandra there to hold his hand as he slipped into anesthetic unconsciousness.

Medical practices were improving but, by the standards of the late 20th century, the risks to life from both the environment and therapies remained horrific. Even young fit adults could be at grave risk from the simplest of injuries, as statistics from the United States revealed. As late as 1918, 46 percent of all the fractures treated in the U.S. Army led to permanent disability, usually from amputation; one in eight proved fatal. The only treatment for tuberculosis was still long periods of bed rest, good feeding and attentive nursing, usually provided in sanatoria, deliberately built in isolated places to prevent infected people from passing on their affliction. The cold, clean air of mountains was thought to be beneficial, so that many of the most famous sanatoria were clustered in regions such as the Alps.

Other major areas of health, particularly mental health, remained clouded by primitive prejudice among the general public and the medical profession alike. Deafness, blindness, squints, dumbness, epilepsy, left-

HOME OR HOSPITAL A British mother in 1946 greets her new baby, born at home. From the mid-century onwards, hospital deliveries became the norm in Britain and the U.S.

handedness and sexual precocity were all at times identified as signs that the sufferer was in some way mentally retarded.

Do-it-yourself

Doctoring could also be expensive. In many cities around 1900 the most common case heard before the local courts was that of a practitioner suing a patient for non-payment of fees. These fees, combined with general ignorance about health matters, drove millions of people to self-medication. The barely literate poor throughout the industrial world were credulous readers of newspaper advertisements for nostrums that claimed to cure even life-threatening conditions such as syphilis. Among the multifarious remedies

PILL PUSHERS In the 1900s expensive doctors' bills encouraged people to seek advice from pharmacists, and to trust the claims of the makers of patent medicines.

suggested for the condition known as neurasthenia—really a catchall for any mysterious ailment—included the Heidelberg Electric Belt. Strapped around the waist, the belt promised to "restore manly vigor" through the application of a mild electrical current. Many panaceas were nothing other than souped-up forms of narcotics. One putative cure for consumption owed its "therapeutic" kick to opium and chloroform.

There was also a widespread preoccupation with "inner cleanliness," notably in Germany and English-speaking countries—the French were more preoccupied with the state of their livers. Weekends, when one could stay close to home and a bathroom, were favored times for the purgation of adults with senna pods or cascara sagrada (the dried bark of the cascara buckthorn) and of children with licorice powder or Californian syrup of figs.

A revolution in America

The United States at the start of the century was the richest country on earth, but it still suffered periodically from horrifying afflictions. Bubonic plague hit San Francisco in 1900, returned in 1907, when it also broke out in Seattle, appeared in New Orleans in 1914 and 1919 and erupted in Los Angeles in 1924. In 1905 more than 1,000 people died during a single outbreak of yellow fever in New Orleans. Hookworm,

A DOG'S LIFE

In 1914, the year the First World War broke out, the French-born surgeon Alexis Carrel carried out the first successful heart surgery—on a dog.

meanwhile, was endemic throughout the impoverished South, as was pellagra—a skin disease caused by a deficiency of niacin, a B-vitamin found in yeast, liver and milk.

Things did improve. In 1900 the leading causes of death in the United States were tuberculosis, influenza, pneumonia, heart disease, and infant diarrhea and enteritis. By 1922, the incidence of TB, flu and pneumonia had more than halved; the incidence of infant diarrhea and enteritis had fallen by more than two-thirds; and deaths from diphtheria and typhoid had been all but eliminated. This transformation was due, at least in part, to a revolution in medical training.

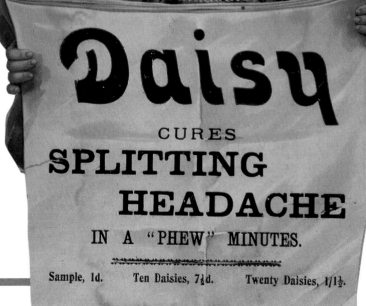

Daisy

CURES

SPLITTING

HEADACHE

IN A "PHEW" MINUTES.

Sample, 1d.   Ten Daisies, 7½d.   Twenty Daisies, 1/1½.

THE FOURTH HORSEMAN OF THE APOCALYPSE

After the most bloody war to date in human history came pestilence—possibly from a pig farm in Iowa. The great influenza pandemic of 1918–19 killed more people in 18 months than the Great War did in four years of unrestrained slaughter. A conservative estimate puts the figure at 21 million, about 1 percent of the entire population of the world. In countries that had taken part in the war, many families who may have already lost a son in the slaughter found themselves confronted with yet more loss at home.

In the United States one person in four caught it and 550,000 died—more than all the nation's military losses in Vietnam, Korea and both World Wars added together. Spain, with a population less than a fifth as large as the United States lost almost as many. In India a staggering 12 million died—one in 25 of the population. In sparsely populated Alaska one in 12 died; in the south Pacific one in five. And in Russia, torn by civil war, influenza deaths compounded the horrors of a four-year typhus epidemic that carried off 3 million.

The killer was a unique virus before which doctors were helpless. Unlike many maladies which prey on the old, the young, the feeble and the malnourished, the 1918 flu virus seemed almost to target fit young adults in the prime of life. After 90 men died in a day at an overcrowded military base, Camp Devens outside Boston, army surgeons opened the chests of the dead to find lungs corrupted to the consistency of "red currant jelly." American servicemen called it the "Spanish Lady." British soldiers knew it as "Flanders Grippe." In Japan it was known as "Wrestler's Fever."

White cotton masks were widely worn to protect against infection. In San Francisco they were made compulsory. But they were quite futile (although they did cause a sharp drop in deaths from measles, whooping cough and diphtheria). In New South Wales church services, auctions and race meetings were banned; theatres, billiard halls and library reading rooms were closed. One small town in Arizona made it a criminal offense to shake hands.

City life was crippled. In Philadelphia so many operators went down that the telephone system ceased to function; with 500 policemen in bed, the streets went unpatrolled. Gravediggers struggled to bury more in a week than they normally did in a month. But, by the summer of 1919, the great influenza pandemic—brief, global and anonymous—had passed as mysteriously as it had arisen.

In the 50 years before 1914 an estimated 15,000 American physicians had been obliged to pursue postgraduate studies in the German-speaking world. As late as 1910 an investigation of 155 North American medical schools reported that only one—Johns Hopkins in Baltimore—was up to European standards. A $600 million program was launched to put things right. Full-time professorships of clinical medicine were established at universities and by the mid 1920s America had some of the finest medical schools in the world.

Out of evil . . .

War or the threat of it helped to raise public awareness of health. Even in the late 19th century, the Germans and French, with their conscript armies, had been alarmed by the poor health of the recruits emerging from their growing industrial cities. In Britain, the puny physical shape of many of the recruits during the Boer War of 1899–1902 sparked an intense debate about "national efficiency." The first fruits of this concern in Britain included free meals in elementary schools and compulsory medical examinations of all their pupils. One of the few beneficial con-

sequences of the First World War was its dramatic effect on standards of health education on both sides of the conflict. Across Europe and North America, millions of men were drilled not only to fight the human enemy but germs as well; the rules of individual and collective hygiene were a fundamental part of their training.

The First World War also led to advances in methods and organization. The military concern with record-keeping accustomed doctors to making fuller and more regular records of their patients' case histories when they returned to civilian practice. They likewise got used to having the services of a professionally staffed laboratory at their disposal. Experience of transporting and treating wounded men would carry over into peacetime with better ambulance and emergency services for victims of industrial accidents. The widespread use of X-rays, to detect pleurisy and pneumonia as well as in surgical

FIGHTING FLU Clerks in New York in 1918 wear masks in an effort to avoid catching influenza.

cases, sharpened the expertise of radiologists. Blood transfusion became a routine procedure that no longer required the supervision of a highly skilled surgeon.

As artillery fire was by far the most common cause of casualties, leading to horrendous disfigurements and disabilities, surgeons focused their efforts on developing better reconstructive techniques and technicians on constructing better artificial limbs. The recognition of shell shock as an illness did much to raise the prestige of psychiatry. Venereal disease, which in peacetime had a seventh of the British army in India regularly out of action at any one time, was tackled by blunt "education," the distribution of condoms and treatment with Paul Ehrlich's arsenic-based drug, Salvarsan.

In the postwar period major companies built on this wartime progress by providing medical care for their employees and their families, believing that it raised productivity and morale and cut down malingering. The French railway system employed some 1,500 doctors to care for a labor force which, with its dependents, numbered 600,000.

In this new age the prestige of medicine rose considerably. Patients came to expect more from their doctors, but they also held them in awe formerly reserved for clergy.

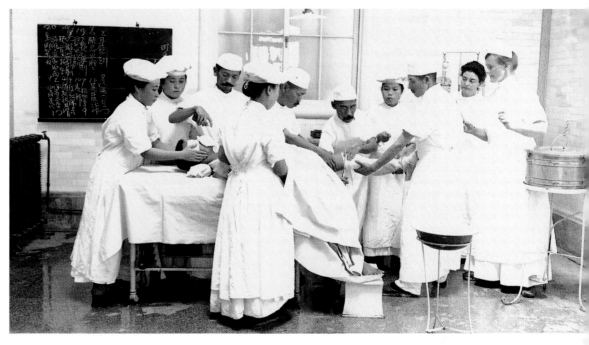

While the priest or minister became the butt of popular mockery in an increasingly secular age, the doctor was rarely derided. School curricula reinforced the heroic image of medicine by recounting the life stories of such titanic figures as Edward Jenner (pioneer of vaccination), Joseph Lister (antiseptic surgery), Florence Nightingale (nursing education), Robert Koch (bacteriology) and Louis Pasteur (microbiology).

The enhanced public standing of the medical profession greatly increased its political clout in such matters as nutrition,

COMPACT CARE   This ingenious 1928 German sidecar ambulance was designed for use with a motorcycle.

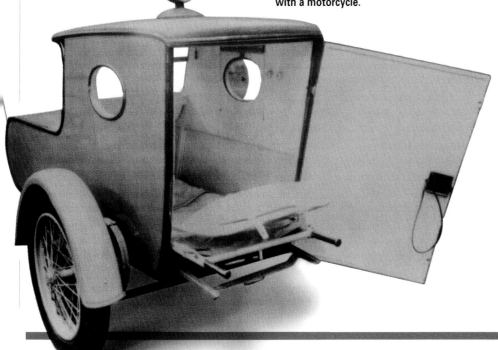

PRICE OF GLORY   A casualty of the Russo-Japanese war of 1904-5 has a limb amputated in a Hiroshima hospital. The nurses on the right were probably seconded from Britain, Japan's ally.

housing and working conditions. In capital cities leaders of the medical profession were earnestly consulted by government ministers and hobnobbed with celebrities. At the other end of the social scale, in rural communities, it was often the local practitioner who lived in the best house and was the first to have a telephone and automobile. These conveniences enabled him to cope with a much-increased caseload, and also marked him out as a person of consequence.

The advance of medical science

Outside Germany, medical research before the First World War had been almost exclusively in the hands of physicians and surgeons. During the 1920s, however, the German-style multidisciplinary approach, drawing on chemists and physicists as well as medics, spread to other countries. Dramatic advances in biochemistry and sciences such as bacteriology followed, producing a series of seemingly miraculous new treatments.

Insulin for the treatment of diabetes was first synthesized at the University of Toronto in 1922. The importance of this achievement was recognized at once and earned the researchers F.G. Banting and J.J.R. Macleod the 1923 Nobel prize for medicine. In Germany I.G. Farben, the chemicals giant, made a major breakthrough in 1932 with the creation of Prontosil, the first man-made drug capable of attacking bacterial infections such as meningitis, pneumonia, and rheumatic and puerperal fever.

The most important medical revolution to emerge from the Second World War was the use of antibiotics—naturally occurring substances (in, for example, fungi) that are capable of destroying bacteria. These had been known about since the start of the century, and the most famous, penicillin, had been discovered by the Scotsman Alexander Fleming as early as 1928. But it was not until the mid 1940s that drug companies learned how to isolate and prepare antibiotics in large quantities. The impact first of penicillin, then of streptomycin and other antibiotics was huge, taking the sting, so it appeared, out of such dreaded diseases as pneumonia and tuberculosis.

As medical experts seemed to be eliminating many of the scourges of earlier centuries, so any revelation of the limitations of their powers became that much more terrifying. Infantile paralysis—poliomyelitis—was an example. A viral infection which could paralyze or kill, polio was particularly virulent in attacking the very young, although older people could also get it. In one year—1952—polio struck more than 58,000 Americans. An Australian outbreak in 1937 led the panic-stricken authorities in neighboring New South Wales to take extraordinary measures of self-protection. Police reinforcements were rushed to patrol interstate crossings, airports, stations and wharves. Children traveling interstate were isolated for 21 days on arrival at their destination.

ANTISEPTIC After seeing amputees die of infection, the 19th-century surgeon Joseph Lister pioneered the use of a carbolic-acid spray to combat postoperative infections.

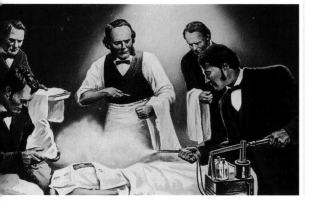

LIFELINE A US medical orderly in the Second World War administers plasma to a casualty. Since then, field transfusions have drastically reduced the death rate from major wounds.

The United States' most famous victim was its future president, Franklin D. Roosevelt. In the summer of 1921 the fit and active 39-year-old, who had run for vice-president the year before, was stricken with the disease while on holiday and for a time he was left nearly totally paralyzed. Determined to recover the use of his legs—which, however, he never did—he spent several winters in Florida, swimming in the warm sea there, and became a regular patron of the mineral baths at Warm Springs, Georgia, where he later established a charitable foundation for the care of polio sufferers. He also returned to politics, though the stigma attached to disability was such that he had to disguise the full extent of his paralysis. For public appearances he had to be propped up, usually by his two sons, one on each side of him, as he imitated a kind of rolling walk to the podium or his seat. Nearly no news photographs exist showing Roosevelt in a wheelchair.

Polio was again endemic in the United States in 1942–53, peaking at 33,344 cases in 1950. Effective vaccines, developed separately by the Drs. Jonas Salk and Albert Sabin, and a massive inoculation program, ended this curse from the mid 1950s.

THE CREDIT FOR PENICILLIN

The discovery of penicillin by Sir Alexander Fleming has long been considered one of the triumphs of modern medicine. In fact, however, Fleming, working at St. Mary's Hospital in Paddington, London, discovered penicillin in 1928 quite by chance and regarded its bacteria-killing qualities as little more than an interesting curiosity.

A decade later two Oxford researchers, Australian Howard Florey and German-Russian refugee Ernst Chain, took a new interest in Fleming's discovery and, having produced small quantities of penicillin from a mold of brewer's yeast, used it successfully to treat child patients under threat of death from certain kinds of infection. They published their results in the British medical journal *The Lancet* on August 28, 1940. Four days later, Fleming turned up in Oxford with renewed interest in his discovery.

During the Second World War, though Florey had proved the clinical efficacy of penicillin against germ infections, he was unable to synthesize it in large enough quantities for the military to use in treating wounds. It was giant American drug companies who produced large quantities of it just in time for the Allied invasion of Normandy and the Soviet advance into eastern Europe, thus saving thousands of lives.

In 1945, Fleming, Florey and Chain shared the Nobel prize for medicine for the discovery of penicillin, though the Oxford team could not bring themselves to speak to Fleming at the award ceremony.

DESIGNING GENES

In September 1990, a four-year-old girl suffering from a rare genetic disorder called ADA deficiency became the world's first recipient of gene therapy—using the genes in human DNA to repair cells. Gene therapies are now in development to help combat such diseases as AIDS, cystic fibrosis, and cancer.

Beyond the bedside manner

By mid-century doctors were more and more becoming mini-scientists. Their predecessors in 1900 had been proficient in diagnosing dozens of diseases, but had no idea how to cure many of them. In such cases, a doctor's chief skill had been to inspire confidence in the patient and then trust to the body's own repair mechanisms to do their work, assisted by an appropriate diet and careful nursing.

A convincing bedside manner had then been a basic asset in the physician's professional armory, to the extent that a certain calculated theatricality was not only permissible

GRIN AND BARE IT   A reluctant youngster from Buenos Aires receives an injection during a 1956 polio epidemic in Argentina.

but desirable—one was, after all, treating a patient not a disease. At the start of the century, a handbook for practitioners had advised them always to carry a thermometer, not merely to provide information on which to base their diagnosis but also as an "aid . . . in curing people by heightening their confidence in you." However, as science came to provide doctors with an ever-increasing range of antibiotics and other drugs, which really could cure illnesses, medical training tended to downgrade such sensitive social skills.

Paradoxically, this trend away from the use of psychological skills in medicine paralleled a growing awareness of the importance of psychology in its own right. At the start of the century, the Viennese physician Sigmund Freud had published his ground-breaking work, *The Interpretation of Dreams*. In the years that followed—against considerable opposition from conventional opinion—he developed his theory that certain forms of mental illness or neurosis are due to the sexual conflicts of early childhood which have never been properly resolved. Later, his former disciple, the Swiss Carl Gustav Jung, researched into

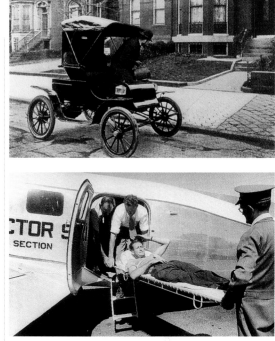

MERCY MISSIONS   An English doctor on a house call in 1907 (top) and Australia's flying doctor service in action (above). Doctors were among the first professionals to make use of the century's improvements in transport.

such areas as character types, coining the terms "extrovert" and "introvert" in the process. During the same period, a range of treatments was devised, and often discarded, for coping with more serious disorders such as schizophrenia and manic depression. Electric shock treatment was used in the mid-century, though it was later discredited. From the 1950s, drugs such as lithium were found effective for treating manic depression.

A new age

The power of medicine as a social institution reached its apex around the third quarter of the century. In 1967 Dr. Christiaan Barnard, leading a team of 20 surgeons, performed the world's first successful heart transplant operation at the Groote Schuur Hospital in Cape Town. The patient was a grocer, Louis Washkansky, with an incurable heart condition, and the transplanted heart came from an accident victim. Washkansky died 18 days later—from double pneumonia—because drugs administered to stop his body rejecting the heart had also destroyed his immunity mechanism. A second operation the next year was more successful with the patient surviving just over a year and a half. Twenty years later heart-transplant patients were routinely surviving for five years or more and successful kidney, liver and lung transplants were becoming relatively commonplace. In 1997, 2,284 heart transplant operations were performed in the United States, with a combined survival rate of 95.8 percent.

Meanwhile, another seeming miracle had come in 1978 when the first "test-tube baby" was born in Britain. An egg from the mother had been fertilized in a test tube using sperm from the father and then implanted in the mother's womb. Subsequently, *in vitro* fertilization became increasingly common for infertile parents, though it raised a number of thorny ethical and legal problems which led some countries to ban certain forms of it. Many countries, for example, prohibited surrogate motherhood when the fertilized egg is implanted not in the mother's womb but in another woman's.

Now, it seemed, doctors could both cheat death and manufacture life. They were intervening in people's lives in other new ways, too, thanks to some wholesale redefining of what sickness meant. Such conditions as alcoholism and drug abuse came increasingly to be regarded as treatable illnesses, rather than as purely moral or character failings. Surgery could even be used, not merely to save life, but also to improve on it—with enough money, surplus fat, an undersized bosom, a large nose, or a sagging neckline could all be corrected surgically.

MYSTERIES OF THE MIND While Jung (above) and Freud probed the complexities of neurosis, the usual treatment for sufferers from serious psychiatric illnesses was incarceration. An American doctor in the 1920s stands with a patient diagnosed as insane (left). At the start of the 21st century, much remained to be learned about mental illness.

Power over the public imagination was matched by power over the public purse. Expenditure on health came to absorb an ever-increasing portion of every advanced nation's spending. In the United States, for example, allowing for population growth and inflation, it rose seven-fold between 1940 and 1975. By the 1990s, many Western European countries were spending more than 10 percent of their gross national product on health care. The act of giving birth, for example, which still commonly happened at home around 1940, had become routinely a hospital procedure, involving teams of specialists using sophisticated but expensive equipment. The development meant that thousands of babies' lives were saved, but the increased cost was considerable.

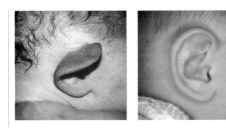

WE CAN FIX IT The deformed ear (above left) of this baby girl, born in 1995, was surgically corrected within days of birth.

The tide turns

In the end, medical science's very success helped to produce its own crisis. Doctors, surgeons and scientists continued to push back the frontiers of what was understood about health and disease and what could be done to alleviate or even banish suffering. From the 1960s, for example, thousands of people with arthritic hip joints were granted a pain-free life by an artificial hip-replacement operation.

In the following decades a stream of new technology, from body-scanners to the use of lasers, transformed doctors' and surgeons' ability to diagnose and treat illness.

As the century drew to its close, the power of medical science to achieve seeming miracles had not abated, yet there was a definite crisis in healthcare in advanced countries. The sheer spiralling cost of it was a major concern for governments anxious to trim their budgets. People's very expectations of medicine could lead to a corresponding sense of disillusion or at least disappointment when it seemed to fail them. No cure for cancer had yet been found.

The advent of AIDS, mysterious and seemingly inexorable in its onslaught, served as a brutal reminder that there were still very real limits to what doctors could do. In the United States, there were 630,000 known diagnosed cases of AIDS in 1997, with 30.6 million cases reported worldwide, and more than 390,000 known deaths in the U.S. (since 1980), and 11.7 million worldwide. The mere fact that many common diseases were no longer killers and therefore that people were living longer had opened the gates to previously rarer ailments: for instance, post-menopausal diseases such as osteoporosis, which had not been such a problem 100 years ago, simply because fewer women survived for many years after the menopause.

At the same time, scientific advances could also yield disturbing results. Advances in genetics promised new ways of treating hereditary diseases from cystic fibrosis to

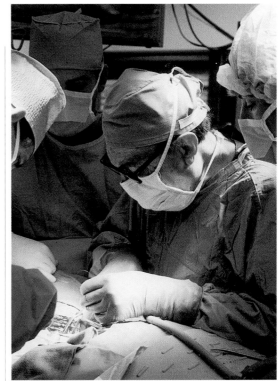

HEART MENDER By the 1980s open heart surgery had become a standard procedure, and angioplasty—the insertion of a tiny balloon into an artery using a miniature video camera— could be done under local anesthesia.

muscular dystrophy, but they also raised ethical conundrums about how far we should go in tampering with the genetic codings of fellow human beings.

Even some of the achievements of earlier decades were being thrown in doubt. By the end of the century TB was once more on the increase, even in Western countries, and so, on a worldwide scale, was malaria, thought to have been largely contained by insecticides and antimalarial drugs.

By the early 1990s the anopheles mosquito, the carrier of the malarial parasite, was becoming resistant to the insecticides, and in many parts of the world the parasite itself was becoming resistant to the drugs. In the mid-1990s a drug derived from the wormwood shrub offered new hope, proving effective against the newly resistant parasites. But this presented a commercial problem. The drug had been used for centuries in traditional Chinese medicine, so no drug company could apply for a patent on it. Without a monopoly that a patent would provide, no company could be sure of earning sufficient profits to make it worth their while to produce the drug relatively cheaply and in large quantities. The drug was still unavailable as the decade ended.

MINOR MIRACLES Louise Brown (left), the first test-tube baby, celebrates her second birthday in 1980. Also in the 1980s, a young patient awaits an X-ray (above).

THE ALTERNATIVES From the traditional healer to moxibustion (right)—Chinese treatment in which herbs are burnt on acupuncture needles—natural therapies now exist alongside Western medicine.

WATER BABIES These 1990s babies swim with eyes open and without fear. In recent years many have turned to "natural birthing"— immersing the expectant mother in a warm pool to imitate the conditions of the womb— believing it to lessen the trauma of the baby.

Another significant trend across the Western world was the growing interest in alternative therapies. Some women were even willing to experiment with new techniques when giving birth—the birthing pool, for example, with the baby emerging not into the air, but into a pool of water kept at blood temperature.

In the United States, an estimated one-third of the population has tried some form of alternative medicine, from acupuncture to osteopathy. By the mid 1990s, the number of practitioners was growing year by year, reaching over 300,000 by 1997. In part this represented a return to the notion of the medical practitioner as healer rather than scientist, treating the mind and body as a whole—"holistic medicine" was a popular catchphrase. It was also a reaction against the use of drugs which in occasional, well-publicized cases proved to have dangerous side effects. "Natural" treatments, such as herbal or homeopathic remedies, were seen to be much safer. In fact, this was open to doubt. Some homeopathic remedies were known in certain circumstances to lead to digestive problems, for example, and a lack of regulation in some countries meant that woefully underqualified practitioners occasionally set up in the healing business, sometimes with fatal results.

Nonetheless, the popularity of "complementary" medicine continued to grow in advanced countries, and the attitude of orthodox medicine, initially scornful, if not downright hostile, tended to soften as doctors recognized the benefits of the holistic approach.

The century that had seen such astonishing advances in medical science, transforming the power of the doctor and surgeon to heal as well as diagnose, had also brought reminders of the limits of their powers and the possibility that healing, or at least the alleviation of problems, could be effected in other, subtler ways.

OPERATING ON A BEATING HEART

Jerome Groopman, writing in The New Yorker, describes a remarkable new development in heart surgery:

"In an operating room at Boston's Beth Israel Deaconess Medical Center, a heart is being repaired. For the most part, the surgical team is following the standard steps of a coronary-bypass operation: the patient's breastbone is sawed through in a straight, vertical line, a steel retractor is inserted and ratcheted back to expose the chest cavity, and the bleeding edges of the incision are stanches with an electric cautery...Then the pericardium, a fibrous sac that encases the heart, is slit open with a scalpel, and the heart itself, pulsating and slick, is exposed to view.

"Billy Cohn, the attending surgeon, peers into the chest cavity...Cohn is preparing to do something that until recently would have been inconceivable—operate on a beating heart..."Look at this heart beating happily," Billy Cohn says to his team in the operating room. [Assisting senior surgeon] Ron Weintraub mounts a long metal rod on a steel retractor that clamps on either side of the gaping chest cavity, and he lowers it to just millimeters above the beating heart, then fixes it in place by tightening a knob on the retractor. Now Cohn takes a plastic stabilizer and connects it to the bottom of the rod, deftly adjusting its rectangular aperture so that it sits over the atherosclerotic artery. He checks that the two bracing sutures he had earlier passed through the heart muscle are tight under the diseased artery. Then he ties them around the plastic rectangle, fastening it firmly onto the surface of the heart...Even as the rest of the heart thrashes away in the exposed cavity, the...stabilizer has grabbed on to one small area and is holding it steady...

"I move behind a sterile barrier and observe the patient's face. It is peaceful and ruddy, as if he were napping...By noon, the operation is over. Three diseased coronary arteries, including one on the underside of the heart, have been bypassed."

THE WAY WE WORSHIPPED

RELIGION HAS CHANGED MANY OF ITS FORMS BUT RETAINED ITS TRADITIONAL ROLES: TO INSPIRE, CONSOLE, UNITE—AND DIVIDE

On Monday, July 31, 1905, at 8:30 in the evening, Reverend R.J. Bowen began a service at Shell Beach mining camp near Ladysmith, British Columbia. About half the congregation of 200 or so were in little boats moored within earshot of the beach. Accompanied by the lusty singing of a

MAKING DO American worshippers gather for an outdoor meeting. New communities had to wait to gather funds before they could build "proper" church buildings.

"Welsh Choir" and the reedy piping of a concertina, the congregation sang "There is a Fountain Filled with Blood" and heard a passage of scripture which was clearly aimed at the younger members of the impromptu congregation: "Remember Thou the Creator in the days of thy youth." Then they listened to a sermon, sang two more hymns and dispersed after a blessing from Bowen. An eyewitness recalled: "Everyone present seemed thoroughly interested in the proceedings . . . The singing was very moving."

Ladysmith at the beginning of the century was a very new community. Like thousands of other small frontier towns across the world, it was steadily building up a regular church congregation. A Church of England parish had been organized there in 1901 and services were held in Ladysmith itself and in outlying communities, such as Shell Beach, whenever the busy minister could fit them in. The services were important events for many local people because they were proof that the camps were truly

becoming proper communities with all the usual communal trappings—such as a church, or at least church services.

In Ladysmith itself, the services were at first held in a building which doubled as Parish Hall and Sunday School. A constant round of social events organized by the Ladies of the Guild served the purpose of fund-raising for a proper church and a community building. These included a Strawberry and Ice Cream Social, a High Tea followed by a concert and dance, a Fancy Dress Carnival, a Sherry and Ice Cream Social (admission 10 cents) and moonlight boat cruises "with musical accompaniment." Another useful source of funds was a tennis court, where young businessmen played from eight until nine in the morning before starting work and the ladies played midmorning, when their chores were done.

Unfortunately, despite their best endeavors, the people of Ladysmith did not raise enough for their goal. By 1909, they had $1,538.05 toward a new church that needed an estimated $4,000 to build. In 1910 plans for a place of worship were therefore shelved in favor of altering the "temporary" buildings housing the Church School. A vestry, organ loft, octagonal chancel and

DEDICATED LIVES Life in closed religious communities, such as that of the Shakers of Mount Lebanon, New York, has continued to appeal to a small minority of believers.

FLOWER OF FAITH The perennial poppy symbolized sacrifice and renewal to millions of Allied troops of the First World War.

Gothic windows would be added and the gasoline lamps replaced with electric lights. A "proper" St. John's was not finally dedicated until 1944.

Religion and community were firmly entwined in 1900, and would remain so for much of the rest of the century. Churches of different denominations sponsored choirs, youth groups, and even sports teams. Religious organizations such as the Salvation Army, founded in 1878 by the Englishman William Booth, did pioneering work in bringing soup, welfare and the Gospel to the urban masses.

In many parts of Europe this entwining spread into politics. Catholic-Protestant antagonism brought Northern Ireland to the brink of civil war at various points. Some historians have even contended that the violence endemic to the American Old West was largely caused by Catholic-Protestant antagonism, and not by frontier machismo. In much of Continental Europe sectarian rivalry was less significant than struggles over the relationship between the Roman Catholic Church and the state. Fiercely anticlerical feeling existed in France, Spain, Portugal and Italy—especially among men, who often still approved of their womenfolk and children going to church. Whereas in England the vicar was frequently a figure of fun, in southern Europe the priest could be an object of hatred as well as respect.

In the United States, denominational allegiance was strong, and remained so. Protestants predominated overall in 1900, but with regular congregations of 12 million there

ONWARD CHRISTIAN SOLDIERS Army-style drills and uniforms attracted city lads to Boys' Brigades. The idea was to steer the boys safely from childhood to young adulthood.

were twice as many Roman Catholics as there were members of the largest Protestant denomination, the Methodists. By the end of the century, Catholics, thanks to a high birthrate and Hispanic immigration, remained the largest single denomination and the Baptists had displaced the Methodists as the biggest Protestant group. America also had more Jews—nearly 6 million—than the rest of the world put together.

Despite differences and divergences between nations and continents, definite patterns were obvious. Religious commitment and participation were stronger in rural areas and small towns than they were in big cities, among women than among men, among the old than among the young. This was true as the century opened; it would remain broadly true as it drew to a close.

The Great War

Though both the Allies and the Germans claimed to be marching under God's banner,

MAN-MADE MIRACLE? A cartoon offers a mock-scientific explanation of how troops might have been deceived into seeing the "Angel of Mons."

the First World War probably did more for superstition than for religion. Clergy on both sides of the conflict urged their countrymen to arms as a duty and prayed fervently for the blessings of the Almighty on their efforts—only the Quakers stood out almost solidly against war fever. Superstitions flourished among men at the front who experienced

AN AMERICAN PIONEER

The first U.S. citizen to be canonized as a Roman Catholic saint was Frances Xavier Cabrini (1850–1917). The Italian-born Mother Cabrini founded the Missionary Sisters of the Sacred Heart to work in China but was directed by Pope Leo XIII to "go west, not east." Working mainly among neglected Italian immigrants she founded 67 mission houses in cities stretching from Buenos Aires to Rio, Chicago, Paris, and Madrid. Naturalized as an American citizen in 1909, she was canonized in 1946.

daily the arbitrariness of sudden and terrible death at the hands of a machine-gunner sweeping no-man's-land experimentally, or a grenade lobbed over at random from an opposing trench, or even a shell from one's own side falling short. Fatalism was the most common attitude, summed up in the belief that if a bullet "had your name on it" you were marked to die. This curious notion may have been a garbled Christian version of a folk-belief, common among Indian or Turkish Muslim troops, that at the hour appointed for death a leaf, inscribed with the name of the soul in question, falls from the Tree of Life in Paradise.

The most extravagant myths were fostered by a popular press eager for sensation but bamboozled out of hard news by military censorship. One such was the story of the "Angel of Mons"—variously an angel with a flaming sword, a squadron of angels on horseback, even a troop of medieval bowmen, which had supposedly intervened in the Battle of Mons on the Allied side. After the Angel of Mons came the statue of Our Lady at Arras. Located atop a church tower used by observers to direct artillery, the statue became a natural target for German gunners who succeeded in knocking her over until she hung at a perilous angle, apparently suspended on the brink of self-destruction. When Our Lady falls, Arras falls—so the rumor ran. The generals prudently ordered sappers to wire the Virgin securely in place.

SING OUT! In the Salvation Army, founded by William Booth (right), music and free prayer characterize worship.

When the war finally ended, there was the need to remember. Despite the revulsion many ex-servicemen felt at what they had seen and been through, acts of remembrance at war memorials throughout the former combatant countries were treated with almost universal reverence. The inhabitants of tiny French hamlets would gather round the local memorial and, as the youngest child piped out the names of the fallen, murmur respectfully in ragged chorus *Mort pour La Patrie.* Nations erected memorials at battlefield sites on the Western Front associated with their troops—the South Africans at Delville Wood; the Canadians at Vimy Ridge; and the Americans at the Argonne Forest. Throughout the century millions who had little use for formal religion or its rituals continued to experience the annual act of remembrance as a moment each year when the realm of the sacred came close to their hearts.

Hitting the headlines

After the First World War, although politicians devoted far less time to discussing religious topics than they had done a generation before, religious leaders and organizations continued to pronounce on public affairs and the popular culture of the day. Birth control was denounced, for example, not only by Roman Catholics but, until 1930, by Anglicans too. In the 1920s, fashions such as jazz, the Charleston, and short skirts were

POLAND'S PAPAL PILGRIM

The foreign travels of the Polish Pope John Paul II have called forth astonishing scenes of fervor. In June 1979 he made a particularly moving trip—his first to Poland since his election as Pope, described here by a reporter for the British *Daily Telegraph*:

"Pope John Paul II, who left Krakow as an archbishop seven months ago, returned to Poland at the weekend as the first leader of the Roman Catholic Church ever to set foot in a Communist country.

The 59-year-old Polish-born Pontiff stooped to kiss the ground after stepping from his Alitalia Boeing 727 jet in Warsaw's scorching sunshine.

Then, as every church bell in the city and surrounding villages rang, he declared: 'I come as a pilgrim . . .'

The visit, subject of months of tough negotiations between Church and State, is an historic event for Poland's 30 million Catholics who have clung tenaciously to their faith, despite 35 years of Communist rule. . . .

The formal opening was followed by an ecstatic welcome as the Pope drove seven miles in an open float through the city streets [for a Mass in] St. John's Cathedral in Warsaw's old city. . . .

The crowd, estimated at between 900,000 and two million people, packed 20 deep against metal barriers all along the route. Plain-clothes police had to haul several of the marshals off the long red carpet laid out for the Pontiff from the tomb of the unknown soldier to Victory Square. The marshals, who were supposed to be holding the crowd back, dashed in front of the Pope and threw themselves at his feet, seeking blessings.

Admission to the Mass was by ticket only, but one determined nun scrambled between a marshal's legs."

condemned from the pulpits of all denominations as incitements to immorality.

Individuals, too, made the news in their attempts to influence history. In Germany in the 1930s, a minority of Protestants broke away from the Lutheran mainstream to form a separate church, the Confessing Church, which was one of the few church groups of any description that dared to speak out against the Nazi persecution of Jews. One of its leading figures was the theologian Dietrich Bonhöffer, who became an active member of the German anti-Hitler resistance during the Second World War. He paid for this opposition with his life when the Nazi authorities found documents linking him to a failed plot to assassinate the Führer. He was executed on April 9, 1945.

Another priest who came to prominence in the interwar years was Father Charles Coughlin. Ordained a Roman Catholic priest in Detroit, Coughlin began broadcasting sermons and talks to children in 1926. As the United States plunged into Depression, the Michigan-based priest's pronouncements became more and more political and ever more extreme. He lambasted Roosevelt's New Deal policies and made vitriolic denunciations of Jews, Wall Street capitalists and communists, all of whom he blamed for the Depression. In 1934 he launched a National Union for Social Justice which recruited 5 million members within two months, but his efforts to win a seat in the House of Representatives proved a fiasco. Undeterred, he continued to preach his message of hate until his magazine *Social Justice* was eventually banned from the mail for violating the

TELL THE WORLD
A tireless evangelist, Billy Graham, seen here in 1977, has preached to mass audiences throughout the world.

BORN AGAIN Two thousand converts are baptized by Jehovah's Witnesses at a beach resort in west London in 1951.

1917 Espionage Act; in 1942 the Church hierarchy belatedly ordered him to stop broadcasting.

The language of faith

In 1909, the American black educator Booker T. Washington visited London's East End and watched a street preacher in action: "He was a young man, fresh from college, and he was making a very genuine effort . . . I observed that the people listened respectfully to what he had to say . . . It was only too evident, however, that he was speaking another language than theirs . . . After listening to this man I thought I could understand the great success which the Salvation Army at one time had among the masses . . . it picked its preachers from the streets . . ."

Street preaching, when it was well done, was a vital way of recruiting for the churches at the start of the century. Later, radio and television offered powerful new means of evangelism, while the careers of gifted platform preachers such as the Southern Baptist minister Billy Graham were confirmation that live, face-to-face communication could still yield impressive results. He preached in his first evangelistic campaign in 1946 and 50 years later was still rousing thousands at skillfully organized rallies. He has been the friend of presidents and has taken his message, based on a call to repentance and conversion, all around the globe, from Moscow to Buenos Aires, Paris to Singapore.

Outside the orthodox Christian mainstream, the Jehovah's Witnesses, originally founded in the 1870s by the American Charles Taze Russell, perfected the technique of door-to-door evangelism, armed with batteries of pamphlets and magazines. Denying the divinity of Christ and preaching the imminence of a final day of judgment, they spread remarkably from the start of the 1940s when they had just 106,000 members worldwide. By 1995, they had more than 5 million.

The language of faith, rather than the channels through which it was communicated, remained a preoccupation for many religious organizations. Most experienced a tension between traditionalists, who regarded their accustomed forms of Scripture and worship as inviolable, and modernizers, who saw an urgent need to reframe the Gospel message in the language of the present. In 1901 a proposal to publish the Gospels in modern Greek provoked such serious riots in Athens that the head of the Orthodox Church resigned and the government

TV, SCANDAL AND THE GOSPEL

"Why should the Devil have all the best tunes?" asked William Booth, founder of the Salvation Army, who shrewdly saw how military-style brass bands could be used to draw crowds and drown out hecklers at the same time. A century later America's "televangelists" applied the same thinking to the century's most powerful medium. Their priorities, however, were often rather different from those of the ruggedly upright Booth. A 1986 analysis revealed that America's top ten TV evangelists spent between 12 percent and 42 percent of their airtime appealing for funds. In 1987 Oklahoma-born Oral Roberts warned his supporters that God might "call Oral Roberts home" if they failed to come up with $8 million. A donation from a Florida racetrack owner saved God the trouble.

TV saved Oral Roberts, but not some of his fellows. Also in 1987, a sex scandal caught up with South Carolinan Jim Bakker of PTL (Praise the Lord) Television. In the same year PTL, which had major housing and theme park interests and $70 million of debts, was forced into bankruptcy. In 1988 Jimmy Swaggart, who had denounced Bakker as "a cancer on the body of Christ," was forced to admit having visited a prostitute—after being confronted with photographs of the encounter. This spate of disclosures not only damaged all televangelists, guilty of sexual or financial impropriety or not, but brought an unexpected bonus to "regular" churches, which took the opportunity to distance themselves by claiming squeaky-clean standards of accountability and disclosure.

STAND BY YOUR MAN Jim Bakker poses with his wife Tammy. He confessed to adultery with a church secretary and payment of hush money.

fell. At the end of the century, in post-communist Russia, Orthodox priests who tried using modern Russian instead of the almost unintelligible Church Slavonic in their services were treated with profound suspicion by their fellows.

Nonetheless, the importance of Scripture in both the Christian and Jewish traditions ensured that new translations of the sacred writings were undertaken. In the 1920s the

SOLIDARITY A Polish Catholic confesses to a priest. Through decades of alien communist overlordship, the Church helped to maintain the strength of Polish national identity.

HOLY FATHER Pope John XXIII gives the traditional blessing—*Urbi et Orbi* "To the City and the World"—after his coronation.

German Jewish scholars Martin Buber and Franz Rosenzweig produced a masterly translation into modern German of the Jewish Bible—the Old Testament. Christian scholars used insights from the study of ancient texts to present the Bible in language that was fresh, and later "non-sexist". In 1946, after 17 years' work by 22 scholars from 44 Protestant denominations, the Revised Standard Version of the New Testament was published in the United States to replace the American Standard Version of 1901. It sold a startling 26.5 million copies the first year. Roman Catholic scholars in Jerusalem published the Jerusalem Bible in

1956, a translation into French that was later retranslated into numerous languages.

A new pentecost

From the Albanian-born Mother Teresa working among the destitute of Calcutta to the Polish Pope John Paul II, the first non-Italian pontiff in nearly half a millennium, the Roman Catholic Church has produced a crop of remarkable figures in the 20th century. But more significant probably than any individual was its Second Vatican Council that, from 1962 to 1965, transformed just about every aspect of catholic life. The Council was called by an unlikely revolutionary, Pope John XXIII, elected as a *papa di passaggio*, "interim pope," in 1958 when he was already 76. Until then he had never identified himself with reform movements in the Church, yet he was to unleash the most thorough-going changes Roman Catholics had experienced since the days of the Reformation and Counter-Reformation in the 16th and 17th centuries. His papacy lasted fewer than five years but they were enough to make him one of the best-loved popes of modern times.

In calling the Council, his avowed purpose was to "bring the Church up to date." In the process he had the rare honesty to admit that the Church needed new life—a "New Pentecost"—breathed into it. Despite vehement opposition from some cardinals, who hoped to delay plans until the old man died and they could be conveniently forgotten, he won his way, presiding before his death over the Council's first session in the autumn of 1962.

During its lifetime the Council abandoned the Church's traditional line of denouncing members of other Christian denominations

INTERNATIONAL MISSION Mother Teresa—possibly the world's best-known Christian—was born an Albanian, but dedicated her life to the poor of Calcutta.

SACRED CIRCLE Catholic bishops gather in synod at Rome. Roman Catholicism remains the world's dominant form of Christianity.

as heretics and instead offered the hand of ecumenical friendship. It also expressed its regret for the anti-Semitism of its past. Within the Church, the Council encouraged greater participation by lay people and approved the use of vernacular languages rather than Latin in the liturgy. Catholic clergy in the United States began to include some English prayers in their services as early as 1964. By Easter 1970 the entire Mass was being said in English, Italian, Spanish and other vernacular tongues—despite the opposition of ultra-traditionalists

CHOSEN PEOPLE For Jews, Jerusalem's Wailing Wall (left) is a place of pilgrimage, prayer—and lamentation. Religious observance (above) lies at the heart of traditional Jewish family life.

such as the French Archbishop Marcel Lefebvre (later excommunicated).

Horror and rebirth

For Judaism, the 20th century has been marked by two events: one appalling, the other the fulfillment of a long-held dream. The Nazi Holocaust cost the lives of some six million Jews in German-occupied territories between 1933 and 1945. The foundation of the state of Israel in 1948 fulfilled the Zionist dream of a return to the Holy Land, which had emerged in the 19th century, partly in response to growing anti-Semitism in many regions of Europe.

Both events helped, in their different ways, to sharpen Jewish people's awareness of their identity. However, in many instances this was a cultural rather than a religious phenomenon. Even in Israel there were frictions between those who saw their religion as an all-embracing way of life—which affected everything from what they ate to how they dressed and worked—and "secularized" Jews for whom their Jewishness was more a question of national or cultural identity. Outside Israel many Jewish religious leaders publicly lamented declining attendances at synagogues and the increasing

numbers of Jews who were marrying outside the faith. In the United States, the intermarriage rate is over 50 percent; the title of one recently published book—*The Vanishing American Jew*—neatly articulated the fears of many Jewish religious leaders.

For all that, Judaism, which had suffered in mid century one of the worst traumas of its long and often troubled history, was in many ways stronger at the end of the century than it had been for hundreds of years. In the United States, the Jewish community commanded a respect and authority out of all proportion to its numbers—nearly six million. The state of Israel, despite continuing conflicts with its Arab neighbors, has seen its population expand with immigrants from Russia, and continues to thrive.

The spread of Islam

In 1900 the relatively few English-speaking people who knew what Muslims were generally referred to them as Muhammadans—a deeply offensive term to believers, since it implied worship of their Prophet, rather than of God. *Mohammedanism*, a standard survey by the eminent Sir Hamilton Gibb, published in 1949 by the Oxford University Press, did not change its title to *Islam* until a revised edition appeared in 1968. If the experts could display such insensitivity, what hope was there of greater understanding among the general population?

The long territorial separation of Islam and Christendom was ended by the unravelling of the European colonial empires and the growth of international migration in the years following the Second World War. By the late 1990s, there were nearly 8 million Muslims in North America and nearly 32 million in Europe.

While most Muslim migrants learned the languages of their adopted countries, only a small proportion of them became so culturally assimilated that they abandoned their religion or their identity as Muslims. More usually, they established mosques: at first in convert-ed private houses then, as they prospered, in former churches or other premises. With foreign support, usually from oil-rich countries such as Saudi Arabia or Kuwait, they have established specifically Muslim schools, segregated by sex, where children could pursue a full-time education with a curriculum organized on Islamic principles.

A woman's place

In 1900 most religious bodies assumed that a woman's place in church was either in prayer

THE WORD Muslim girls in Western countries (left) have fought for the right to keep their heads covered. Study of the Koran (below) lies at the core of a strict Muslim education.

TO BE A BLACK PILGRIM

LATE CONVERT Malcolm X belatedly abandoned Black Muslim beliefs to embrace the universal non-racialism of orthodox Islam.

Malcolm Little (1925–65) saw his family home burned down by a Ku Klux Klan mob. At the age of 21, imprisoned for burglary, he converted to the Black Muslim—or Nation of Islam—faith, an American variant of Islam preaching strict personal discipline and the segregation of blacks from whites. Discarding his "white slave name" in favor of the anonymous Malcolm X, he became a close lieutenant of the Nation of Islam's leader Elijah Muhammad after serving his seven-year sentence.

He was a brilliant platform speaker and won a devoted following among Black Muslims, but his bitter invective against whites earned the hatred of many other Americans. When he dismissed the assassination of John F. Kennedy as a "case of chickens coming home to roost," even Elijah Muhammad realized he had gone too far and suspended him from duty. Malcolm X responded by forming his own breakaway movement and decided to undertake a pilgrimage to Mecca—the *hajj*. This experience changed his life. The essence of *hajj* is the common submission of people of all races before the majesty of God. Adopting the name El-Hajj Malik El-Shabazz, the former Malcolm X converted to conventional Islam, renouncing his anti-white racism. Black Muslims denounced him as a traitor and threatened his life. Shortly afterwards he was shot dead at a rally. His posthumously published *Autobiography* made him a hero to black youth.

or polishing the pews. Women were invariably more regular in their attendance at services, usually outnumbering men by roughly two to one. They organized fund-raising events, arranged flowers, and taught Sunday School. But the leading of acts of worship was a male prerogative. Only the Quakers and Salvation Army treated women as anything like the equals of men in such matters.

The admission of women to the ordained ministry in Protestant churches has occurred piecemeal—and at the cost of creating a major obstacle to the forging of closer links with the Roman and Orthodox churches. In 1958 the Evangelical Church of the Palatinate in West Germany and the Lutheran Church in Sweden both voted to admit women to ordination. In 1969 the Church of Scotland admitted its first woman minister. British Methodists voted to follow their example the following year.

In the world-wide Anglican community the struggle for women's ordination was particularly protracted. The first women to be admitted to the Anglican priesthood, Joyce Bennett and Jane Hwang Hsien Yuen, were

ordained in Hong Kong in 1971. In the following year, 11 more were ordained in the United States. This step had, by 1977, provoked the formation of a breakaway Anglican Church in North America, which claimed to be the true heir to the Anglican tradition. Women have also struggled to gain

FERVOR Evangelical and Charismatic churches have evolved a style of liturgy emphasizing involvement and spontaneity.

FAITH AND HOPE A scientific age still sees thousands flock to Lourdes in the French Pyrenees each year, as here in the 1980s, to pray for healing or to refresh their faith.

recognition as clergy in the Jewish faith. Although not permitted to be ordained by the religion's Orthodox denomination, women are becoming involved in the administration of synagogues, and there are more than 350 women rabbis leading synagogues in the Reform and Conservative movements. Indeed, women now outnumber men in many rabbinical schools across the country.

Cults and sects

The 20th century has seen the birth of a range of sects and cults from Rastafarianism to the Holy Spirit Association for the Unification of Christianity ("Moonies"). Christianity has seen the growth of Pentecostalism and the Charismatic movement within the mainstream denominations, both emphasizing "speaking in tongues," healing and other miraculous phenomena. Spiritual hunger among the young and the disoriented found a diversity of outlets, such as transcendental meditation and the Hare Krishna sect in the 1960s, and the "New Age" movement in the 1980s—a mélange of the occult, the tribal, and eastern inspired devotees to try drumming, dancing, dowsing, casting runes—and even sniffing trees.

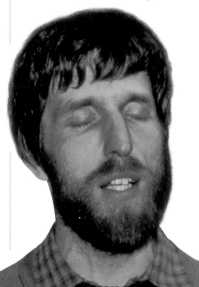

stricken; in Portugal a major new shrine was established following a vision of the Virgin at Fatima in 1917. The black clergyman and civil rights activist Martin Luther King, Jr., won the Nobel prize for peace in 1964; the Catholic nun Mother Teresa won it in 1979; the Dalai Lama received the award in 1989.

Church attendance may be falling in the Western world, but this does not mean that organized religion has been failing to develop in other ways. Few become hermits but thousands go on "retreats" to pray and meditate. More people are meeting for prayer in each other's houses than since early Christian times. If millions came to reject religion as divisive or irrelevant, millions more continued to turn to it for solace in this world and for salvation in the next.

CONVERSION AND CONTINUITY Members of the Hare Krishna sect celebrate their faith on the streets of Berlin (below) and Hindu women maintain their faith at a temple in London (bottom).

WISDOMS OF THE EAST

One of the features of the 20th century has been the willingness of Westerners—especially intellectuals and the young—to investigate, rather than dismiss, Asian religions and philosophies. This may have arisen partly from disillusionment with conventional Christianity, partly from the inspiration of spiritual personalities such as Gandhi and the Dalai Lama.

In Christmas Humphrey, a senior British judge, orthodox Buddhism found an eloquent spokesman, as did Sufism, a mystical strand of Islam, in the essayist Idries Shah. The Lebanese-American Khalil Gibran, a self-professed disciple of the English mystic William Blake, reached millions through his lyrical meditations on love and death, of which *The Prophet*, first published in 1923, is best known.

During the 1960s Hindu spirituality exerted a particular influence, most notably in the world of pop music and entertainment. The Beatles made a much-publicized pilgrimage to India to sit at the feet of the Maharishi Mahesh Yogi and absorb the principles of transcendental meditation. Saffron-robed Hare Krishna missionaries became a regular sight in Western cities. American film star Richard Gere became a devotee of Tantric Buddhism.

The spiritual impact of these eastern currents was, however, probably less profound than their influence on music, costume design, fashionable decor and the cause of vegetarianism. In 1998 two feature Hollywood films, one starring teen heart-throb Brad Pitt, chronicled the life of the Dali Lama.

Anyone tempted to view the 20th century as the era in which traditional, organized religion faded away in the industrialized world, however, should consider its continuing impact on politics and culture, social and sexual behavior, and the solidarity of communities. Millions have continued to flock to Lourdes in southern France to pray for intercession by Our Lady on behalf of the

A START IN LIFE

EDUCATION, AT ONE TIME THE PRIVILEGE OF THE FEW, IS NOW REGARDED AS A BASIC HUMAN RIGHT FOR ALL

THE WAY TO SCHOOL The satchel of a Berlin schoolchild in 1910 almost dwarfs its owner. In most countries, schools aimed at maintaining the social order.

The child was all-important. The aim of education should be to build on a child's existing interests, to stimulate, encourage, and help them to develop. The teacher should not be a drillmaster, forcing pupils to learn by rote and imposing tasks. Rather he or she should be a mentor, working with pupils, helping them to find their own ways through the different fields of learning. The purpose of schooling was, as far as possible, to encourage children to grow and reach their full potential in every area of their lives. These were not the ideas of a 1960s radical, but of John Dewey, a respected American philosopher at the University of Chicago. He published his theories in two books that first appeared in 1899 and 1902.

As societies have been transformed during the 20th century, so has education, though practice has often lagged behind theory. A character in the Irish-born George Bernard Shaw's 1907 play *Major Barbara* confidently asserts that "nobody can say a word against Greek; it stamps a man at once as an educated gentleman." In most advanced countries in 1900, stamping was essentially what schooling was about: rote-learning in the classroom, Greek and other classical subjects for the (predominantly male) elite, basic literacy and numeracy for the masses. Portraits of monarchs or presidents and rituals such as regular parades around the national flag instilled patriotism. The social order depended on hierarchy and deference, and although there were many dedicated and inspiring teachers, and pupils who benefited from their lessons, most education systems were aimed primarily at buttressing that order.

Change was inevitable but came quite gradually. Among the visionaries was the Italian Maria Montessori, founder of the worldwide system for teaching young children that now bears her name. In 1907 she established her first Casa dei Bambini (Children's House) in Rome's San Lorenzo slum quarter. Scorning conventional classrooms which ranked children in rows, "like butterflies mounted on pins," Montessori focused on providing children with concrete learning experiences that harnessed their curiosity. She used beads, rods, cylinders and slabs of wood of different sizes and colors to encourage the basic skills of coordination and perception fundamental to more complex learning tasks. Skeptics were confounded by the sight of infants as young as three, uncoerced and rapt in concentration on their

BOOK LEARNING Smartly uniformed middle-class German schoolchildren in the 1920s study a schoolbook. Old-fashioned drills and teaching methods were still very much the norm in the interwar years of the Twenties and Thirties.

HELPING HAND In many countries, such as the Netherlands, the churches played—and still play—a key role in public education.

tasks for up to an hour at a time. Later, the interwar years saw a burst of small experimental schools set up by other reformers such as the Scotsman A.S. Neill and the Dutch Kees Boeke. They similarly focused on the need to fit the education to the child, rather than the child to the education. Though their short-term impact was limited, many of their ideas would be picked up later by more mainstream reformers.

By mid-century structural change was definitely on the agenda. Modern economies needed a workforce that knew more than just the basics of reading, adding and subtracting. The GI Bill, passed in 1944, provided $14.5 billion in funds for education, allowing more than half of all American World War II veterans to attend college or technical school. In 1949–50, more than twice the number of degrees were conferred as ten years previous, and schools renovated and expanded to accommodate the flood of eager new pupils. In Great Britain, the Education Act of 1944 made education up to secondary school compulsory for all; the French authorities raised the age at which children were permitted to finish their schooling from 13 to 16.

In education, as in most other areas, the 1960s and early 70s brought a ferment of ideas. In the universities of France, Germany, and the United States, students demonstrated against the Vietnam War and the apartheid regime in South Africa, but they also demanded a greater say in the running of their own courses and institutions. German universities, for much of the century a bastion of conservatism, were overhauled following a decision of the Federal Constitutional Court in 1973 that allowed students an important decision-making role.

At the same time, those in authority were asking questions about the place and pur-

TOP OF THE FORM Prizewinners line up at a French primary school in 1947. A generation later, educational theorists often condemned school prizes as elitist and divisive.

PLEASE, MISS A Pittsburgh classroom in 1947. The books may have been antiquated, but schools took pains to instill patriotism—a portrait of Washington and the flag were part of nearly every American class-

PLEASE, MISS A Pittsburgh classroom in 1947. The books may have been antiquated, but schools took pains to instill patriotism—a portrait of Washington and the flag were part of nearly every American class-

FENCING FOR HONOR

Well into the 20th century, rapier duels (*Mensuren*) were a part of life at German universities. The British commentator William Harbutt Dawson described the practice:

"Virtually all the students' associations, except the theological, require their members to engage in a series of *Mensuren* . . . There is no danger in the exercise, though the weapons used frequently inflict severe wounds, which leave their mark for life. For safety's sake the hands, eyes, neck, and breast are protected . . . The face and skull are thus the parts really exposed to the cuts of the glittering blade. At every *Mensur* a medical student is present . . . He discharges his duty well, and many are the stories of the surgical feats which are performed in emergencies of this kind—of how nose-ends and ear-tips are gathered expeditiously from the ground and replaced so skillfully as not to betray the temporary excision. . . ."

pose of education in modern democratic societies. Deference was less important; adaptability and a supply of research workers and middle-grade specialists were much more important. New teaching methods were widely adopted, often along the lines detailed by Dewey, Montessori and other earlier reformers. The old two-track approach—one set of schools for the ruling class, another for the ruled—was increasingly abandoned or modified in favor of more comprehensive education.

Them and us

Comments from the school inspectors' log books in the English industrial city of Salford around the turn of the century paint a dismal picture: "Classrooms are insufficient—four for 450 pupils—and one is without desks"; "The children are well behaved and under industrious if not very intelligent instruction"; "The staff here must be strengthened at once, both in numbers and qualifications."

Standards and conditions in 1900 varied across the advanced world. In Britain, one observer reckoned that after a generation of compulsory elementary schooling, a fifth of the working class was still totally illiterate and another fifth virtually so. Within the schools, classrooms were either, according to the season, fetid with the sweat of verminous juvenile bodies or freezing to all but the fortunate few who sweltered by the single stove. Apart from the basics of literacy and numeracy, slum children were taught stories from the

Bible, history based on the lives of the kings and queens of England and geography that celebrated the fruitful bounty of the British Empire. They sang hymns; other than that, their contact with music was minimal, and their contact with science or art or organized sport non-existent. Class-bound attitudes

prevailed in England, where most elementary schools actively discouraged individual ambition, sure to be a cause only of disappointment or, worse still, of discontent.

In Germany, the scene was in many ways more encouraging, though also more rigid. Elementary schooling was compulsory for all, and for the mass of children this meant the *Volksschule* from which they graduated at the age of 14. Volksschule was free, with a curriculum tightly directed by central government. In its way, it provided a rounded education including a concern for body and spirit. As well as the basics of reading, writing and arithmetic, an important emphasis was

THEIR MASTER'S VOICE Kaiser Wilhelm II and his empress gaze down on schoolchildren in German East Africa. Teaching in such schools stressed the superiority of Western culture.

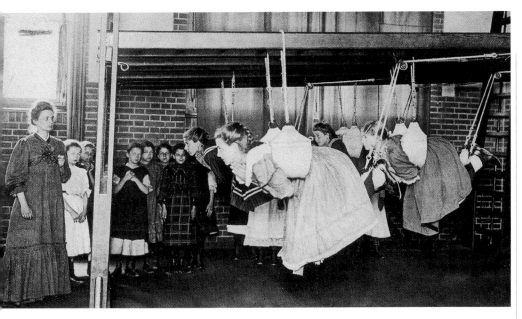

THEORY BEFORE PRACTICE German girls learn to swim without actually getting wet. Physical education for girls was often accepted only hesitantly.

placed on gymnastics and religion. Boys were trained for manual laboring jobs, girls for the domestic sphere. The education was practical —but strictly limited. Even in class-conscious England, a bright working-class child could at least hope for a scholarship to the local grammar school (for boys) or high school (for girls), and thence maybe to the heights of a university education. In Germany, there was little chance of a child progressing from a Volksschule to a secondary school, let alone university. The cycles of the Volksschule and the various kinds of secondary school were deliberately kept out of step with one another.

The best a working-class boy could hope for was "continuation school" that would further his vocational training. The German authorities wanted a disciplined, well-trained, able-bodied workforce—and by and large they got it, and kept it in its place.

The new utopians

Of the prophetic educators working in the first half of the century, none was more influential than Maria Montessori. The first woman in Italy to graduate as a doctor, Montessori initially focused on the problems of children with learning difficulties. She was a professor at the age of 26, lecturing on hygiene, teaching methods and anthropology. Later, in her Case dei Bambini, she applied to average, but disadvantaged, children the methods she had developed to overcome the difficulties of the handicapped. The outstanding success of her methods set her on a 40-year globetrotting career of lecturing and advising that took her

TWO NATIONS Boys from Eton—Britain's most exclusive private school—make their way to a cricket match in 1934. London slum children have their lessons out of doors in a 1937 heat wave.

throughout Europe, India, and the United States. Her core belief about human learning was summarized in the title of the last of her many books—*The Absorbent Mind*.

Another major influence on later progressive education was the example of a very small number of much-publicized experimental schools. Almost all of these were private, established in the aftermath of the First World War. Their founders were idealists who rejected what they regarded as narrow, nationalistic and authoritarian teaching methods which they blamed for the carnage of the war and the willingness with which millions had meekly gone to their deaths.

At the *Werkplaats* (workshop) in Bilthoven, near Utrecht in the Netherlands, Kees Boeke and his English wife Beatrice Cadbury (from the Quaker chocolate-manufacturing dynasty) decided to educate children using Quaker pacifist principles. The Boekes believed that children not only have a natural love of the direct and the spontaneous, but desire order and method as well. The school proved highly successful and produced a number of offshoots. Boeke's British equivalent was A.S. Neill, who originally founded a community school at Hellerau, near Salzburg, before relocating at Leiston in Suffolk, England, in 1927. The school "began as an experiment and became a demonstration." Neill, greeted by the children of Summerhill with the chant "Neill! Neill! Orange Peel!" made something of a speciality of dealing with "difficult" children, many of whom were the offspring of wealthy Americans, who had been rejected as failures or disruptive by more conventional establishments. He spent hours with such charges giving what were called "private lessons" but were in fact sessions of psy-

chotherapy. Summerhill children were encouraged to evolve their own disciplinary rules through discussion and consensus and to enforce them through communal sanctions. Learning was regarded as a matter of discovery rather than instruction. The impact of these experimental schools was delayed by the onset of the Depression of the 1930s,

CHILD'S PLAY The teaching method devised by Maria Montessori was widely adopted, as in this school (above) for the children of British munitions workers in the First World War.

which affected nearly every nation in the world; the huge disruption caused by the Second World War, especially in Europe; and the urgent need for a straightforward, unsophisticated reconstruction in the postwar decades.

SELF-DISCIPLINE At Summerhill School in the mid 1960s, the charismatic A.S. Neill created a community in which children were encouraged to make their own rules.

Education for democracy

In theory at least, the United States had the most democratic education system at the start of the century. Though not all of their countrymen agreed, figures such as John Dewey firmly rejected the dual-track system accepted as natural in Europe. In a democracy, they maintained, there could be only one sort of school common to all. Separate provision for the children of the leisured and the laboring classes lead inevitably, in Dewey's words, to "a division of mental and moral habits, ideals and outlook . . . a plan of social predestination totally foreign to the spirit of democracy."

The key to the American system was the neighborhood high school. After 1910, children did six years at elementary school from which they could graduate to junior high school for three years, then senior high school for another three. In many of these schools, the emphasis was not merely on transmitting names and dates, but on instilling character and important life skills. In 1918, the National Education Association issued an influential report that suggested seven basic areas in which a high-school education should be concerned: health, family life, vocation, citizenship, the worthy use of leisure time, ethical

BE PREPARED

STARTING AS A SUMMER CAMP ON AN ISLAND OFF THE SOUTH COAST OF ENGLAND, THE SCOUTS GREW INTO A HUGE WORLDWIDE MOVEMENT.

During the second Boer War of 1899–1902 the South African city of Mafeking was besieged for 217 days by a large Boer force. When the city was finally relieved London went wild with delight, and the commander of the Mafeking garrison, Colonel Robert Baden-Powell, became a national hero overnight. Returning to England to become inspector general of cavalry in 1903, Baden-Powell was intrigued to find that his army handbook, *Aids to Scouting*, was being used to train boys in woodcraft. In 1904 he was asked to review the 21st anniversary parade of the church-based Boys' Brigade, whose members dressed in uniforms and learned basic army drills. Baden-Powell approved but began to think he could come up with something more appealing to the average boy, something to get him out of church halls and into the fresh air of the countryside, away from the squalor and temptations of city life.

The Boer War had revealed appalling levels of fitness among Britain's young men. The sight of slope-shouldered lads hanging around street corners while they waited for the pubs to open seemed to many not just a social disgrace but a threat to national security. Baden-Powell shared this view passionately, having a soldierly contempt for "loafers" and "shirkers" who were invariably, in his word, "pale, narrow-chested, hunched-up, miserable specimens, smoking endless cigarettes."

Believing that the thing to do was to catch boys before they had acquired idle or vicious habits, he organized a summer camp at Brownsea Island, off the Dorset coast, in 1907. For ten days boys, divided into patrols of Curlews, Ravens, Wolves, and Bulls, crawled through gorse, raced through pine woods, cooked their own food, sang campfire songs and, exhausted and exhilarated, slept out under canvas. The huge success of this experiment inspired Baden-Powell to write another manual, *Scouting for Boys*. Published in 1908 in six weekly parts, it became the textbook of the world's most successful youth movement.

In writing it Baden-Powell drew not only on his experience as a military scout but also on his conduct of the siege of Mafeking, when he had used boys too young to carry a rifle to serve as runners, carrying messages and ammunition to the defenders of the city's perimeter. Such lads, characterized by a keen sense of duty, a willingness to volunteer, cheerfulness, resourcefulness, determination and "pluck," became the model for Boy Scouts, who should grow up to be "good citizens or useful colonists."

In 1910, Baden-Powell retired from the army to devote himself full time to the Boy Scout movement and join his sister Agnes in founding the Girl Guides. By 1911 the movement had grown so fast that a rally could assemble 40,000 members in Windsor Great Park, to be inspected by King George V himself. In 1920 the first international Boy Scout Jamboree was held in London and Baden Powell—"B-P"— was hailed as Chief Scout of the World. Half a century later there were Boy Scout organizations in 110 different countries.

WELL TURNED-OUT The uniform, seen here in 1925, was a major expense for would-be scouts.

character, and "fundamental processes" such as reading, writing and basic arithmetic.

How much of this schooling was free and how much compulsory varied from state to state. How good the schools were also varied—in urban areas many were overcrowded and understaffed. Nonetheless, the ideal, even if it was not always lived up to, was that there should be roughly equal educational opportunities for all regardless of background or wealth. The greater social equality accorded to women in North America than to those in Europe meant that the education of girls was taken almost as seriously as that of boys.

In most European countries, the debate about dual-track versus single-track education did not really get started until well after the Second World War—and was still raging in many places at the end of the century. This largely revolved around the question of selection. By the postwar decades, the old class priorities were less important, but it was still taken for granted in most systems that children deemed suitable for higher education should be separated out at some point be-

tween the ages of around 11 and 15 and sent to special schools or put into special "streams" where they would be prepared for college. The rest of the children would be given various levels of technical or vocational training.

Sweden, which was largely spared the traumas of the mid century, had gone farthest in adopting progressive pedagogy into mainstream education between the 1930s and 50s and attracted eager pilgrims from Germany, France, and Britain. In 1962 it became the first European country to abolish the distinction between "academic" schools

FACES OF DEMOCRACY A science class in 1900 (below), high school girls dressed for their graduation "prom" in 1922 (top), swearing allegiance to the flag in 1970 (right). The high school has been a cornerstone of American democracy in the 20th century. Below right, a graduate at New York University thanks his mom.

and "non-academic" vocational ones in favor of a unified system. Schools in Europe began to experiment with comprehensive education, which instead of removing the more talented children and placing them in special "advanced" schools, aimed to keep pupils of varying degrees together in the same schools for as long as possible. It was believed that 11 was far too young for a definitive selection to be made. Keeping the pupils together for longer allowed those of less obvious ability more time to develop.

Co-education also became increasingly the norm. Most U.S. high schools had taken both girls and boys since the start of the century. The same was true in most of Scandinavia—the Norwegians introduced co-education in 1896. In Britain co-education was common in primary schools but not in secondary schools until after the Second World War. In France the girls went to separate *lycées* (secondary schools), which until the Second World War taught a different

OPPORTUNITY FOR ALL Pupils at an English non-selective comprehensive school participate in a geography class in 1992 (above). First introduced in the 1960s, the debate on the merits of comprehensive education still raged in the 1990s.

curriculum from boys' schools; girls did not learn Latin or Greek and studied mathematics to a lower level. The curriculum for girls and boys was standardized after the war, but separate *lycées* continued until 1975.

Going to college

Education was opening up, and that applied to higher education as well. At the turn of the century American books on "success" had generally told their readers that going to college was a waste of time, except for people who were already rich and did not have to worry about making a living.

By 1968 findings suggested that the opposite was true: it was calculated that those with elementary school education could expect average lifetime earnings of $196,000. A further stint at high school followed by attendance at university tripled that figure to around $586,000. By 1993, statistics showed that the average college graduate earned nearly 90 percent more than the average high-school graduate.

Higher education expanded hugely across the advanced world, particularly after the Second World War. From being a hallmark of the elite and those in a handful of learned professions, such as medicine

of all American adults, were enrolled in such schools. In all advanced countries, the old hard core of classical, literary and scientific courses was expanded to include new ones on subjects ranging from computer studies to sociology, psychology to politics.

New ways, old problems

In many ways, the innovative trends that marked education in the 20th century reached their high-water mark in the 1960s and early 70s. Old school buildings were giving way to light and airy modern ones. Inside the classroom the rigid barriers between

THE COLUMBIA PROTESTS

1968 was a year of student uprising. In France, students rioted in Paris, erecting barricades in the streets and clashing with police. In the United States, protests turned violent on campuses across the nation. Columbia University was a hotbed of such student radicalism. The school had built a large gymnasium in the midst of impoverished black Harlem. Protesting the University's "imperialist intrusion," the campus chapter of SDS (Students for a Democratic Society) planned a protest rally on the morning of April 23. Jeff Shero, one of the founders of SDS, was there:

"A petition was to be carried into Low Library in defiance of an order banning indoor demonstrations. A line of jocks blocked the marchers, and they returned to the center of campus. What looked like another failure of the left was saved by the impromptu idea of marching to the gym construction site in Morningside Park. With a frustrated energy, the demonstrators began tearing down the chain link fence surrounding the property, and when the friendly local police were called in to protect the property and apprehend the culprits, fighting ensued. Arrested demonstrators were freed from the clutches of the police, and several police were knocked into the mud puddles. It was the first hint that the mood was beginning to change...

That night students and community people from Harlem poured in...Just before six o'clock the whites streamed out of the building and headed for Low Library. A window was smashed, and students hurried by the startled security guards who sat at their desks and made only feeble protests. Quickly, and with a sense of awe at being in the inner sanctum, students took over [Columbia President] Grayson Kirk's executive office and tightly barricaded the doors. Everyone expected the police to arrive in force at any moment. Between the frantic periods of scurrying irrationality, when people dashed about accomplishing nothing, frozen moments...gripped the suite. People lived in ten-second spurts. Later in the day when the police hadn't come, the mood changed to liberated jubilation. The President's sherry and cigars were broken out, the mood was festive—the peasants had taken over the palace."

PRIVILEGED POSITION? Despite efforts to broaden student recruitment, the universities of Oxford and Cambridge retained a mystique of exclusivity.

and the law, it became a passport to success in a whole range of careers, and increasing numbers of people aspired to it. By the late 1960s, the number of graduates per year in the United States had almost doubled since 1850 to around the 800,000 mark. By the late 1980s four American parents out of every five said they wanted their children's formal education to go beyond high school.

Universities and colleges were transformed accordingly. Long-established institutions, such as Oxford and Cambridge in Britain and the Ivy League universities in the United States continued to thrive, but a whole range of other institutions were either created or expanded. In Britain new universities and polytechnics—offering university-level courses in both technical and general arts and science subjects—broadened the options for those seeking higher education from the 1960s. In the United States, new schools proliferated and old schools adapted to accommodate the growing trend of adult education. In 1995, more than 76 million older students, 40 percent teacher and pupil were giving way to a more relaxed relationship. Increasingly, it was realized that pupils should be encouraged and stimulated rather than merely drilled. Opportunities for higher education were blossoming for generations whose parents would have been lucky to complete a satisfactory secondary schooling. The post-Second World War "baby boom" was by now

COME AS YOU ARE In recent decades student life, as at Frankfurt University here, has emphasized spontaneous self-expression.

feeding through to the universities and colleges, swelling their numbers to unprecedented levels. Students were a force to be reckoned with, politically and in every other way. When student riots in Paris in 1968 came close to toppling President Charles de Gaulle, it was a telling symbol of the newfound power of Western-educated youth.

It was a relatively short-lived heyday. As Western economies faltered with the oil crisis and rising inflation of the mid to late 70s, much of the confidence and sense of ever-expanding opportunities that went hand in hand with the educational revolution of the previous years began to break down. Factors such as the high-tech revolution also meant that economies were now changing faster than ever. As well as providing children with a good basic education, countries had to organize themselves so that adults could retrain as appropriate to meet the new demands. In many countries education and training became a political battleground.

On the one hand, the reforming impulse continued, and much work needed to be

CONFRONTATION Student power showed itself in 1968 in anti-Vietnam demonstrations at New York's Columbia University (top) and at Berkeley (above).

done. Seven years after the 1954 Supreme Court ruling of Brown vs. Board of Education, which abolished the policy of "separate but equal" in American schools, four Southern states still had yet to integrate

THE COST OF COLLEGE

The cost of a college education in the United States has skyrocketed in the last several decades. In 1930, the average cost of a public four-year college—room and board included—was $730. In 1990, that number was $5,289. Tuition and room and board at a public institution in 1930 was $960; in 1990, $15,165.

LUNCHTIME IN TOKYO Increasingly, advanced countries use their schools to improve child health through nutrition, exercise and medical check-ups.

a single public school. During the 1970s, these states were gradually, and sometimes grudgingly, desegregated. These struggles to admit disadvantaged students into the classroom were mirrored by the nation's contem-

LEARNING STYLES From the large class in a Russian school (below) to an Australian farm boy learning by radio (bottom), different situations demand different approaches.

poraneous battle over affirmative action. In 1978, the Supreme Court ruled that state schools could not set aside a fixed quota of seats in each class for minority groups. However, the court did allow that a student's race could be considered an asset in improving a school's diversity. Exactly how much diversity was necessary, and how much salutary, continues to be a point of contention. Nevertheless, these controversies heightened American's sensitivity to issues of race and ethnicity in the classroom, and many began to examine history, literature, art, and music courses for signs that they were "sexist" or marginalizing the achievements of African-Americans, Native Americans and other non-whites. During the 1980s and 1990s such disputes were extended into a general debate on "political correctness."

At the same time, there was soul-searching about standards. New teaching methods were more imaginative than the old ones, but many commentators in countries where they had been tried felt that the pendulum had swung too far and that the basics of literacy and numeracy were being forgotten. A 1983 report of the U.S. National Commission on Excellence in Education pulled no punches: "If an unfriendly foreign power had attempted to impose on America the mediocre educational performance that exists today, we might well have viewed it as an act of war . . . We have in effect been

committing an act of unthinking, unilateral educational disarmament."

How countries responded to such crises varied markedly. In the United States, efforts were made to impose higher standards for those wishing to become teachers, and higher pay was recommended for those who qualified. Eager for more direct control over their child's education, some parents even turned to home-schooling. In 1998, 1.5 million American children were educated at home, either by their parents, or by private tutors. In England, a centralized National Curriculum started to be imposed for the first time in 1989, followed by national testing at the ages of 7, 11, and 14. Sweden at the same time was introducing a program of radical decentralization, devolving responsibilities away from central government to the regions. Questions abounded. Had comprehensive education been a failure? Should selection and the old "academic" grammar schools and the like be reinstated? How much subject specialization was healthy, and how soon should it be applied? What was the place of religion in the classroom? How important is diversity? How much choice should parents have in deciding which schools their children attend? If the answers to these questions still seemed out of reach, one thing was sure: education, the key to success in a rapidly changing world, looked set for many further transformations.

WORK—OR PLAY? The fascination of computer technology can both stretch gifted children and seduce reluctant learners, while economizing on direct teacher time.

LEISURED SOCIETY

PROVIDING PLEASURE FOR THE MANY WAS TRADITIONALLY THE PROFESSION OF THE FEW—FROM MUSICIANS TO INNKEEPERS, FROM JUGGLERS TO COURTESANS. MASS AFFLUENCE AND COMMUNICATIONS HAVE TRANSFORMED ENTERTAINMENT INTO THE WORLD'S FASTEST-GROWING INDUSTRY, SPAWNING THE CINEMA AND THE CD, JAZZ MUSIC AND THE JACUZZI, AND DEFINING THE CENTRAL PURPOSE OF WHOLE COMMUNITIES, FROM LAS VEGAS TO LAS PALMAS.

REST AND RELAXATION

THE "LEISURE INDUSTRY" HAS BECOME A PROVIDER OF NOVEL EXPERIENCES, REFRESHING ENJOYMENTS—AND MAJOR EMPLOYMENT

Twentieth century travel was hitched to the automobile, benefiting from the blessings of freedom and mobility the car bestowed on its passengers. By 1929, there were more than 4 million cars in the United States, speeding along the newly constructed national highways, trekking to national parks or just taking a Sunday spin. Small hotels sprang up along roadways to accommodate these new travelers. In California in 1926, an enterprising innkeeper named Arthur Heinerman was momentarily discouraged when the name of his establishment, the Milestone Motor Hotel, would not fit on his entrance sign. Through a clever abbreviation, he came up with the term "motel," and another classic American institution was born. Tourism is now no longer merely a pastime; it is big business. In the United States, the world's second most popular tourist destination behind France, domestic travelers spend $383 billion a year, while foreign globetrotters add another $90 billion.

Throughout the century, one destination whose appeal remained constant was the seaside. From the cheerful throngs milling along the boardwalk and piers of Atlantic City at the start of the century to the rows of roasting northern Europeans lining the beaches of Spain and Greece in the 1990s, vacationers have kept faith with the seaside and its tonic virtues. Styles have changed, and the decorously clad bathers of 1900 would stare in amazement—and most probably outrage—at the bronzed flesh and skimpy attire of late 20th-century sun worshippers. But for millions of people in the developed world, vacations are still virtually synonymous with beaches and the seaside, as they were for the working and middle classes

MAIDENLY MODESTY Bathing beauties (right) dare partial exposure of the limbs. Bathing machines, hats and sunshades on the beach at Ostend (below) around 1900 reveal a preference for sea rather than sunshine.

alike in much of industrialized North America and Europe at the beginning of the twentieth century.

In Britain, which had pioneered the seaside holiday in the 19th century, 55 percent of English people were taking day excursions to the seaside by 1911 and 20 percent were taking vacations there that involved staying overnight. Britain's Brighton and Blackpool had their transatlantic counterpart in Atlantic City, New Jersey, where visitors could stroll along 5 miles of boardwalk, eating taffy (a candy) and buying picture postcards imported from Germany. Nearby Ocean City had been founded by Methodist ministers and was firmly against the sale of liquor, making it a favored location for religious conventions and the family vacations of the ultra-respectable. Germans had a selection of Baltic resorts such as Binz, Lohme, and Sellin on the island of Rügen; Belgians frolicked on the North Sea beaches of Ostend and Nieuwpoort-Bad. By July 1912 the French *Revue hébdomadaire* was able to assert that "50 years ago the person who took a vacation stood out. Today a person stands out if he does not take a vacation." Meanwhile, the superrich of all nations patronized high-society watering spots from Newport, Rhode Island, to Nice in France.

THE SEASIDE—ENGLAND **The classic 1950s seaside family holiday, whether at England's Blackpool (below) or in America's Atlantic City (right), enshrined such rituals as the donkey ride and the ice cream stand.**

THE SEASIDE—FRANCE **High-fashion bell-bottom trousers emphasize the importance of elegance rather than family fun at Juan-les-Pins in 1930.**

Blackpool lights

In Britain at the start of the century, tourists from the industrial and textile factory towns would flock to nearby beaches during "wakes weeks" in July and August. Wakes were originally celebrations to mark the dedication of a parish church, but they had become secularized and extended into complete breaks in the collective life of tight-knit mill communities. What had once been a "holyday" was now a "holiday"—a trend that would extend across the industrialized world. Employers accepted a complete shutdown of their factories because it reduced disruption from casual absenteeism and gave them time to arrange annual repairs and maintenance work. The drunken revels that punctuated these weeks in preindustrial times gave way to whole towns cleared out and echoing, as workers headed en masse for the coast. As one man reminisced, "In place of the fair, we see hundreds of people carrying boxes and bags on their way to the railway station for a few days at the seaside."

Their most popular destination was Blackpool, on the country's western coast. Blackpool courted these vacationers with a series of impressive innovations and spectacular attractions. It was the first town in Britain to have an electric trolley, and five years after the construction of the Eiffel Tower, Blackpool built a rival tower of its own. The town boasted three separate piers,

REST CURE Patients at Baden-Baden in the 1930s pass long hours chatting or strolling to and fro—or watching others do so.

the newest of which had a bandstand and no fewer than 36 shops. In 1912, the town took advantage of the new technology of electric power to inaugurate its famous illuminations, creating an attraction that extended its season well into autumn. By 1914, Blackpool had 4 million visitors each year, and the figure reached 7 million by 1939.

Taking the waters

For Europe's elite, unenthusiastic about sharing sand with the hoi polloi, there was the inland spa. There the moneyed class could lounge, "take the waters" and undergo therapeutic cures. Germany's Baden-Baden and Homburg were especially popular, as was Aix-les-Bains in France. However, as the century progressed, the popularity of European spas among the wealthy declined, partly as a result of medical skepticism, partly because of competition from exclusive warm-climate beach and yachting resorts such as Puerto Banus in southern Spain. Baden-Baden, which had 15,000 hotel beds in 1900, had just 4,000 by 1990; the grand Hotel Kaiserhof had given way to a supermarket. But, thanks to the generous German health insurance system, some 300 spas in Germany did continue to survive, attracting about 9 million visitors a year for an average stay of two weeks. Both patients and doctors in Germany believe in the effectiveness of natural remedies. Rest cures at spas are used for rehabilitation (after heart attacks, strokes and so on), as well as for the treatment of chronic diseases. Research in Germany showed that after a rest cure, the patient's absence from work through illness, and the cost of their medical treatment, fell by 60 percent.

In the United States, the place for the rich to congregate on holiday was Newport, Rhode Island, a resort community dedicated to conspicuous consumption, populated by railroad barons and oil magnates. To lodge in one of the town's many hotels, though, was considered déclassé; better to build a second home there—the more lavish the better. These homes were referred to, with more than a bit of false modesty, as "cottages." William Vanderbilt spent $11 million dollars (nearly a quarter of a billion in today's dollars) for his "cottage"—Marble House, a res-

BE PREPARED For these rich Berliners in 1908, travel meant bulky trunks to ensure you had appropriate attire for all occasions.

idence with all the subtlety of Versailles. His brother, Cornelius, summered at The Breakers, a four-story, 70-room villa in the style of a 16th-century Genoese palace. Once these palaces were built, the men and women of Newport spent their days walking along the beach, horseback riding, or playing tennis and polo, and their nights attending extravagant soirees.

A place to stay

In 1928 the English hotelier Sir Francis Towle observed somewhat despondently that great hotels were rather like battleships—they became obsolete every 20 years or so. The history of hotels in the 20th century has tended to confirm this maxim.

The typical major hotel of 1900 was notable for its spacious public rooms, its exclusive restaurant and its extensive banqueting facilities. Its staff would almost all have been natives of the country in which it was located, with the exceptions perhaps, in the most expensive establishments, of the manager, the maître d'hôtel and the chef. They might come from Switzerland, France, or Italy, or at least have been trained in one of those countries whose hotels offered the most rigorous apprenticeship.

The guests, apart from a sprinkling of rich globetrotting Americans and British, would have come overwhelmingly from the country where the hotel was located. Wealthy guests in those days stayed for lengthy periods—usually weeks, often months, sometimes years. Many came as whole families. For both these reasons the rooms—or suites—of those who took up residence were spacious and elegantly furnished, commanding fine views of seashore, lakes, or mountains.

During the interwar period the layout and appointments of leading hotels began to change in response to new patterns of travel and recreation. Elevators, central heating and en suite bathrooms were increasingly regard-

SUNSEEKERS In 1930s Monte Carlo (above), vacationers under a beach umbrella take a break from the new fad of sunbathing. Below, at the same time, Miami Beach became a haven during the winter months for a wide range of tastes and pocketbooks.

SIMPLY THE BEST Thomas Cook, inventor of modern tourism, created a business that was synonymous with calm competence from Jerusalem (above) to the farthest locales.

ed as essential by the elderly and invalid— and by Americans, who additionally looked for telephones in their rooms and a newsstand in the foyer. The craze for new dances, such as the high-kicking Charleston in the 1920s, made a permanent professional band desirable. Thanks to the influence of Hollywood movies, wealthy socialites also wanted a cocktail bar and a night club. Young people wanted tennis courts and a swimming pool, both for the sake of genuine exercise and to give them an excuse to slip into newly fashionable sportswear.

The hotels of the late 20th century had changed again. In the United States, chains of cheap, clean, modest hotels sprang up across the country. The first Holiday Inn was built in 1952; by 1997, there were some 1,119 nationwide. Luxury hotels also experienced significant transformations. The high cost of prime locations had encouraged the construction of narrow, multistory buildings. The only ground-floor area likely to have grown bigger was the foyer, needed to handle a much higher turnover of guests, many of whom were traveling for business rather than pleasure. To cater to their demands, hotels not only provided conference and meeting rooms, but also international telephone, modem and fax links.

In their off-duty moments guests could browse in the shopping arcade, take a sauna, use the fitness center, or just relax in their rooms watching TV and consuming the contents of a refrigerated mini-bar while an

automatic trouser press restored their slacks to pristine condition. The vast majority of guests stayed only for a few nights, often just one. Their rooms, if air-conditioned and abundantly equipped with gadgets, were usually compact. The large hotel had ceased to resemble a battleship, or even a luxury liner; it had become the terrestrial equivalent of the jumbo jet.

Packaged paradise

Modern packaged tours, which until after the Second World War remained very much the domain of the British and Americans, are essentially the invention of one man: the Englishman Thomas Cook. He began it all in 1841 by chartering a train to take 500 fellow Baptists, neighbors and friends to hear a lecture against the evils of alcohol. Half a

century later, in 1902, Thomas Cook and Son was praised as one of "the three most competent organizations in the world"—the other two being the German army and the Roman Catholic Church.

By 1914, 150,000 Americans were arriving in Europe each year. American Express, which issued the world's first travelers checks in 1891, established itself in Europe to challenge Cook's for a share of this lucrative market. By the end of the Second World War there were 139 American Express offices overseas. Cook's responded by looking for new business down market and launched a range of Popular Tours, for people "prepared to travel abroad under less luxurious conditions than those of our Select Conducted Tours." These provided second-class travel and accommodation and left clients to arrange their own excursions.

The First World War put the emerging travel industry into temporary eclipse, but it bounced back in the 1920s when people were eager to put the horrors of the recent past behind them. Surplus Army trucks were converted into sightseeing motor coaches to cash in on the demand for excursions. Their success inspired the manufacture of purpose-designed motor coaches, an innovation that was to transform tourism. Cook's used the new coaches to transport clients on six-day tours of the European battlefields. It also began to offer half-hour rides in converted Handley-Page bombers and made confident predictions about the future

TRAVELER'S DELIGHT After the First World War, motorized coaches opened up new fast-paced excursions and touring vacations to a new breed of traveler.

SKY HIGH

AIR TRAVEL HAS MADE TOURISM A GLOBAL INDUSTRY WHILE REVOLUTIONIZING VACATIONING IN LARGE COUNTRIES LIKE THE UNITED STATES AND AUSTRALIA.

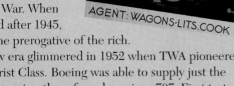

AIR AFRIQUE REGIE
VISITEZ L'AFRIQUE EN AVION

AGENT: WAGONS-LITS.COOK

Civil aviation began in Germany in 1910, using airships. By 1914 airships had carried 34,228 passengers the equivalent of four times round the globe without a single injury. The first scheduled passenger air service using planes was established in 1914 in St. Petersburg, Florida. Passengers were flown—one at a time—20 miles across Tampa Bay.

Efforts to develop passenger services began after the First World War, when surplus military aircraft became available and discharged pilots sought employment flying them. There was such a glut of trained and talented aviators—and so few commercial planes for them to fly—that one World War I ace quipped that the greatest risk in being a post-war pilot was not crashing, but starving to death from lack of work. Opportunities emerged gradually. In 1919 the first international services began—Paris-Brussels, London-Paris, and Toulouse-Barcelona-Tangier. Cabins were unheated, unpressurized and noisy. In the United States, where luxurious long-distance rail travel was widely available, there were no regular passenger air services until 1926. Then Americans opted for a "flying bus" approach, aiming to compete with the railroads in reliability and cheapness.

A London-Cape Town service began in 1932, and a San Francisco-Hawaii service soon followed in 1935. The first stewardesses appeared in 1930, eight trained nurses, all under 25 years old, for a United Airlines flight. Landing strips were rare, so flying

HIGH LIFE This 1936 Pan-Am Clipper airliner (below) carried 40 passengers. Its German counterpart offered luxury dining (right). By 1970 (below right) airliners carried many more people—but the service was rather more basic.

JUNGLE JAUNT Airlines were promoting "safari" holidays in Africa as early as the 1930s.

boats were preferred. From 1935 onwards, however, more air strips were built and the Douglas DC-3 (Dakota) supplanted the flying boat as the workhorse of civil aviation. PanAm established the first transatlantic service in 1939, but this was suspended following the outbreak of the Second World War. When civil aviation resumed after 1945, air travel remained the prerogative of the rich.

The dawn of a new era glimmered in 1952 when TWA pioneered a new concept—Tourist Class. Boeing was able to supply just the plane for this type of service: the safe and spacious 707. First testflown in 1954, the 707 could carry 219 passengers. In 1958 more than a million passengers crossed the Atlantic by plane, surpassing the number travelling by ship for the first time.

The 707 was superseded by the 747 "jumbo" in 1969. Capable of carrying more than twice as many passengers as the 707, the 747 brought long-haul flying within the reach of even modest budgets. Its internal cabin length of some 40 yards was just about the distance flown by Orville Wright on his historic first powered flight in 1903.

HELLO, CAMPERS! Adult vacation camps on both sides of the Atlantic brought modern management to the leisure business, providing a standardized product at a bargain price.

of air travel: "Space will be annihilated, the cities of the world will be brought within the reach of all." In 1927 Cook's arranged the first-ever escorted tour by plane—from New York to Chicago to see Jack Dempsey fight Gene Tunney for the world heavyweight title.

Tourism was suddenly recognized by bankers and politicians as an "industry" and one with immense potential for European countries replete with attractive scenery and historic sites. As one visionary speculated as early as 1923: "it is even possible that the part ultimately reserved for the British Isles in the scheme of the international division of labor will be that of a playground and park and museum to exercise the youth and soothe the declining years of the strenuous industrial leaders congregated on either side of the Pacific Ocean."

Not all were content with this emerging new scheme of things. In Italy, where Mussolini really had eased the travel agent's life by making the trains run on time, upper-class European visitors were horrified to find themselves rubbing shoulders with compatriots the very sight of whom made them shudder: "the most awful people with legs like flies who come into lunch in bathing costumes." Novelist F. Scott Fitzgerald was just as disgusted with the

AWAY FROM IT ALL
The development of skiing as a fashionable sport in the early part of the century transformed remote mountain communities into prosperous resorts.

behavior of his fellow Americans abroad who displayed "the humane values of Pekinese, bivalves, cretins, goats."

For the beneficiaries, rich and not so rich, of the new tourism, there were many new choices, including all kinds of specialist packages. Bermuda and Cuba were being colonized as winter playgrounds; it was possible to book special vacations for golfers, skiers, and daredevils who wanted a balloon ascent over Mont Blanc. By the 1920s one could go trail riding in the Canadian Rockies or travel to Timbuktu in a Tin Lizzie. The discovery of Tutankhamun's tomb in 1922 sparked a renewed rush to Egypt. Idealists organized trips to Bolshevik Russia to inspect the workers' paradise, archaeologists to Lascaux in France to see newly discovered prehistoric cave paintings.

The "great outdoors" exercised a growing appeal, and would continue to do so for the rest of the century. In May 1903, Theodore Roosevelt took a break from his presidential duties and joined preservationist John Muir, the founder of the Sierra Club, for a guided tour of one of America's most stunning natural sites, California's Yosemite Valley. Inspired by breath-taking vistas and the rugged environment, Roosevelt joined Muir's campaign to protect these national treasures; he was enthusiastically supported in his efforts by railroad barons, who realized that the creation of national parks would spark an interest in travel that would ultimately fatten their own purses. Their calculations were right. By 1986, America's 30 National Parks, historic sites, protected shores, rivers and trails were attracting 364

WANDERLUST The growth of youth hostels in the 1920s and 30s helped to spread the German cult of hiking and made "rucksack" (literally "back sack") an English word.

million visitors every year, and raising billions of dollars in profit.

One of the earliest and most popular of these parks was Yellowstone, sprawling over almost 3,500 sq. miles of Wyoming, Montana and Idaho, and offering an abundance of rare plant and animal life. As early as 1872 it had been established as a major ecosystem to be protected from disturbance. By the 1890s the

national park concept had spread to Canada, South Africa, Australia, and New Zealand. Europe then started creating its own national parks, starting with Sweden in 1909. The interwar period brought Argentina, Chile and Japan into the national park movement. In Europe, the outdoor traveler was also assisted by the emergence of youth hostels, providing affordable housing for itinerant guests. Hostels first appeared in Germany before World War One, catering to the students taking walking or cycling excursions in the Black Forest. They continued to spread throughout the Continent and can still be found in almost every nook and cranny of Europe.

The interwar decades also introduced a new attraction to the seaside holiday. Where

NATURAL WONDERS In 1872 the United States began the creation of national parks to preserve areas of wilderness—but not, as this Redwood in Yellowstone shows, from all forms of commercial intrusion.

earlier generations had shrouded themselves against the sun, fearing the harmful effects of too much exposure to its rays, the opposite now came to be the rule. Sunbathing was becoming all the rage, and remained so until the depletion of the ozone layer towards the end of the century renewed fears of excessive exposure. Devotees of the new fad clustered in the mushroom-growth cities of Florida— "the Riviera of America."

Cheap and cheerful

The Depression of the 1930s meant a bleak time for the travel business. The very rich, however, cushioned from the inconvenience of poverty, continued to take luxury cruises. The demand for air travel also continued to grow. By 1939 it was possible to go "Round the World in Thirty Days."

But the real growth came at the low end of the market, with the opening of the first major commercial "holiday camp" at Skegness on the east coast of England in

1936. This venture was the brainchild of the former traveling showman Billy Butlin. He was following a path first trodden by high-minded socialists and teetotalers before the First World War, when campers had slept in tents or huts made from old trolley cars.

Billy Butlin accommodated his campers in neat rows of chalets and gave them three sit-down meals a day and free entertainment for the price of a workman's weekly wage. By 1938 his experiment had proved so successful that Cook's had sunk $1 million into creating a rival establishment at Prestatyn on the North Wales coast. By 1939 Britain had more than 100 holiday camps in operation, capable of accommodating half a million people each season. In Nazi Germany, the *Kraft durch Freude* (Strength through Joy) organization sponsored similar camps.

As in the 1920s, the ending of war in 1945 inaugurated a boom in travel. But this time the boom just went on booming. In 1950 a million Britons went abroad and 200,000 North Americans visited Britain. The mass of people in war-shattered continental Europe had yet to catch the travel bug, but that too would shortly change. In 1950, Gerard Blitz from Antwerp went a step farther than Billy

FLYING FASHIONS

Germany's first airline, Deutsche Luft-Reederei, began its service in 1919 with open cockpit biplanes – obliging passengers to don flying suits, helmets, goggles and fur-lined boots and gauntlets.

Butlin, replacing Butlin's "cheap'n'cheerful" formula with one combining romance and simple elegance. Using U.S. Army surplus tents for accommodation, Blitz advertised an informal holiday camp on the Spanish island of Majorca. A staggering 2,600 people, most of them French, responded to his invitation. Club Méditerranée was born.

Blitz knew what he was offering: "Today's luxury is not comfort, but open space. Adventure is dead and solitude is dying in today's crowded resorts. But if you can no longer go on holiday alone without finding yourself in a crowd, it ought to be possible to go off in a crowd in order to find yourself alone. The individual . . . needs a very flexible holiday community where at any moment he can join in, or escape . . ." Within 20 years of its birth 350,000 "Club Med" clients were

LUXURY TRAVEL ON THE QUEENS OF THE ATLANTIC

The Cunard line built its reputation as a transatlantic carrier around the motto "Speed, Comfort, Safety." Senior officers were strictly instructed to avoid "racing, rivalry or risk-taking." Having never lost a life at sea, the company prospered as a passenger carrier until faced with cut-price competition. Its response was to move up-market and focus on providing travelers with unashamed luxury aboard two of the most famous ships in the world—the *Queen Mary* (launched in 1934) and the *Queen Elizabeth* (1938). In 1938 the *Queen Mary* made the fastest Atlantic crossing to date in 3 days, 21 hours, 48 minutes and then held the Blue Riband—the award given to passenger ships holding the record for fastest crossing—until 1952, when the title passed to the SS *United States*.

During the Second World War both Queens served as troopships, each carrying up to 15,000 servicemen, ten times their normal complement of passengers. Their destinations included the Middle East and Australia and they had to rely on their speed to keep them safe from attack. Both were modified to fit their unaccustomed role. On the *Queen Elizabeth* the dance salon became a hospital ward and the Turkish bath became an X-ray room.

The heyday of the Queens came in the decade after 1945, when liners rather than planes were still the most popular way of crossing the Atlantic and the two great ships ran a back-to-back weekly service between England and New York. Along with thousands of postwar refugees and migrants travelling tourist or cabin class, regular voyagers aboard the Queens included well-known celebrities such as Bob Hope, Noël Coward, Marlene Dietrich, Fred Astaire, Gary Cooper, Cary Grant, Bing Crosby, Bette Davis, and Liberace.

At the peak of their popularity the Cunard fleet of 12 ships carried between them more than a third of all transatlantic passengers. Airline competition then forced a reassessment and the Queens were reallocated to cruising. Too big to berth in many ports, they became major loss makers. *Queen Mary* was sold (1967) to become a tourist attraction, combining hotel facilities with a maritime museum, in Long Beach, California. *Queen Elizabeth* was refitted to become a floating university but caught fire and sank in Hong Kong harbor (1972), to be broken up later for scrap. The Queens' successor, the *QE2*, launched in 1969, is now the only liner to offer a transatlantic service, although even that is not a regular one.

A WORLD APART The cruise liner represented the ultimate in luxury but has been forced by airline competition to redefine its market appeal.

being accommodated in pseudo-Polynesian villages located in Tunisia, Morocco, Israel, Spain, Italy, Yugoslavia—and Tahiti itself.

The French, meanwhile, took to *le camping*. In 1950 a million French people went on camping vacations. By 1990, 5 million did so, mostly at sites renowned for their comfort and efficiency. Having part of the Alps in their country, some 4 million were able to take skiing vacations. In the United States, "recreational vehicles," or RV's, allowed restless men and women to enjoy camping excursions in the comfort of their own home. Over 400,000 RV's were sold in the U.S. alone in 1995. The French also owned more second homes than any other nation in Europe. Many families of relatively modest means were thus able to imitate the wealthy middle classes of the previous century by deserting sweaty cities each summer to relish the fresh air of the countryside.

While European holiday patterns began to change from the 1950s—partly due to short-haul flights—in the U.S. mass motoring was enabling suburbanites to renew contact with real or imagined rural roots. Millions of Americans were drawn to the majesty of the Grand Canyon and the Rockies, and the love of their new roomy, air-conditioned automobiles made them all the more eager to go.

SUNSPOTS Mass-migrations from northerly climes to sun-soaked beaches, like Miami Beach (above) with its highly developed hotel industry, are now a well-established tradition—although fears of skin cancer and other health concerns have modified the trend.

By 1965, 114 million people worldwide were traveling abroad. Spain now relied on tourism for 40 percent of its export earnings. The UN designated 1967 as International Tourist Year and endorsed a resolution recognizing it as "a basic and most desirable human activity, deserving the praise and encouragement of all peoples and all governments." The British broadcaster Malcolm Muggeridge opined that "tourism today is a more dynamic force than revolution . . . Thomas Cook and the American Express . . . unite the human race." By 1972 tourism was the world's single biggest international business. Fifteen years later it was not only the biggest but the fastest-growing. In 1988, 355 million tourists traveled abroad and twice as much was spent on tourism as on the international arms trade.

Adventure and honeypots

The very fact, in 1900, that millions of ordinary families could get a break at the seaside ensured that many of the wealthy and adventurous wanted to go somewhere else Outfitted by such reputable firms as Abercrombie & Fitch, many took

THEME DREAM With new technologies, the travelling Victorian fairground has evolved into a fantasy world providing every manner of entertainment.

hunting vacations in Africa, bringing back big game as their souvenir-spoils. As the century progressed, this need to go off the beaten path has evolved into a new brand of adventure tourism. By the 1950s it was possible to go in a group to Nepal, in a safari Cape-to-

Cairo, or round Cape Horn in a square-rigger. The first package tour to Mount Everest was organized in 1970, although the tourists confined themselves to the lower slopes. Cheap international air travel, meanwhile, was bringing everywhere from the Andes of South America to the islands of Indonesia within the reach of youthful backpackers.

Nowadays, some are still content to go on safari in Kenya or scuba-diving off an island in the Indian Ocean—and then return to a five-star Western-style hotel each evening. But there are others who are lured by the prospect of crossing Greenland by dog-sled or of meeting "Stone Age" peoples in New Guinea or on the Amazon. Doggedly seeking spectacle, solitude or the exotic, these pioneering tourists of the late 20th century have ensured that almost nowhere, except perhaps Antarctica, can now be regarded as remote. Fragile ecosystems are, ironically, now threatened by the frequent visits of even those who recognize and treasure their fragility.

Whole cities have become what the travel trade calls "honeypots," attracting swarms of free-spending visitors. In Venice one person in four is directly employed in catering to their demands. The noise and bustle they generate make the city ever less worthy of its proud title—*La Serenissima* ("the most serene"). Florence, Versailles, Memphis, and

VIRTUAL REALITY? A Las Vegas hotel offers its guests a flirtation with Egypt – without all the time-consuming bother of having to travel there.

Stratford-on-Avon are similarly in thrall to the sightseer. Benidorm, an insignificant Spanish fishing village in the 1950s, had a permanent population of 25,000 some 30 years later—except in summer, when it welcomed a million seekers after sun, sea, sand and sangria. The islands of Corfu, Majorca, Tenerife and dozens of others in the Mediterranean, Atlantic, and Caribbean have similarly become tourist-dependent.

Some centers have become honeypots by design. These include the Disneylands in California and Florida and outside Tokyo and Paris, which aim primarily at families with young children. Others are coastal enclaves, such as Acapulco in Mexico and Konya in Turkey, which have been allocated massive

MODERN TRADE In past centuries, Venice prospered by controlling East-West commerce. Now it lives by peddling culture, romance and nostalgia.

state funding for roads, sewage systems, hospitals, recreational facilities and the other bits of infrastructure geared to tourist needs.

Some capital cities have become honeypots almost by default as the numbers of vacationing tourists have been swelled by business travellers or students filling in spare hours by visiting the sights. In 1994, New York attracted 36.4 million domestic and 6.6 million foreign visitors; more than 2 million people clamber up the Empire State building each year. These guests have generated some 268,000 jobs in the city, and added $20 billion to its economy. Cities like New York, London, and Paris are big enough to take on yearly invasions of 20 million people without being overwhelmed. But smaller sites risk overloading themselves, as the veteran travel writer Jan Morris observed: "I went to the coast of Maine and found its old seaports swamped by Collectible Shoppes, Sea'n'Surf restaurants and Davy Jones Boutiques. I went to the Caribbean island of St. Maarten, and found its old Dutch waterfront garishly dominated by duty-free shops for cruise passengers, I went to the Côte d'Azur and ran away again."

GOING OUT, STAYING IN

FROM MUSIC HALL TO MOVIES TO TV—OUR NOTION OF AN EVENING OUT (OR IN) HAS BEEN TRANSFORMED DURING THE 20TH CENTURY

The moving image more than anything else has transformed entertainment in the 20th century. A night on the town in 1900 meant just that. Only large cities offered commercial entertainment on a regular basis—and the bigger the city, the bigger the choice. Berlin, which doubled its population between 1900 and 1914, had no fewer than 33 theaters and four opera houses. Elsewhere, Montmartre in Paris, New York's Broadway, London's Strand and Leicester Square, all were synonymous with pleasure. But these places were so famous largely because they were so few.

Already, however, a new force was starting to make itself felt: the "bioscope" or cinema. The first public demonstration of "moving pictures" had taken place in Paris in 1895 before an audience of 34, who were only mildly impressed by the novelty. By 1907, however, the United States alone had 3,000 "nickelodeons"—charging a nickel, with accompaniment from harmonium-like organs called melodeons. By 1910 the U.S. had 10,000 such theaters; a quarter of all New Yorkers saw at least one show a week. The silent screen gave way to the "talkies" after 1928; then, after the Second World War came the all-invading television. Ready-made entertainment, provided by nationally or internationally acclaimed stars, was no longer the prerogative of the great cities. The movies had brought it to the street corner or town square; television brought it directly into the living room.

Homemade fun

At the start of the century, most Americans still lived in small towns or on farms. They could gather only at the general store, in a church hall or on each other's porches, to while away idle hours with gossip and homemade music, unless their isolation was interrupted by a traveling "tent show," circus or

FUN OF THE FAIR Jumbo leads the circus parade into an American town. Tobogganing without snow offers fun at Munich's *Oktoberfest*.

"showboat" presenting popular melodramas. The *fiestas*, *festas*, *fêtes* and feasts of the Church year were occasions for jollification in Europe, with parades, firework displays and much feasting and drinking. In Germany such celebrations were especially strong in the Rhineland and Bavaria. Munich's celebrated *Oktoberfest*, spread over 16 days, was dominated by serious consumption—of 40 roast oxen, 500,000 chickens and nearly 8 million pints of beer.

In Britain the music hall was in its heyday, though it could hardly compete with the pub. London had the most halls, more than 60— but even that meant only one music hall for over 100,000 people. Nationally there was one pub for every 300 people. In France, where alcohol was even more central to working-class leisure, there were three times as many outlets per head as in Britain. A trip to the vaudeville hall—or in British cities the music hall, in Paris the *café-concert*, in Berlin the *Kabarett*—meant getting dressed up and paying for a trolley ride to the city

PARISIAN PLEASURE Paris was renowned for its saucy cabarets, of which the most famous was the Moulin Rouge (Red Mill), founded in 1888 and still thriving in the 1930s (below).

center. For this reason, the best customers were young, employed men reveling in the few years before early marriage relieved them of their spare cash. At the end of a working day that often began at 6 a.m., most married working men were content to stroll to their corner bar for a few relaxing drinks. Taverns and bars offered not only alcohol but cheery company, music and laughter, cards and dominoes, and a brightness and warmth that contrasted with the dingy, cramped and chilly homes they would totter back to.

Observers were concerned by the phenomenon of solitary drinking, to be observed in the lowest dives in many working-class districts. The condition was memorably portrayed by the French painters Degas and

HAVE A SWIG The local bar was often a place of mirth and music. The many hours of keeping patrons entertained—and drinking— inspired musical forms, from ragtime to jazz.

Toulouse-Lautrec. Historians have explained the solitary drinker as a reaction to the decline in traditional festivals in big industrial cities, the loss of craft skills which had once been a source of self-respect, and the increasing monotony of work governed by machinery —coupled with increased leisure and income, which meant time to fill or to kill.

The top end of the entertainment market, meanwhile, was dominated by the huge spending power of the "idle rich." In 1905, James Hazen Hyde, the heir to the Equitable Life Insurance fortune, threw a fancy dress

ball, complete with an orchestra, a ballet troupe, an imported French actress, three suppers, and lavish decorations, evoking the theme of Louis XV. At a time when the average yearly pay hovered around $500, the bill for this event was rumored to be $200,000.

In 1901, there were over 4,000 millionaires in the United States; in Great Britain, there were some 250,000 males of property, "without trade or profession." Such people could seek their pleasures, not weekly, but nightly, dining at Maxim's in Paris, Delmonico's in New York or the Savoy Grill Room in London, before applauding the performances of a new breed of international superstar represented by Sarah Bernhardt, Isadora Duncan, Ellen Terry, or Nellie Melba. Other hits included the Hungarian-born Franz Lehár's operetta *The Merry Widow* and the Russian Sergei Diaghilev's Ballets Russes.

STARS AND SUPERSTARS
Classical actresses like Sarah Bernhardt (left) and improvisational dancers like Isadora Duncan (top) were idolized on both sides of the Atlantic. German cabaret artists such as Betty Berane (above) often used props and gesture to overcome language barriers One of the most popular comic actresses of the century was Fanny Brice (right), the singing comedienne who headlined the *Ziegfeld Follies.*

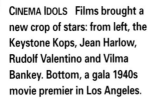

CINEMA IDOLS Films brought a new crop of stars: from left, the Keystone Kops, Jean Harlow, Rudolf Valentino and Vilma Bankey. Bottom, a gala 1940s movie premier in Los Angeles.

The silver screen

Even before 1914, people started flocking to movie theaters. Unlike the music hall, it was untainted by smut or strong drink. Even respectable women could go to see "moving pictures." Captions carrying dialogue or narrative links required a minimum literacy in the audience. The unlettered brought their offspring as translators. Robert Roberts, who grew up in the slums of northern England, recalled that "when picture gave place to print on the screen a muddled Greek chorus of children's voices rose from the benches, piping above the piano music only to falter when confronted with an unfamiliar long word."

France was the biggest pre-1914 producer of motion pictures, its industry dominated by the former magician George Méliès. His quirky, fantastical films such as *A Trip to the Moon* (1902) and *Conquest of the Pole* (1912) entertained growing worldwide audiences. From the expanding U.S. industry came epic dramas such as D.W. Griffiths' *The Birth of a Nation* (1915), the first movie shown in the White House, and the crazy antics of Mack Sennett's Keystone Kops.

The interwar years brought the cinema's golden age. Already in the early 1920s the silent screen had generated a cluster of superstars, from the comics Charlie Chaplin and Buster Keaton to the romantic husband-and-wife team of Mary Pickford and Douglas Fairbanks, the vampish Pola Negri to the sex symbol Rudolf Valentino. The German horror film *The Cabinet of Dr. Caligari* (1919) sent shivers down audiences' spines with its tale of the mad, murderous head of an insane asylum. Sergei Eisenstein's *Battleship Potemkin* (1925) stirred them with its celebration of the Bolshevik revolution of 1917.

Gradually, motion pictures overhauled other forms of entertainment. In the United States, nickelodeons gave way to "picture palaces" seating not a few hundred but 2,000 or more. New York's biggest, the Roxy, could take 5,889. The typical movie-goer was young, female, urban and working class. Many went two or even three times a week. In 1920, Americans bought 100 million movie tickets a week—nearly one for every American man, woman and child; movie stars were regularly awarded six-figure salaries.

By now Hollywood, whose sunny climate and ample labor market made it an ideal movie-making location, dominated the commercial film business, and the coming of sound in 1928 confirmed its supremacy. The year before, *The Jazz Singer*, starring Al Jolson, was the first movie with sound.

What were called the "talkies" would carry American culture into the far corners of the English-speaking world and beyond. As the New York *Morning Post* declared: "If the United States abolished its diplomatic and consular services, kept its ships in harbor and its tourists at home, and retired from the world's markets, its citizens, its problems, its towns and countryside, its roads, motor cars,

counting houses and saloons would still be familiar to the uttermost corners of the world . . . The film is to America what the flag was once to Britain. By its means Uncle Sam may hope some day, if he is not checked in time, to Americanize the world."

Escapism was always one of the chief appeals of motion pictures. A 1925 advertisement for Paramount showed that the studios understood this clearly: "All the adventure, all the romance, all the excitement you lack in your daily life are in—Pictures." Romances were the most popular type, followed by lavish musicals. Hollywood obliged; nine out of ten films featured romance as the main plot

STUDIED CRAZE Professionals demonstrate the Lindy in a New York ballroom, 1941. Dance crazes were invented and promoted by music publishers who relied on the sale of sheet music well into the 1950s.

or a major subplot. Men favored Westerns and gangster movies. A stream of classics emerged, from musical blockbusters such as Busby Berkeley's *Gold Diggers* films to the raunchy humor of Mae West in *I'm No Angel* (1933), from the sultry decadence of the

SIMPLY SHOCKING! New, more daring dance crazes have followed one another, including (left to right) the tango, black bottom and jive.

German import Marlene Dietrich in *Blue Angel* (1930) to the wistful mystery of her Swedish-born rival Greta Garbo in *Queen Christina* (1933), from the cool elegance of Fred Astaire and Ginger Rogers in *Flying Down to Rio* (1933) to the Boy's Own frolics of Ronald Colman in *The Prisoner of Zenda* (1937). Perhaps the greatest year in movie history was 1939. Two movies were released that year that were to have an enormous and lasting hold on the American imagination: *The Wizard of Oz* and *Gone With the Wind*.

Movie-makers elsewhere coped with the competition as best they could. In films such as Jean Renoir's *Grand Illusion* (1937), French directors offered more intellectual subject matter, treating movies as an art. The Germans followed the same path until their filmmakers were diverted to propaganda work by the Nazi regime. The British excelled in films that drew on local nuances of language and manner, or historical traditions, as in comedies and costume dramas. They also produced some notable thrillers such as the early Alfred Hitchcock classic, *The Thirty-nine Steps* (1935).

Dance mad

The most typical patrons of the movie theater—young, urban working girls—were also the most enthusiastic supporters of another craze, the dance hall. Here again, the

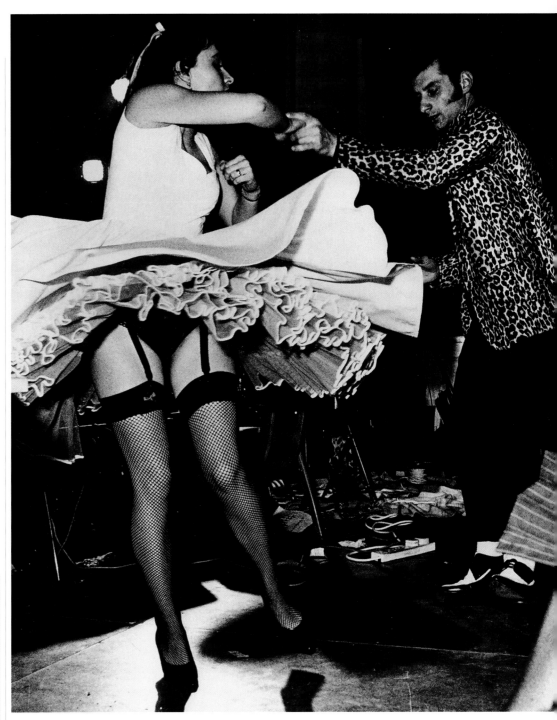

SHOW OFF! The dynamism and daring of rock and roll in the 1950s was accentuated by the flamboyant clothes of the time.

Americans set the pace. Even before the First World War, jazz and syncopated rhythms had started to cross the Atlantic to Europe, and America had established itself as the source of vibrant new dances such as the cakewalk, grizzly bear, and turkey trot.

In 1913, the comedian Harry Fox devised the foxtrot for a Broadway review, the Ziegfeld Follies—based on the Parisian Folies-Bergère. At the same time, the sensuous tango, originating in the slums of Buenos Aires, was sweeping all before it. The 1920s brought many more new steps as short-skirted "flappers" and their male partners

danced the nights away. In hotels and restaurants professional dancing couples instructed clients in the latest steps. In the United States there were grueling marathons where the object was to keep on dancing until all other couples had collapsed. One brother and sister kept dancing for an incredible 3,327 consecutive hours! On the eve of the Second World War, the athletic jitterbug first hit European dance floors from the United States, a taste of

---

A SCHOOL OF LIFE AT THE MOVIES

For Polish-born Kate Simon, growing up in New York's Bronx between the wars, the cinema was an education:

"The brightest, most informative school was the movies. We learned how tennis was played and golf, what a swimming pool was and what to wear if you ever got to drive a car. We learned how tables were set, 'How do you do? Pleased to meet you,' how primped and starched little girls should be, how neat and straight boys should be, even when they were temporarily raga-muffins. We learned to look up soulfully and make our lips tremble to warn our mothers of a flood of tears, and though they didn't fall for it (they laughed), we kept practicing. We learned how regal mothers were and how stately fathers were, and of course we learned about Love, a very foreign country like maybe China or Connecticut.

"It was smooth and slinky, it shone and rustled. It was petals with Lillian Gish, gay flags with Marion Davies, tiger stripes with Rudolf Valentino, dog's eyes with Charlie Ray."

the many dance crazes to come, including swing, the jive, and the twist.

Sporting lives

In the twentieth century, sports—both playing them and watching them—provided men and women with yet another outlet for exhausting their energy, if any was left over after the fox-trot and jitterbug. Football, baseball, basketball, soccer, and tennis all vied for the attentions of spectators around the world. By 1900 in the United States, football had evolved into a brutally rough game, often played between rival colleges, eager to knock their opponents senseless. In the 1905 season, 18 players died from injuries sustained during games, and the following year, President Roosevelt intervened, demanding immediate rule changes to make the game safer. In 1913, progress was made toward that end when an obscure school named Notre Dame and its wiry end Knute Rockne revolutionized the game with the forward pass.

But it was baseball that was truly the "national pastime." With baseball already established as a professional sport for a quarter of a century, in 1903, the first World Series took place, the Boston Red Sox beating the Pittsburgh Pirates five games to three. Baseball saw its share of great athletes in the century's early years, but its first real superstar, and one of its greatest players ever, was "the Babe." In an era when the home run was

CASH OR CACHET? Professional sportsmen like this baseball player (left) came to earn big money, but these English girls (below) probably thought of tennis as a social asset.

a rare event, George Herman Ruth clocked 714 round-trippers, and almost single-handedly turned the New York Yankees into a sports dynasty.

Americans also enjoyed boxing, though at the turn of the century it was still outlawed in several states. In 1910, the nation flinched as

THE SULTAN OF SWAT

In 1931, Babe Ruth demanded a salary increase to the princely sum of $80,000. When confronted with the fact that he would earn more than the president, Ruth replied, "Well, I had a better year than he did." Ruth was probably right: he had hit 49 home runs that year, while Herbert Hoover was booed by fans when he threw out the first ball at the World Series.

Jack Johnson, the black champion, dashed the Great White Hope, Jim Jeffries, in the 15th round. The century would witness many more brilliant African-American pugilists and heroic athletes; the nation thrilled to watch Muhammad Ali "float like a butterfly and sting like a bee"; Jackie Robinson broke baseball's color barrier in 1947, playing second base for the Brooklyn Dodgers; Jesse Owens silenced the Nazis at the 1936 Berlin Olympics, winning four gold metals under the Fuhrer's nose; basketball big-man Bill Russell dominated the middle for the Boston Celtics in the 60s, and in the 90s, Michael Jordan took the sport to new heights. Women also distinguished themselves as superb athletes. Mildred "Babe" Didrickson excelled in basketball, billiards, swimming, tennis, track and field, and golf; Wilma Rudolph won three track gold metals at the 1960 Olympics, and

TEEING UP Cartoonists in the interwar years poked fun at women playing traditionally male sports such as golf.

at the Los Angeles Olympics of 1984, 16-year old gymnast Mary Lou Retton scored a perfect ten, and won the hearts of Americans everywhere.

Other countries had their own favorite athletic pastimes, each reflecting their national characters. From decades of touring their own countryside, the French became master cyclists, and the Tour de France, first established in 1903, quickly became a national institution. Germany, with an emphasis on *Kraft durch Freude* (strength through joy), became pre-eminent in gymnastics. Britain, in sport as in society, was divided along class lines. Rowing, squash, tennis, and equestrian

sports such as polo were largely the prerogative of the elite, as were sports involving travel or major expense, such as yachting and mountaineering. Croquet and golf had their following largely among the middle class. Soccer and rugby were proletarian games. The entire world, though, was astonished on March 6, 1954, when Roger Bannister, a 25-year old medical student from England, became the first runner to break the four-minute mile.

Hi-tech sport

From the 1920s onwards advances in technology created new sports and had a profound impact on existing ones. Night games in baseball became possible when, in the 1930s, electric lights were installed in many stadiums. Motor racing emerged from its infancy to be joined by rally driving, speedway, dirt-track racing, and go-cart racing. Radio, and later television, created mass audiences among sports fans too far away to be there in person at Wimbledon, Yankee Stadium, or Churchill Downs. Baseball and football, lending themselves so naturally to

LEADER OF THE PACK The final phase of the 1991 Tour de France. Cycling has won a passionate following in mainland Europe.

detailed commentary, came to rely increasingly on their association with broadcasting and the business interests that controlled it. In 1970, the garrulous Howard Cosell first

BIG GAME Football—followed enthusiastically at both the collegiate and the professional level—featured such athletes as Johnny Unitas of the Baltimore Colts, below, passing in 1970.

COMPETING FOR GLOBAL GLORY: THE OLYMPIC GAMES

The Olympic games have regularly brought together more people from more countries than any other event—with the exception perhaps of the annual pilgrimages of Muslims to Mecca. In spite of this record, the Olympics have also included some notable disasters. The Paris Olympics of 1900 lasted for five months and were so disorganized that many competitors did not even know what they were taking part in. Sprints were run downhill. Discus and hammer-throwers in the Bois de Boulogne kept hitting the trees. The Parisian waiter who won the marathon was suspected of taking short cuts through back alleys.

RECORD-BREAKERS In four Olympics American Ray Ewry (above) won ten golds for standing jumps. The Olympic spirit survived Hitler's attempt to turn the 1936 Berlin games (right, below) into a Nazi showcase.

The St Louis Games (1904) were financially out of reach for most Europeans. Of the 625 competitors, 533 were American and 41 Canadian. The London Games (1908) were better run. They took place in a brand-new 70,000-seat stadium at White City, the largest in the world. For the first time countries were limited to 12 competitors for each event and winners were given gold medals. The Stockholm Games (1912) were the first to combine efficiency with hospitality. The Swedes made useful technical innovations, such as electric devices to make timings as accurate as possible.

War scuttled the 1916 games planned for Berlin and the defeated nations were pointedly not invited to Antwerp in 1920. In the interwar years events such as standing jumps, tug-of-war and rugby were dropped from the Olympic schedule and new ones admitted—weightlifting, yachting, ice hockey, speed skating, canoeing and basketball. Winter Games were staged from 1924 and the number of events for women increased. Taking an Olympic oath (1920), flying the Olympic flag (1928) and lighting an Olympic flame (1936) were added to the opening rituals.

During the postwar decades the games were held outside Europe or North America for the first time. The number of competing nations increased. In Rome (1960), 83 nations competed and a member of the Emperor of Ethiopia's bodyguard, Abebe Bikila, became the first black African to win a gold—in the marathon, barefoot. He repeated this triumph in Tokyo (1964). At Barcelona (1992), 169 nations took part. Cuba, which had not participated since 1980, won 31 medals, coming fifth in the overall table. By then many purists were complaining that the modern Olympics' lofty vision had been clouded by professionalism, advertising, sponsorship, and the demands of television. The games had become a mega-business—risky but potentially rewarding. Montreal in 1976 had budgeted for costs of $310 million and ended up facing a bill for $1.4 billion. By contrast, Los Angeles in 1980, thanks to the backing of sponsors like General Motors and Xerox, showed a $200 million surplus. By the 1996 Atlanta games, commercialism had reached the point where, as disgusted commentators pointed out, the logos of the sponsors were often more prominent than the five-ring logo of the games themselves.

announced Monday Night Football for ABC; in 1982, 40 million fans tuned in for Super Bowl XVI, the fifth largest audience in American television history. In 1993, five networks paid a whopping $4.38 billion for rights to televise the National Football League games for four seasons.

In the last decades of the century, many of the most popular activities in the advanced world were now non-competitive, health-oriented and even narcissistic. These included jogging, aerobics, fitness training and body-building. Between 1970 and 1984, some 400,000 Nautilus exercise machines were sold, membership at gyms and health clubs soared, and the fitness business turned into a $750 million industry. Others required a level of income unimaginable to ordinary families even a generation before. In the France of 1960 there were just 20,000 people sailing dinghies on weekends; by 1990 there were more than 30 times that number.

A quiet night in

As homes became more comfortable, more spacious, warmer and better lit, they became more popular as a place for entertainment and a focus for leisure. Before 1914, family get-togethers, especially at birthdays and weddings, or religious holidays, were often enlivened by singing round a piano or playing charades. Fortunetelling was much favored at all-female gatherings. A 1910 issue of the British magazine *The World and His Wife* featured 15 "impromptu laughter-making games" for winter parties. These included threading needles at speed, flipping a cork off the neck of a bottle while walking past it and picking up dried peas with two pencils.

Some families kept up the 19th-century custom of reading aloud from a novel in the evenings. There was also an abundance of periodicals, many of them illustrated, for individual perusal. In the United States, where the literacy rate was over 90 percent, readers could enjoy literary magazines such as *Harper's Monthly* and *The Atlantic*,

GONE FISHING In contrast to the thrill of competitive sport, fishing—one of the most popular of all sports—allows fans to enjoy the tranquility of a quiet day in the open air.

WORK OVER? WORK OUT Male staff of a British Columbia paper mill work out. In an increasingly sedentary age, getting fit and staying fit are growing obsessions.

McClure's and *Collier's*, which published the works of such eminent writers as William Dean Howells, Mark Twain, and Henry James, and serialized novels by many European authors. Women could glean *Ladies' Home Journal* and *Cosmopolitan* for fashion and cooking advice. In Britain, authors like Jack London, H.G. Wells, Joseph Conrad, and Rudyard Kipling enthralled devoted fans. The adventures of Sherlock Holmes in *Strand Magazine* were at the

height of their popularity at the start of the century, and continue to captivate readers.

The less bookish played with train sets or constructional toys if they were boys, Kewpie or Raggedy Ann dolls if they were girls. Collecting picture postcards, most of them printed in Germany, and mounting them in elaborate albums was another popular pastime. The busy-handed occupied themselves by making rag rugs or

READ ALL ABOUT IT

In 1900, when the flow of immigrants into the U.S. was at its height, over 1,000 foreign-language newspapers were on sale in America. At the same time sports-crazy Londoners could choose from no fewer than 25 local papers devoted to their passion.

using their skills of embroidery, fretwork or rafiawork to create knick-knacks for use as gifts or decorations in the home. The card games whist and bridge were socially acceptable amongst the middle and upper classes, although some strict churchgoers still regarded all card games as tantamount to reading "the devil's books." Older men often indulged in harmless outbursts of petty malice by trouncing each other at chess, dominoes or checkers. Many enjoyed puttering in the garden or vegetable patch, and those stuck in apartments perfected the art of growing plants in window boxes and on rooftops.

Between the wars, radios and cheap phonographs reinforced the attraction of the home at the expense of the local bar. This was especially true among the unemployed and couples with children, who had little cash to spare for going out. For the better-off it was an era of crazes. Mah-jong, a Chinese gambling game, was regarded as chic in the 1920s. An American version of the game was created in 1922, and in one year sold 1,600,000 sets. Chinese manufacturers, overwhelmed by the demand, ran out of calf shinbones to make the tiles, and had to get fresh supplies from Chicago slaughter houses. Crossword puzzles became an obsession through-

out the English-speaking world. The board game Monopoly swept all before it in the mid 1930s.

Radio was the most universal source of home entertainment and dance-band music the most popular form of programming. By 1930 Denmark had the highest level of radio ownership, followed by the U.S. and Sweden

In Britain, the government-controlled British Broadcasting Company (BBC), created in 1922, developed a strong public-service ethos. Under the leadership of its first Director-General, John Reith, the BBC's mission was to inform, educate and entertain —in that order. In the United States, where at the end of the 30's, 85 percent of the population owned a radio, advertisers pressed stations to reverse this commitment. Shows like "The Lone Ranger" and "Amos and Andy" attracted millions of listeners, and potential consumers, each week. A distinctive new form of radio serial, based on the saga of

GUESS WHO? The oldest and simplest games, like Pin the Tail on the Donkey, are often the best and never lose their popularity. Squeak, Piggy, Squeak requires the blindfolded child to identify his "victim" by sound alone.

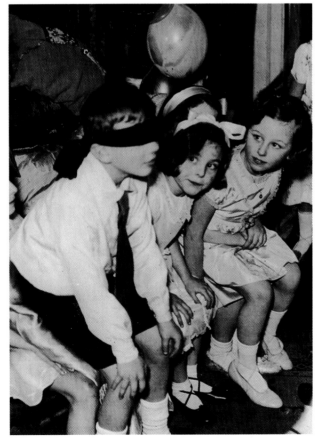

THE GOOD OLD DAYS? Televisions in the 1950s were cumbersome affairs. Before the arrival of satellite and cable, network programs had to appeal to wide audiences.

an imaginary family, emerged under the patronage of various companies plugging household products, most typically washing powder—thus the "soap opera."

The box in the corner

After the wireless came television. TV services began experimentally in the mid 1930s but did not start in earnest until after the

BIG BUDGETS As TV won mass audiences and improved its technology, more money was spent on series such as *Dallas* (right) or *M*A*S*H* (below) or remote broadcasts of sporting events and public occasions.

Second World War a decade later. Televisions then sold faster than any other consumer durable in history. By 1954 half the households in America had one and so did a quarter of all homes in Britain and Canada.

TV output soon became the despair of cultural critics and even some within the industry. As early as 1961 America's TV watchdog, Newton Minow of the Federal Communications Commission, denounced American broadcasting as: "A vast wasteland—a procession of game shows, violence, audience participation shows, formula comedies about totally unbelievable families . . . blood and thunder . . . mayhem, violence, sadism, murder . . . and, endlessly, commercials . . . screaming, cajoling, and offending."

The earliest TV programs assumed that viewers had a limited attention span and imitated the old vaudeville format of unconnected "turns" or "spots." Other genres soon emerged—the celebrity chat show, the big money quiz show (such as *Wheel of Fortune*) and the formula drama (*Ironside, Colombo, Cannon* and countless others), in which the central character, a detective, lawyer, doctor

THE IMPACT OF ROOTS

In January 1977, America was glued to the TV set for eight consecutive nights as people from all walks of life were mesmerized by "Roots," the 12-hour epic about slavery in America. The program was a brutal and riveting adaptation of Alex Haley's best-selling family history. It starred newcomer LeVar Burton in the lead role as the young African, Kunta Kinte, brought in chains to America. The program gave Americans an understanding of the tyranny of slavery as never before; it also gave birth to a new entertainment form —the miniseries—which was to become a television staple for years to come.

FANTASY FUN The cast of
Monty Python's Flying Circus satirize the
taste of one television presenter, Alan
Whicker, for exotic locations.

or teacher, encounters a different guest star in each weekly episode. Sports coverage attracted a large male audience while entertainment variety shows like Ed Sullivan's "Toast of the Town" and Milton (Uncle Miltie) Berle's "Texaco Star Theater" appealed to the entire family.

In the United States, the Public Broadcasting System (PBS) was established in 1969 to raise programming standards, often by importing productions from Britain. PBS won a limited but loyal following for such diverse offerings as the classic *Forsyte Saga*, based on John Galsworthy's Edwardian novels, and the surreal *Monty Python's Flying Circus*. The establishment of international audiences for quality drama and natural history series encouraged co-production across national frontiers. The sumptuously produced *Brideshead Revisited*, a dramatization of the novel by the English writer Evelyn Waugh, was made by a British commercial company Granada, drawing on finance from an American PBS station, a German national network and the Exxon oil corporation.

Language barriers were readily crossed with the use of dubbing and subtitles—though as with films in the interwar years the traffic was mostly one-way, from the English-speaking world to the rest. *Dallas*, the everyday story of Texan oil tycoons, became a national obsession in the socialist Islamic republic of Algeria—everybody there apparently understood family rivalries and the abuse of wealth and power. *Yes, Minister*, which reveled in revealing the manipulative machinations of British bureaucracy, was well received in China as an accurate exposé of how the People's Republic actually worked. And a number of Mexican and Brazilian soaps found a ready market in post-Soviet Russia.

In the 80s and 90s, television found its most popular programming not in fictional worlds, but in the inimitable circus of everyday life. Talk and tabloid shows, from Johnny Carson's, to Oprah Winfrey's to Jerry Springer's, dominated the air-waves; real-life dramas, like "Cops" and fictional ones, like "NYPD Blue" claimed to take the viewer behind the scenes. The 80s' most popular comedy, "The Cosby Show," featured a middle-class African-American family whose normalcy was its defining feature; in the 90s, hit sitcoms like "Seinfeld" could even take "nothing" as subject matter and keep its audience laughing—real life was that funny.

Pop and rock

As TV was entrenching itself in the world's living rooms, popular music was turning into "pop." In the 1940s the big bands still held sway, producing music by adults for adults. In the 1950s solo artists like Frank Sinatra, Ella Fitzgerald, Perry Como and Nat King Cole began to command the adult market, while younger talents, such as Pat Boone, Elvis Presley and, in France, Johnny Halliday appealed to a booming teenage

OL' BLUE EYES TV has enabled cabaret and concert artists like Frank Sinatra to reach simultaneous audiences of tens of millions.

market demanding "rock'n'roll." Jazz and country-and-western added mainstream appeal to their established cult followings. New genres developed, such as bluegrass and rhythm and blues. The huge growth of the music business was reflected in the sales of individual hits. In 1946 and 1947 around 20 records reached the million mark in the United States; a decade later the figure was over 100. Released in 1984, Michael Jackson's album "Thriller" would sell nearly 50 million copies in ten years. Individual commercial radio stations flourished by serving specific musical markets; by 1953 there were 270 American stations focusing their output on the black community alone.

YEAH! YEAH! YEAH! By the 1960s groups such as the Beatles (below), embodiments of the newly emerging "youth culture," inspired an almost religious fervor in their fans (left).

BEATLEMANIA! THE "FAB FOUR" HIT NEW YORK

In February 1964 Tom Wolfe chronicled the arrival of the "Fab Four" for the *New York Herald Tribune*:

"By six-thirty a.m. half the kids . . . were already up with their transistors plugged in their skulls . . . You could turn anywhere on the dial . . . and get the bulletins: "It's B-day! . . . The Beatles left London 30 minutes ago! . . ." By one p.m. about 4,000 kids had finished school and come skipping and screaming into the international terminal at Kennedy Airport. It took 110 police to herd them. At one-twenty p.m. The Beatles' jet arrived . . . To get a better look, some of the kids came plunging down the observation deck, and some of them already had their combs out, raking their hair down over their foreheads as they ran . . . some of the girls tried to throw themselves over a retaining wall. The Beatles left the airport in four Cadillac limousines . . . Five kids in a powder blue Ford overtook the caravan on the expressway, and as they passed each Beatle, one guy hung out the back window and waved a blanket . . .

"At the Plaza Hotel there were police everywhere . . . The Plaza was petrified . . . Every entrance to the hotel was guarded. The screams started as soon as the first limousine came into view . . . The kids were still hanging around the Plaza hours after they went inside . . . A policeman came up and one of them yelled, 'He touched a Beatle! I saw him!' The girls jumped on the cop's arms and back . . . There were goony smiles all over their faces."

By the 1960s music in the hands of groups and singers such as the Beatles, Rolling Stones, Bob Dylan and Joan Baez had become the pivotal feature of a youth culture that expressed itself in dance crazes, "way out" fashions and drugs. The Vietnam War and the massive expansion in the proportion of young people at college across the developed world made music more socially engaged, critical of existing society and confrontational towards authority in all its forms. The nihilistic, self-loathing Punk movement of the mid 1970s marked the most extreme expression of this trend.

Down at the flicks

As television came to monopolize family entertainment and pop music became central to youth culture, motion pictures seemed to be facing terminal decline. The 1950s had their share of stars, notably Marilyn Monroe and James Dean, whose cult status in both cases was confirmed by early tragic deaths—aged 24 in a car accident for Dean, aged 36 of an overdose of

MOVIE MAGIC *Cleopatra* with Elizabeth Taylor was a box-office flop but inspired stamp designers in Mali. More financially successful movies were *The Godfather* (right) and *The Graduate* (below).

sleeping pills for Monroe. Even so, by 1956 the major Hollywood studios were producing less than half as many feature films each year as they had in 1946. A decade later only one film in ten was profitable. Grudgingly, some studios survived by churning out formula weekly Westerns for the despised television screen. (Earlier, Warner Brothers had refused to allow the word "television" even to be mentioned in their films.)

In 1963 *Cleopatra*, made for 20th Century Fox at a cost of $40 million and starring Elizabeth Taylor and Richard Burton, nearly bankrupted the studio and flopped at the box office. After that Hollywood began to abandon the strategy of competing with television by producing stupendous spectacles or special effects, such as Cinemascope, which could not be reproduced on the small screen.

The fact that good movies did well if they were good movies was painfully rediscovered. *The Sound of Music*, made in 1965 for $8 million, grossed $78 million in North America alone.

The real turnaround came in 1967 when *The Graduate*, starring Dustin Hoffman, and *Bonnie and Clyde*, with Warren Beatty and Faye Dunaway, drew young people back into the theaters. Audience figures turned up again for the first time in 20 years. In 1968 Hollywood finally abandoned the hallowed Production Code which for decades had established standards of taste, decency and social acceptability. Films became more violent, more sexually explicit—and often more original in content and treatment.

The next year *Easy Rider*, made for a mere $400,000, grossed $25 million. In the

same year *Midnight Cowboy*, directed by an Englishman, John Schlesinger, became the first 1960s movie to win the Academy Award for Best Film without being based on a musical. Widely acclaimed films like *The Godfather* (1972) and *Schindler's List* (1993) proved that it was perfectly possible to combine quality with profits.

But mega-blockbuster hits like *Jurassic Park* (1993) and *Titanic* (1998) showed that some special-effect wizardry couldn't hurt either. And as the century ended, independent film-makers, with old equipment and funding by credit card, were producing some of the outstanding films of the day. Soon, the independents would mount award shows and film festivals that rivaled the mainstream efforts, and would soon become mutimillion-dollar players in the entertainment world.

**1900s buzzwords:
nickelodeon, suffragette,
chauffeur, hamburger**

1900

The World Exhibition and the second Olympiad are held in Paris. The first escalator for public use is demonstrated at the exhibition. The Paris **Métro** is opened and motorized ambulances are introduced, also in France.

PALACE OF GLASS The Horticultural Pavilion at the Paris exhibition.

Hamburgers are first sold in New Haven, Connecticut.

The first **Zeppelin** airship—designed by the retired German army officer, Ferdinand, Graf von Zeppelin—makes its maiden flight from a floating hangar on Lake Constance.

Harvey Samuel Firestone founds the **Firestone** Tire and Rubber Company in Akron, Ohio.

1901

In the United States, **Oldsmobile** becomes the first motor manufacturer to turn out more than ten cars a week.

The first **Nobel** prizes are awarded, under terms laid down in the will of the Swedish inventor of dynamite, Alfred Nobel. The first winner of the prize for physics is the German Wilhelm Röntgen, discoverer of the X-ray.

The first electric **hearing aid** is patented in the U.S. In Britain, the first practical **vacuum cleaner** is invented by Hubert Cecil Booth, a bridge engineer.

The first **body-building** contest is held in the Royal Albert Hall, London.

1902

The **Pepsi-Cola** and **Texaco** companies are founded.

Beatrix Potter's *The Tale of Peter Rabbit* is published in Britain. A **wax disc** of the Italian tenor Enrico Caruso singing "Vesti la giubba" from the opera *I Pagliacci* sells over a million copies.

Berlin's **U-bahn** (Underground) opens.

1903

Richard Steiff invents the **Teddy Bear**, named for U.S. President Theodore "Teddy" Roosevelt.

The Boston Red Sox win the first **World Series**. The first **Western** movie, *Kit Carson*, opens—it has a running time of 21 minutes.

The Wright Brothers achieve **powered flight** at Kitty Hawk, North Carolina. In Detroit, farmer's son Henry Ford founds the **Ford** Motor Company.

The first **Tour de France** cycle race takes place.

1904

Some 150,000 people use the first section of the New York **subway** on its opening day.

The Fédération Internationale de Football Association (**FIFA**) is set up in Paris.

The **tea bag** and the **caterpillar** tractor are pioneered in the U.S. The domestic **Thermos** flask is marketed in Germany. The Parisian jeweller Louis Cartier invents the **wristwatch**.

Premiere of **J.M. Barrie**'s *Peter Pan*.

1905

The Pittsburgh-based firm H.J. Heinz markets **baked beans** in Britain.

The first **nickelodeon** opens in Pittsburgh. New York sees the first gallery dedicated exclusively to **photography**.

The electrification of London **Underground** is completed. In France, **oxyacetylene** welding, intelligence tests and factory production of aircraft are pioneered.

1906

Permanent hair weaves, taking 8 to 12 hours, introduced in England.

The first **Mozart Festival** is held in Salzburg. The first **animated cartoon** is released in the U.S.

1907

The Australian Arbitration Court establishes the concept of the **basic wage**.

The Shell Oil Trust is founded, and the **Boy Scouts** movement established.

First **helicopter** designed and flown by Frenchman Paul Cornu.

1908

Filming of *The Count of Monte Cristo*, one of the earliest story-telling movies, is completed in **Hollywood**. The next year a former tavern on Sunset Boulevard is converted into Hollywood's first film studio.

The Ford Motor Company begins production of the **Model T**. Buick and Oldsmobile merge to create **General Motors**.

Disposable **paper cups** are introduced by a New York company.

U.S. newspaper advertisements offer householders the chance to buy an upright vacuum cleaner for $70 after ten days' free trial. The man behind this scheme is a former harness-maker from Ohio, W.H. **Hoover**.

The first international meeting of **psychiatrists** is held at Salzburg.

1909

The General Electric Company produces the first electric **toaster**.

Frenchman Louis **Blériot** flies the English Channel.

**1910s buzzwords: ace, chow,
civvies, dud, red tape, rookie,
shell shock, vamp**

1910

The **tango** craze sweeps the United States and Europe. The 5,000 seat Gaumont Palace, the world's largest movie theater, opens in Paris. Also in France, fluorescent **neon** lights are introduced.

Father's Day is first celebrated in Spokane, Washington.

Iodine proves useful as a disinfectant and antiseptic.

1911

The first **Indianapolis 500** auto race is held.

The **Olivetti** company is founded in Italy.

The U.S. introduces **white lines** to mark the middle of roads. The US Army adopts the **Colt .45** automatic pistol.

1912

American Albert Berry makes the first **parachute jump** from a plane—the aircraft is flying at a height of 1,500 ft. A London-Paris **airmail** postal service is introduced.

Morse Code's **SOS** is adopted as international distress signal.

Manhattan delicatessen-owner Richard **Hellmann** sells his ready-made Blue Ribbon Mayonnaise in wooden containers.

Coco **Chanel** opens her first salon in the resort of Deauville, France.

1913

Grand Central Station in New York is opened—it is the world's largest railway station. The **Panama Canal** is completed linking the Atlantic and Pacific oceans.

NO 5 Coco Chanel, *marquise* of the perfume bottles (*flaconnerie*). Eugene Sandow (background), American apostle of body building.

The first **crossword** puzzle is published in the *New York World*.

The first home electric **refrigerator** is marketed in the United States.

The Ford Motor Company's moving **assembly line** reduces production time per vehicle from 12½ hours to 1½ hours.

1914

The **First World War** breaks out in Europe.

Edgar Rice Burroughs' *Tarzan of the Apes* is published. It is the first **Tarzan** book.

1915

The first **tanks** are developed in Britain. The German, Hugo **Junkers**, develops the first all-metal aircraft.

Heatproof **Pyrex** glass is developed in the United States.

FIRST THROUGH The SS *Ancon* was the first ship through the Panama Canal.

1916

Britain introduces **British Summer Time**—clocks are put forward one hour in summer as a measure to "save" daylight and fuel.

The first **self-service** store is opened in Memphis, Tennessee.

The first **birth-control** clinic is opened in the U.S. by Margaret Sanger.

Jeanette Rankin becomes the first **woman member** of U.S. Congress.

American automobile manufacturers introduce **windshield wipers** and the Dodge Company produces the first all-steel automobile bodywork.

Canadian Peter Nissen, designs the **Nissen hut** to house troops.

Lightweight, non-corrosive **asbestos** cement pipes are developed in Italy.

The German company Telefunken begins the mass production of **radio valves**.

1917

The **Trans-Australian** railroad is completed; the last 300 miles being the longest straight stretch in the world.

German soap shortages stimulate the production of the pioneer **detergent** Nekal. The U.S. Navy adopts wind-proof flying jackets with **zippers**.

The annual **Pulitzer** prizes are established for outstanding achievements in journalism and letters. The awards were endowed by the late Hungarian-born journalist and newspaper editor Joseph Pulitzer.

1918

New Mexico store-owner Conrad Hilton buys the Mobley Hotel in Cisco, Texas. Before long he acquires hotels in Waco, Dallas and Fort Worth—the start of the **Hilton** chain.

Outbreak of the worldwide **influenza** epidemic which kills more people than the First World War.

1919

The **jazz** craze spreads from the United States to Europe.

British flyers John Alcock and Arthur Brown complete the first **transatlantic** flight (Newfoundland-Ireland) in 16 hours, 27 minutes.

AT & T introduces the first **dial telephones**.

The **Bauhaus** group is established in Germany to promote modern design.

1920s buzzwords: blind date, bootlegger, flapper, goofy, hooch

1920

The first international **feminist** conference opens in Geneva.

Transcontinental **airmail** services begin between New York and San Francisco.

The U.S. adopts **Prohibition**; the sale of intoxicating liquors remains illegal until 1933.

Marconi establishes the first public **radio station** in the U.S. In Britain, HMV devises the first gramophone **disc autochanger**.

America's Jantzen Company markets the first elastic **one-piece bathing suit**.

1921

The first **Autobahn** is completed in Germany.

The **BCG** tuberculosis vaccine is pioneered in France.

Coco Chanel markets **Chanel No. 5** perfume in France. The first bathing beauty contest is organized for the title **Miss America**.

1922

The **BBC** is founded.

Reader's Digest is founded in the United States.

American **cocktails** become fashionable in Europe. The **dance marathon** craze seizes the U.S. The first improvised **water-skis** are used at Lake Pepin, Minnesota.

The Canadian scientists Frederick Banting and Charles Best successfully treat diabetes with **insulin**.

London's Piccadilly Line introduces the first underground train with **automatic doors**.

1923

Time magazine is first published in the U.S. The BBC introduces daily **weather forecasts**.

The **Charleston** dance craze sweeps America. The American celebration of **Mother's Day** is adopted in Europe.

The first **speedway** motorcycle races are organized in NSW, Australia.

Milky Way and **Butterfinger** candy bars appear; **Warner Bros.** Studio established.

The American LaPlante-Choate Company introduces the **bulldozer**.

1924

The **MGM** motion-picture company and **IBM** corporation are founded.

The German **Leica** company pioneers mass production of a precision miniature camera.

The first **Zeppelin** transatlantic flight takes place, from Friedrichshafen on Lake Constance to New York.

The first **Surrealist** exhibition is held in Paris.

MODERN LINES The surrealist Salvador Dalí with his wife Gala. A tubular chair (background), designed in 1926.

British hairdresser Antoine introduces the **blue rinse** for gray hair.

1925

The Exposition des Arts Décoratifs in Paris popularizes the **Art Deco** style.

The New Yorker magazine begins publication. The world's first **motel** opens at Monterey, California.

1926

Lufthansa airline is founded in Germany.

Lone Scottish inventor John Logie Baird demonstrates **television**.

1927

Charles A. Lindbergh makes the first **solo transatlantic flight** (New York-Paris) in 33 hours, 39 mins.

Pan American Airways is founded. A London-New York **transatlantic telephone** service is inaugurated.

Shingled haircuts become fashionable.

1928

Australia introduces the **flying doctor** service.

Walt Disney produces his first **Mickey Mouse** cartoon, *Steamboat Willie*. Mickey Mouse and later Donald Duck and the dogs Pluto and Goofy entertain growing audiences during the Great Depression.

Scottish researcher Alexander Fleming discovers **penicillin** by accident but fails to exploit its potential.

1929

The **Wall Street Crash** and central European banking crises trigger worldwide depression.

The Anglo-Dutch **Unilever** Corporation is founded, manufacturing margarine, soaps and other fat-based products.

SYDNEY'S PRIDE The Harbor Bridge and, later in the century, the Opera House became Sydney's world-famous landmarks.

The French-born Raymond Loewy founds the bureau that will pioneer **streamlined** industrial design in the U.S. Some of his famous designs include a refrigerator for Sears, Roebuck, automobiles for Studebaker, railway locomotives and passenger carriages and Greyhound buses.

The first Academy Awards are distributed. They are nicknamed the **Oscars**, apparently because an official quipped that the statuettes looked like his uncle Oscar.

Popeye the Sailor and "Lithiated Lemon"—later called **7-Up**—make their first appearance.

The **iron lung** machine is developed in the U.S. for polio victims.

The British Dunlop Company develops **foam rubber**.

1930s buzzwords: dole, fireside chat, jitterbug, New Deal, swing

1930

Uruguay beats Argentina 4-2 to win the first-ever soccer **World Cup**.

PVC and **Scotch Tape** are invented in the U.S.

1931

J. Schick markets the **electric razor** in America and **Alka Seltzer** makes its appearance.

The **Empire State Building** is opened as the world's tallest structure.

Al Capone is found guilty of tax evasion and is sent to prison.

1932

Charles Lindbergh, Jr.—**Baby Lindy**—is kidnapped from his crib—the first "crime of the century."

Existence of **protons, neutrons** and **electrons** is confirmed.

1933

The **Boeing** 247 airliner, capable of cruising at 189 mph, enters regular service.

Monopoly, world's best-selling board game, is invented by Parker Bros. in the U.S.

1934

Dupont introduces **nylon**.

Cat's-eyes road reflectors are invented in Britain.

1935

George **Gallup** pioneers reliable opinion polling in the United States.

Catastrophic **dust storms** devastate American farmlands, forcing mass migrations.

Penguin Books launch the "**paperback** revolution" in Britain.

1936

The first **Butlin's** holiday camp is opened at Skegness, Lincolnshire, on England's east coast.

FLYING HIGH The cover for *Picture Post's* first issue, October 1, 1938.

Ferdinand Porsche unveils the prototype Volkswagen **"Beetle"** and millions of German workers subscribe to savings schemes to buy one— but few will be built until after the Second World War.

Jesse Owens wins four gold medals at the Berlin Olympic games—to Hitler's consternation.

The first **vitamin pills** are marketed in the U.S.

1937

The **Golden Gate** bridge is opened to traffic in San Francisco.

British engineer Frank Whittle builds the first **jet** engine.

The first **magnetic tape recorder** is marketed in Germany.

Nescafé, the first commercially successful **instant coffee**, is made by the Swiss Nestlé Company.

Disney issues *Snow White and the Seven Dwarfs*—the first all-color **cartoon** feature film with sound.

1938

New Zealand introduces a **state medical service**.

The first issue of the **photo-illustrated** weekly news magazine *Picture Post* appears in Britain.

Hungarian Laszlo Biro patents the **ballpoint** pen, using quick-drying printer's ink. America's Du Pont corporation manufactures **nylon** to

---

make toothbrushes; nylon stockings are first sold in 1939.

1939

Pan American Airways begins regular **transatlantic flights**.

Hollywood's "Golden Year" sees premiers of **Casablanca, Gone With the Wind,** and **The Wizard of Oz**.

The **Second World War** breaks out.

1940s buzzwords: blitz, ersatz, gobbledygook, kamikaze, Mae West, POW, walkie-talkie

1940

The **"Jeep"** (General Purpose) four-wheel-drive vehicle is adopted by American armed forces.

The U.S. pioneers **freeze-drying** for food preservation.

1941

The **aerosol** can is developed for spraying insecticides. Massey-Harris manufacture the first **combine harvesters**.

In Britain the RAF's first **jet-powered aircraft**, the Gloster E28/39, has a successful test flight.

WHITE CHRISTMAS Irving Berlin's Christmas musical, starring Bing Crosby, became a holiday favorite.

1942

The Oxford Committee for Famine Relief **(OXFAM)** is founded by Oxford classics professor Gilbert Murray to relieve famine in Greece that kills 350,000.

Napalm is invented in the U.S.

Bing Crosby records Irving Berlin's **"White Christmas."**

1943

The first **kidney dialysis** machine is improvised in the Netherlands.

The **aqualung** is invented in France.

IKEA, the Swedish furniture retailer, is founded.

1944

DDT insecticide is used for the first time on a large scale—to halt a typhus epidemic in Naples.

1945

The U.S. introduces **fluoridation** of water to combat tooth decay.

1946

The **jukebox** craze spreads from the U.S. to Europe. The two-piece **bikini** swimsuit is designed in France.

1947

Christian Dior's lavish **New Look** revolutionizes Parisian haute couture.

The **Dead Sea Scrolls** are discovered in caves in the Judean Desert.

U.S. presidential adviser Bernard Baruch coins the term **"Cold War."**

The **polaroid** camera is demonstrated for the first time. The first **microwave** oven is marketed in the United States.

The Goodyear company pioneers the **tubeless tire**. The **Vespa** motor scooter is launched in Italy.

1948

Scientists at Bell Laboratories invent the **transistor** to replace the vacuum tube.
The modern states of **Israel** and **India** are established.

PENNY IN THE SLOT Postwar American exports to Europe included the jukebox.

The **Velcro** fastener is invented by the Swiss engineer George deMestral.

1949

The maiden flight takes place of the De Havilland Comet, the world's first **jet airliner**.

Scrabble, the word game, is launched in the United States.

1950s buzzwords: beatnik, fallout shelter, station wagon

1950

Diners' Club pioneers the first **credit card**.

The first **kidney transplant** operation is performed in the U.S.

1951

Deutsche Grammophon markets the first 33 rpm **long-play record**. Chrysler pioneers **power-steering**.

Color TV becomes available in the United States.

1952

The airline TWA pioneers **tourist class** flights.

The world's first **sex-change** operation is performed in Denmark.

The first pocket-sized **transistor radio** is marketed by Sony in Japan.

1953

An Anglican clergyman, the Rev. Chad Varah, founds the **Samaritans** organization in London to counsel potential suicides.

The *Kinsey Report* declares that a quarter of American wives are **unfaithful** to their husbands.

1954

Frozen food sales in the U.S. surpass $1 billion a year.

Medical student Roger Bannister becomes the first man to run a **four-minute mile**.

Photochemical **smog** identified in Los Angeles.

Rock'n'roll sweeps the U.S. with The Crew Cuts' "Sh-Boom," Bill Haley and the Comets' "Rock Around the Clock" and Elvis Presley's "That's All Right Mama."

1955

Disneyland opens in California.

Commercial TV begins in Britain. Also in Britain, the **hovercraft** is developed, and frozen **fish fingers** are marketed.

1956

Ampex of California launches the first commercially viable **video recorder**. Long-life stainless-steel **razor blades** are marketed in Britain.

1957

France, Germany, Italy, Belgium, the Netherlands and Luxembourg sign the Treaty of Rome to form the European Economic Community **(EEC)**.

The first **stereo** discs are marketed in the U.S. Also, the **Frisbee** disc-throwing craze sweeps American college campuses.

The U.S. begins underground **nuclear testing** in Nevada.

1958

The lightweight, cheap **aluminum can** is developed in the U.S. **Lycra** artificial elastic is marketed in the U.S. **Nonstick** frying pans are first marketed in France.

The **Honda 50** is launched in Japan—it will become the world's biggest-selling motorcycle.

1959

Alaska and **Hawaii** admitted to the union, making the U.S.A. 50 states big. First **Xerox** copier is introduced.

FALLOUT Cold War jitters brought devices such as the family fallout shelter. Background: the Vespa motor scooter, synonymous with youth and romance.

THE FIRST JAMES BOND FILM!

IAN FLEMING'S

DR. NO

KING OF COOL Sean Connery, the original "James Bond."

Sony markets a transistorized **portable television**. The **Barbie** doll is launched in the U.S.

The four-hour film epic *Ben Hur* wins a record **11 Oscars**.

1960s buzzwords: commune, flower power, gear, LSD, tie-dye, trendy

1960

After being cleared of **obscenity** charges, Penguin Books sell 200,000 copies of D.H. Lawrence's *Lady Chatterley's Lover* on the first day of publication.

Sit-ins begin in Greensboro, North Carolina, and soon spread throughout the U.S.

Surgeons in Birmingham, Britain, develop the first **heart pacemaker**. The **oral contraceptive pill** is marketed in the United States.

1961

Three million copies of the **New English Bible** version of the New Testament are sold in its first year of publication.

The "freedom riders" campaign ends **segregation** on interstate buses.

Chubby Checker inspires the **twist** dance craze.

Miniskirts are shown as haute couture at the Dior and Courreges fashion houses.

Texas Instruments patents the **silicon chip**.

1962

Amnesty International is founded in London to campaign for political prisoners.

The first **James Bond** film, *Dr. No*, comes out.

Lasers are first used for eye surgery. General Motors installs the first **industrial robots**. Canadian thinker Marshall McLuhan predicts that electronic communications will make the world a **global village**.

1963

The first **touch-tone phone** is manufactured and marketed. Kodak launches the **Instamatic** camera using cartridge film.

1964

The 130 mph Shinkansen—**Bullet Train**—service is launched in Japan to link Tokyo and Kyoto.

Ships designed to carry standardized **containers** revolutionize international trade. IBM introduces the first **word processor**.

Beatlemania sweeps the U.S. The world's first **discotheque**—Whiskey-a-Go-Go—opens in Los Angeles.

British youth styles are dominated by designer Mary **Quant** and hairdresser Vidal **Sassoon**. Terence **Conran** opens Habitat housewares store in London.

High-yielding rice strains developed in the Philippines initiate a **"green revolution"** in developing countries.

1965

Watts riots ravage Los Angeles.

The Early Bird **communications satellite** enables the exchange of TV programs between Europe and North America.

Soft **contact lenses** are invented.

1966

TV sci-fi serial *Star Trek* begins.

1967

South African surgeon Christiaan Barnard performs the first **heart transplant** operation.

Rolling Stone first appears.

1968

Student riots in Paris.

1969

Hundreds of millions of people worldwide watch U.S. astronauts **land on the Moon**.

Massive **anti-Vietnam** War demonstrations erupt across the U.S. Some 400,000 attend the **Woodstock** Rock Festival in upstate New York.

Monty Python's Flying Circus is shown on British TV for the first time.

The Anglo-French supersonic airliner **Concorde** makes its maiden flight.

1970s buzzwords: encounter group, jogging, singles bar, streaking, transcendental meditation

1970

Expo '70 in Osaka is Asia's first world fair.

The **Gay Liberation Front** holds its first demonstration in Britain.

The Boeing 747 **jumbo jet** enters transatlantic service.

IBM develops the **floppy disk** for storing computer data.

1971

Intel introduces the **microprocessor**. Texas Instruments markets the

BEAM ME UP *Star Trek*, one of many 1960s institutions that would outlast the decade. Disposable mini dresses (background) were less successful.

---

first **pocket calculator**—weighing some 2½ lb.

The Magi-Mix **food processor** is exhibited in Paris.

1972

Total sales of the Volkswagen **Beetle** overtake those of the Model T Ford.

The **feminist** magazines *MS* and *Spare Rib* appear in the United States and Britain.

1973

An Arab-led oil-price hike provokes a global **energy crisis**.

Tennis star **Billie Jean King** trounces Bobby Riggs in the "Battle of the Sexes" tennis match.

The **Sydney Opera House** is opened.

Supermarkets introduce **computer-coded labels**.

1974

President Richard **Nixon** resigns in midst of the Watergate scandal.

Hank Aaron hits 715th home run, beating **Babe Ruth's** 39-year-old record.

The **IRA** launches a bombing campaign in mainland Britain.

1975

Liquid crystal displays are used for calculators and digital watches.

In the **International Women's Year**, Japanese Junko Tobei becomes the first woman to reach the top of Mount Everest.

1976

Punk style and music emerge in Britain.

America celebrates its **Bicentennial**.

1977

Saturday Night Fever inspires a worldwide **disco-dancing** craze.

The Apple II **personal computer** is launched. The first cheap **autofocus** camera is marketed.

THE VICTIMS A vast quilt was one memorial to those who succumbed to the new plague of AIDS.

1978

Louise Brown, the first **test-tube baby**, is born in Manchester, Britain.

Compact discs (CDs) are first demonstrated.

1979

Canada becomes the first country to operate a **satellite TV** broadcasting service. The **mobile cellular phone** is launched.

The Sony **Walkman** personal stereo is launched in Japan.

The game **Trivial Pursuit** is invented in Canada and sweeps across the U.S. and then the rest of the world.

1980s buzzwords: cellulite, interface, nerd, quality time, safe sex, sound bite, yuppie

1980

The laser-scanning process for reading **bar codes** is perfected by IBM

SINGING FOR THE STARVING Bob Geldof's Live Aid concert built on the success of the Band Aid record.

Rollerblades are invented in U.S. as a summer training tool for ice-hockey players.

1981

First U.S. **AIDS** case is officially recognized by health officials.

The **Rubik's Cube** puzzle (invented in 1974) becomes a global craze.

Some 700 million people worldwide watch the marriage of Britain's Prince **Charles** and Lady **Diana** Spencer.

1982

Rap music becomes the rage in America and Britain. The first **CD players** are marketed in Japan.

HOLE IN THE SKY Satellite images brought proof of ozone depletion.

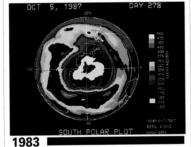

1983

Widespread **anti-nuclear** demonstrations take place in Europe.

1984

Apple's user-friendly **Macintosh computer** is launched.

The **Band Aid** concert and record raises money to relieve famine in Ethiopia.

Michael Jackson's *Thriller* LP is released. It goes on to sell an all-time record 47 million copies

1985

The World Health Organization declares **AIDS** an epidemic affecting the entire globe.

Seventeen-year-old German, **Boris Becker**, becomes Wimbledon's youngest-ever men's singles lawn tennis champion.

The **Home Shopping Network** TV sales channel is launched in the United States.

LAST GUARD East German guards line the Berlin Wall; its fall shortly afterwards marked the end of an era.

1986

The first **heart, lung and liver transplant** is performed in Britain.

Scientists express concern over the **greenhouse effect** and the thinning of the ozone layer.

1987

Televangelist **Jim Bakker** and politician **Gary Hart** brought down by scandals.

A worldwide **stock exchange crash** creates turmoil on Black Monday, October 19.

Solar-powered cars race across Australia from north to south.

1988

Australia marks the **bicentennial** of European settlement.

1989

France celebrates the **bicentennial** of the Revolution of 1789. The **Berlin Wall** is demolished.

Nintendo produces the handheld video **Game Boy**.

1990s buzzwords: smart bombs, double whammy, ethnic cleansing, road rage

1990

West and East Germany are **reunited**.

The **Teenage Mutant Ninja Turtles** craze is at its height.

1991

Operation **Desert Storm** liberates Kuwait after invasion by Iraq. The last **apartheid** laws are abolished in South Africa.

CDs now outsell tapes and records.

1992

Euro Disney amusement park opens near Paris. **Madonna**'s photo-album *Sex* sells 100,000 copies in 12 hours.

1993

Michael Jordan retires—temporarily—from basketball.

Schindler's List wins seven Academy Awards, including Best Picture.

1994

The **Channel Tunnel** is opened.

Nelson **Mandela** is sworn in as the first black president of South Africa.

1995

TV viewers are mesmerized by the televised trial and acquittal of former football-player **O.J. Simpson**.

1996

Bill Clinton elected first two-term Democratic president since FDR.

1997

At 43, **Tony Blair** becomes youngest British prime minister in 200 years.

Diana, Princess of Wales, is killed in Paris car accident.

1998

Linda Tripp turns over tapes she made of her phone conversations with **Monica Lewinsky** concerning sex in the White House.

Mark McGwire hits 70 home runs as he and **Sammy Sosa** both smash Roger Maris's 1961 record.

1999

President **Bill Clinton** is impeached by House of Representatives; acquitted by the Senate.

Michael Jordan retires—again—as NBA's most celebrated player.

INDEX

ACKNOWLEDGMENTS

Abbreviations:
T = Top; M = Middle; B = Bottom;
R = Right; L = Left

3 Ullstein Bilderdienst, L; Corbis-Bettmann, LM; Popperfoto, RM; Hulton Getty, R. 6 Corbis-Bettmann, BL; Dennis Gilbert, Arcaid, BR. 7 TRWIA, L; Corbis-Joseph Sohm, R. 8 Popperfoto, TM; Corbis-Bettmann, BL. 9 Popperfoto, TL; Vintage Magazine Company, BR. 10 Illustrated London News, TR; N. D. Comtec, M; Mary Evans Picture Library, BL. 11 Mary Evans Picture Library, L; Giraudon/ Bridgeman Art Library, ML; Corbis-Bettmann, MR; Fred Mayer/Magnum,R. 12 Corbis-Bettmann, BL, Camera Press, TR. 13 AKG Photo, TR; Corbis-Bettmann, B. 14 Giraudon/Bridgeman Art Library, L; Mary Evans Picture Library, TR; Corbis-Bettmann, MR, BR. 15 Corbis-Bettmann, TL; Popperfoto, MR. 16 AKG Photo, TR; Corbis-Bettmann, L. 17 Hulton Getty, TR. 18 Corbis-Bettmann, T; Popperfoto, B. 19 Corbis-Bettmann, TR, TM; Simon Kenny/Belle/Arcaid, MM; Constantine Manos/Magnum, BL.
20 Corbis-Bettmann, T, ML. 21 Popperfoto, TL; Corbis-Bettmann, MR; Hulton Getty, B. 22 Hulton Getty, TL; Orde Eliason/Link, TR; John Parkin/Link, BL. 22-23 Alex Bartel/Arcaid. 23 Richard Bryant/Arcaid, TR; David Hurn/Magnum, BR. 24 Hulton Getty, TR; Corbis-Bettmann, BL. 24-25 Burt Glinn/Magnum. 26 Corbis-Bettmann, BL; Mary Evans Picture Library, MR. 27 Topham Picturepoint, TL; Corbis-Robert Holmes, BR; Mary Evans Picture Library, ML; Corbis-Bettmann, MR. 28 Illustration by Graham White, reference courtesy of Corbis-Bettmann and Hulton Getty, TL; Michael Nichols/Magnum, BR. 29 Popperfoto, TL; Corbis-Lake County Museum, MR; Corbis-Bettmann, B. 30 Roger-Viollet, TL; Corbis-Bettmann, BR; Alfred Dunhill Archive, BL. 31 Popperfoto. 32 Fred Mayer/Magnum, TR; J. R. Eyerman, Time Inc./Katz Pictures, BL. 33 Clarence Saunders/Library of Congress; Ullstein Bilderdienst, L; Advertising Archives, ML; Anthony Blake Photo Library, MR; Roger-Viollet, R.
34 Corbis. 35 Mary Evans Picture Library, TL; Corbis-Bettmann, MR. 36 Mary Evans Picture Library, TM, BM; Ullstein Bilderdienst, L. 37 Corbis-Hulton-Deutsch, M; Corbis-Bettmann/UPI, BL. 38 Hulton Getty, T; Corbis-Bettmann, B. 39 Topham Picturepoint. 40 Camera Press, L, Corbis-Bettmann, R. 41 Jean-Loup Charmet, MR; The Granger Collection, BR. 42 Corbis-Bettmann/UPI, ML; Cadbury Ltd, BR. 43 Collection of the New York Historical Society, TL; Roger-Viollet, R. 44 Corbis-Bettmann, TL, TR; Corbis-Horace-Bristol, B. 45 Mary Evans, TL; Hulton-Getty, TR; Topham Picturepoint, B. 46 The Granger Collection, T; Corbis, B. 47 Corbis-Ted Strashinsky, T; Corbis, M; Peter Paz/Image Bank, BR. 48 Jon Love/Image Bank, TL; Lou Jones/Image Bank, BL. 49 Topham Picturepoint, TL; Philip J. Griffiths/Magnum, R; Corbis-Julie Houck, BL. 50 Corbis-Hulton Deutsch. 51 Corbis-Bettmann.
52 Ullstein Bilderdienst, TR; Popperfoto,

L. 53 Advertising Archives, TR; Corbis-Hulton Deutsch, ML; Popperfoto, B. 54 Corbis-Bettmann/UPI, L; Mary Evans Picture Library, TM; Corbis-Bettmann, BR. 55 Popperfoto, TL; American Vogue, 1926/Condé Nast Publications, New York, BR. 56 Topham Picturepoint, TL; SuperStock, TR; Corbis-Bettmann, BL. 57 Corbis-Bettmann, BL; Paul Bremen Corbis-Lake County Museum, BM; Vintage Magazine Co., TR; Topham Picturepoint, RM. 58 Robert Opie Collection, TL; Corbis-Bettmann, BL; Hulton Getty, TM; Topham Picturepoint, MR. 59 Advertising Archives,TR, B. 60 Topham Picturepoint, TL; Pictorial Press, R, BM. 61 Pictorial Press, L, M, BR. 62 Advertising Archives, LM; Corbis-Bettmann/UPI, R. 62-63 Illustration by Kevin Jones Associates, B. 63 Camera Press,TM; Corbis-Neal Preston, R. 64 Corbis-Bettmann. 65 Mary Evans Picture Library, TL, ML, BR. 66 G. Spencer Pryse/Public Records Office, TM; Fred Taylor/Public Records Office, M; Robert Opie Collection, TR, B. 67 The Granger Collection. 68 Ullstein Bilderdienst, L; Popperfoto, TR. 69 Corbis-Bettmann, TL; R; Corbis-Lake County Museum, BM. 70 Corbis-Bettmann/UPI, ML. 70-71 Corbis-Bettmann/UPI. 71 Roger-Viollet. 72 Corbis-Bettmann, TL, ML, BR. 73 Corbis-Bettmann, M; B. 74 Hulton Getty, TL; Popperfoto, B. 75 Hulton Getty, BL; Pictorial Press, TL, TR. 76 Anthony Blake Photo Library, TR, B. 77 Anthony Blake Photo Library, TM; Camera Press, TL, TR, BL, BR. 78 Kermani-Liaison/ FSP/Gamma, TL; Chris Steele Perkins/Magnum, ML; Corbis-Keren Su, BR; Corbis-Thomas A. Kelly, MR. 79 Popperfoto; Robert Opie Collection, L; Andreas Springer/Ullstein Bilderdienst, ML; Mary Evans Picture Library, MR; Ullstein Bilderdienst, R. 80 Pictorial Press, TR; AKG Photo, BL. 81 Hulton Getty, ML; Popperfoto, B. 82 L'Illustration/Sygma. 83 Eve Arnold/Magnum, TL; Hulton Getty, M, BR. 84 Keystone/Sygma, B; Robert Opie Collection, M; Corbis-Hulton Deutsch, MR. 85 Ullstein Bilderdienst, TL; Corbis-Hulton Deutsch, B. 86 Eve Arnold/Magnum, TL; Corbis-Bettmann, BM. 86-87 Ullstein Bilderdienst. 87 Hulton Getty, TL, BR. 88 Rotolo-Liaison/FSP/Gamma, TR; Noël Quidu/FSP/Gamma, ML; Hulton Getty, BR. 89 Burt Glinn/Magnum, TL; Corbis-Vince Streano, R. 90 Mary Evans Picture Library, BL, MR. 91 Corbis-Bettmann, TL; Hulton Getty, B. 92 Ullstein Bilderdienst, TL; Corbis, B. 93 Hulton Getty, TL; Mary Evans Picture Library, BR; Süddeutscher Verlag, BL. 94 Corbis-Bettmann. 95 Popperfoto, TR; Ullstein Bilderdienst, BL. 96 Corbis-Bettmann, TR, BL. 97 Corbis-Bettmann, TR, B; Hulton Getty, MR. 98 Camera Press, TR; Corbis-Bettmann, BL. 99 Mirror Syndication International, TL, TM, BL; Corbis-Bettmann, TR; Science Photo Library, M. 100 Corbis-Bettmann, L; John Walmsley Photo Library, TM; Hulton Getty, TR. 101 Corbis-Bettmann, ML, B. 102 Corbis-Bettmann, L; Robert Opie Collection, TM; John Frost Historical Newspaper Service/illustration by Kevin Jones Associates, MR. 103 Eve Arnold/ Magnum, BL; Mary Evans Picture

Library, M. 104 Sygma. 105 Corbis-Bettmann, TL, BR. 106 Keystone/Sygma, BL; Ullstein Bilderdienst, TR. 107 J. P. Laffont/Sygma, R; Frederic Stevens/Rex Features, BL. 108 Frank Spooner Pictures, BL, TR. 109 Frank Spooner Pictures, TL; Abbas/Magnum, BL; Eve Arnold/Magnum, TR. 110 Christoph Henning/Ullstein Bilderdienst, TR; Rex Features, BL; Jon Walter/Katz, M. 111 D. Goldberg/Sygma, TL; Andreas Springer/Ullstein Bilderdienst, MR; Denis Doran/Network, BR. 112 Ullstein Bilderdienst, BL, T. 113 Donald McLeish/Robert Harding Picture Library, T; Lapi/Roger-Viollet, B. 114 Corbis-Charles Harris, Pittsburgh Courier, TL; Ullstein Bilderdienst, B; Corbis-Richard T. Nowitz, M. 115 Süddeutscher Verlag, T; Hulton Getty, BL; Topham Picturepoint, MR. 116 Popperfoto, T; Corbis-Bettmann, BL; Mary Evans Picture Library, M. 117 Mary Evans Picture Library. 118 Corbis-Bettmann, TR, MR, B. 119 John Walmsley Photo Library, T; Corbis-Bettmann, B. 120 Dr M. Mundle, TL, ML; Hulton Getty, BL. 121 Corbis-Bettmann, T; Marc Riboud/Magnum, MR; Ulrike Preuss/Format, BL. 122 Paul Lowe/Magnum, TL; Novosti (London), ML; Steve Strike/Image Library of New South Wales, BL; John Walmsley Photo Library, BR. 123 SuperStock; Popperfoto, L; Sygma, ML, MR; Robert Opie Collection, R. 124 Popperfoto, MR; Roger-Viollet, B. 125 Jean-Loup Charmet, TR; Robert Opie Collection, ML; Hulton Getty, BL; Corbis-Lake County Museum, BR. 126 Ullstein Bilderdienst, TR, M, BL. 127 Hulton Getty, TL; Robert Opie Collection, TR, TM; Corbis-Lake County Museum, MR; Cobis-Bettmann, B. 128 Hulton Getty, TL; Robert Opie Collection, TM, B. 129 Jean-Loup Charmet, TR; Keystone/Sygma, M; Corbis-Lake County Museum, BL; Hulton Getty, BR. 130 Hulton Getty, TL, BR; Robert Opie Collection, BM. 131 Hulton Getty, TR, BL; Robert Opie Collection, TL.
132 Robert Opie Collection, TM, M; Camera Press, BR. 133 Corbis-Morton Beebe, MR. 134 Hiroji Kubota/Magnum, R; Craig Davis/Sygma, BL. 135 Richard Smith/Sygma, TR; Peter Brooker/Rex Features, BL. 136 Hulton Getty, ML; Ullstein Bilderdienst, B. 137 Corbis-Hulton Deutsch, TR; J. A. Grun, Private Collection/ Bridgeman Art Library, M; Sygma, B. 138 Hulton Getty, L; Corbis-Hulton Deutsch, TM; Ullstein Bilderdienst, M; Corbis-Bettmann, BR. 139 Hulton Getty, TL, MR; Robert Opie Collection, TM; Corbis-Bettmann, BR. 140 Corbis-Bettmann, TR; Popperfoto, BR; Ullstein Bilderdienst, BL, BM. 141 Pictorial Press. 142 Ullstein Bilderdienst, L; Hulton Getty, B. 143 Sygma, TL; A. Gyori/Sygma, TR; Corbis-James L. Amos, B. 144 Popperfoto, TL; Robert Opie Collection, M. 144-5 Martin Parr/Magnum. 145 Hulton Getty, TL, BR. 146 Ullstein Bilderdienst, TL; Sygma, M; Popperfoto, BR; Corbis-Bettmann, BL. 147 Hulton Getty, TL; Dennis Stock/Magnum, BR. 148 David Hurn/Magnum, L; Keystone/Sygma, M. 149 Sygma, TL, TM; Pictorial Press, TR. 150 Hulton Getty, TL, M; Jean-Loup Charmet, BR. 151

Victoria & Albert Museum/Bridgeman Art Library; Popperfoto, ML; Corbis-Bettmann, BR. 152 Image Library of New South Wales, ML; Hulton Getty, M; Corbis-Bettmann, BR. 153 Popperfoto, M, BR; Pictorial Press, TM. 154 Hulton Getty, M; The Ronald Grant Archive, TL; Pictorial Press, BL; Corbis-Bettmann, BR. 155 Corbis-Bettmann, TL, TR, BR; Hulton Getty, M.

Front cover: SuperStock, T; Corbis-Bettman, M; Corbis-Bettmann, B.

Back cover: Alex Bartel/Arcaid, T; Mary Evans Picture Library, M; Hulton Getty, B.

The editors are grateful to the following individuals and publishers for their kind permission to quote passages from the publications listed below:
Chatto & Windus, from *Gift From the Sea* by Anne Morrow Lindbergh, 1955. Collins and Brown, from *Motor Mania: Stories from a Motoring Century* by Richard Sutton, 1996. *The Daily Telegraph*, June 4, 1979. From *The New Yorker*, © 1996. From *Newsweek* magazine, © 1969. From *Travels With Charley* by John Steinbeck © 1962 by the estate of John Steinbeck. Victor Gollancz, from *A Wild Herb Soup* by Emilie Carles, trs. by Avriel H. Goldberg. HarperCollins Publishers Ltd., from *Nineteen Sixty Eight: A Personal Report* by Hans Koning, 1988. *New York Herald Tribune*, Tom Wolfe, © 1964 by the New York Times Co. Martin Secker & Warburg Ltd., from *Collected Essays* by George Orwell, © The estate of the late Sonia Brownell Orwell & Secker & Warburg Ltd. Richard Scott Simon Ltd., from *Bronx Primitive* by Kate Simon, © Kate Simon 1982, 1986, 1989. Souvenir Press Ltd., from *Beyond All Pity* by Carolina Maria De Jesus, trs. by David St Clair.